CHARLES LEONARD IRBY
JAMES MANGLES

TRAVELS
IN
EGYPT AND NUBIA, SYRIA
AND
THE HOLY LAND

INCLUDING
A JOURNEY ROUND THE DEAD SEA, AND THROUGH
THE COUNTRY EAST OF THE JORDAN

Elibron Classics
www.elibron.com

Elibron Classics series.

ISBN 1-4021-5787-8 (paperback)
ISBN 1-4021-2211-X (hardcover)

This Elibron Classics Replica Edition is an unabridged facsimile of the edition published in 1844 by John Murray, London.

TRAVELS

IN

EGYPT AND NUBIA, SYRIA, AND THE HOLY LAND

TRAVELS

IN

EGYPT AND NUBIA, SYRIA, AND THE HOLY LAND;

INCLUDING

A JOURNEY ROUND THE DEAD SEA, AND THROUGH THE COUNTRY EAST OF THE JORDAN.

BY

THE HON. CHARLES LEONARD IRBY,

AND

JAMES MANGLES,

COMMANDERS IN THE ROYAL NAVY.

LONDON:

JOHN MURRAY, ALBEMARLE STREET.

1844.

LONDON:
BRADBURY AND EVANS, PRINTERS, WHITEFRIARS.

PREFACE.

On the 14th of August, 1816, the Hon. Charles Leonard Irby and James Mangles, Commanders in the Royal Navy, left England, with the intention of making a tour on the Continent. This journey they were led to extend far beyond the original design. Curiosity at first, and an increasing admiration of antiquities as they advanced, carried them at length through several parts of the Levant, which have been little visited by modern travellers, and gave them more than four years of continued employment.

Soon after their return to England, in the end of the year 1820, they were induced to transcribe a selection of the letters which they had addressed during their absence to their families in England, as the most convenient mode of satisfying the inquiries of numerous friends.

A limited Edition, for private circulation only, was in consequence printed: this was so well received, and the copies were in such request, that Mr. Murray has been solicited, as a small mark of the friendship and esteem of the writers, kindly to accept the copyright, and further to oblige them by giving the book publicity in the more popular form of his Colonial and Home Library.

March, 1844.

CONTENTS.

CHAPTER I.

TOUR IN EGYPT AND NUBIA.

PAGE

Our Party and its objects—Departure from Philæ—Our Boat's Crew—Saracenic Building—Supposed Boundary between Egypt and Nubia—Kalapsche—Its Temple—We are taken for Physicians—Mr. Belzoni bitten by a Water Lizard—Arrival near Koroskoff—Offidena—Arrival at Derry—Nubian Dance—Attempted impositions on the part of our Crew—Pass Ibrim—Researches of former Travellers—Abou-Simbel—The Dongola Caravan—The Mockatem Mountains—Ruins near Farras—Crocodiles—Torpedo—Camelions—Arrival at the second Cataract—Description of the Cataract—Elpha—Further troubles with our Crew—Abou-Simbel—The small Temple—Message from the Cashiefs—Arrival of the Cashiefs—We wait upon them—Presents—Offence taken by Halleel—We engage Labourers—Proceed to the large Temple—Description of the Front—Commence operations—Are abandoned by the Natives—We continue our Labours—The Darfur Caravan—Interruption from Mahommed and Ali Cashief—Arrival of a Mameluke—The Natives refuse to supply us with Provisions—We succeed in reaching the Door of the Temple . 1

CHAPTER II.

Renewed Complaints of our Crew—We effect an Entrance into the Temple—Statues found in it—Colossal Statues in the Front—The Interior of the Temple—Paintings on the Walls—Description of the small Temple—We start on our return—The Cashiefs—Temples at Derry—At Armada—At Sabour—At Offidena—At Dekki—At Garbe Girshe—At Garbe Dendour—Unable to visit the Temple at Kalapsche—Ruins at Hindaw—Temple at Daboude—Present from our Crew—Philæ—General Observations on Nubia and its Inhabitants . . . .

CHAPTER III.

Descent of the first Cataract—Ancient Quarries at Assuan—Visit from the Aga—Elephantina—Koum Ombo—Mountains of the Chain—Temple at Edfoo—Fine Ruins at El Cab—Esneh—Luxor—Tombs of Gourna—Mummy Pits—Magnificent Tomb—The Tombs of the Kings—View from the Summits of the Lybian Chain—Observations on Thebes—Tentyra—Singular Use of the Mummy Cases—Ruins at the Foot of the Mockatem—Arrival at Cairo—Visit to the Pyramids—Observations on Cairo—Massacre of the Mamelukes—Appearance of the Country—The Nile—Travellers in Egypt—Expenses . . 37

CHAPTER IV.

SYRIA.

Departure from Cairo—Route to Jaffa—Al Arist—Haneunis—Gaza—Ancient Khan at Asdoud—Ruins of a Roman Bridge—Jaffa—Singular appearance of the British Consul—Liberality of the Aga—Cesarea—Ruins at Athlite—Convent on Mount Carmel—Acre—Zib—Value of Medical Knowledge—Tyre—Sidon—Lady Hester Stanhope—Bayruth—Tripoli—The Cedars of Lebanon—Baalbec—Arab Village—Latachia—Picturesque Scenery on the Orontes—Heavy Rains—Antioch—Aleppo—Mr. Barker—His hospitality and kindness—Abundance of Game—Proposed Route—Observations on Aleppo . . . 52

CHAPTER V.

PAGE

Departure for Hamah—Letters of Introduction—Caravan from Mecca—Hamah—Khans—Georgian Slaves—Negotiations with the Arabs—Interview with them—Homs—Departure for Palmyra—Arab Camp—Interview with the Arab Chiefs—Arab Feast—Fine View of Palmyra—Disappointment on reaching the Ruins—Description of them—Return to the Arab Camp—Reach Homs—Expenses of our Journey—Traits of the Arabs—Their character for Dishonesty not deserved—Damascus—Sketch of intended Route . . . 73

CHAPTER VI.

Departure from Damascus—Source of the Jordan—Singular Lake—Panias—Abundance of Game—Safot—Its elevated situation—Vermin—Tiberias—Ancient Baths—Lake of Tiberias—Om Keis—Ruins around Tiberias—Bysan—Its Theatre and other Ruins—Ford of the Jordan—The Valley of Adjeloun—The Callah-el-Rubbat—Souf—Remarkable Ruins at Djerash—Agreement with the Benesuckher Arabs to escort us to Kerek—Uproar at Katty—Description of Djerash—Troubles with our Escort—Szalt—Disturbance at quitting Szalt—Escape from the Arabs—Difficulty in fording the Jordan—Nablous—Jerusalem—Visit of the Pilgrims to the Jordan—Future Route—Adventure at the "Tombs of the Kings." 87

CHAPTER VII.

A TOUR TO PETRA AND THE DEAD SEA.

Difficulties attending our proposed Visit to Petra—Our Party—Our assumed Names and Costumes—Departure from Jerusalem—The Mountain of the Franks—The Labyrinth—Tekoa—Hebron—Its Governor—Difficulty in obtaining a Guide—Jellaheen Arabs—Plain of the Dead Sea—Salt Hills—Singular Trees and Plants—Favourable Reception by the Ghorneys—Beautiful Geological Specimens—Stopped by Arabs—The Castle of Kerek—Description of Kerek—Christian Church—Reception at Kerek—Sheikh Yousouf—His openness of Character—Departure from Kerek—The Wahabees—Mahannah—Mote—Ruins at Dettrass—The Wady-el-Ahsa—Ruined Temple—Gharundel—Volcanic Mountains—Shobek—Abon Raschid—His Dispute with the Sheikh of Wady Mousa, who refuses to permit our Advance—Noble conduct of Abon Raschid—View of Wady Mousa—Conferences of the Rival Chiefs—Preparations for Hostilities—Reinforcement from Kerek—Hindi—Failure of Negotiations—The Enemy suddenly withdraw their Opposition 102

CHAPTER VIII.

Wady Mousa—Encampment of the Inhabitants—The Necropolis of Petra—Remarkable Tombs—Narrowness of the Valley—Description of the Architecture—Romantic Pass—Representation of an Altar—Scene of the Murder of thirty Pilgrims—Course of the Stream—Magnificent Temple—Singular appearance of the Rocks—Ancient Authors on Petra—Buildings in the Valley—Houses—Tombs—Visit to the Tomb of Aaron—View from the summit—Strange liberality of the Natives—Compelled to quit Petra—Parting with Abou Raschid—Locusts—Wady-el-Ahsa—Kerek—Mountains of the Franks—Start for the Dead Sea—The Ghorneys—The Oskar plant—The Dead Sea—Salt on its Shores—Lumps of Nitre and Sulphur—Absence of living Creatures—Scene in Ismayel's Tent—Optical illusion—Wady Modjeb—Country of the Amorites—Mayn—Visit to the Hot Springs—A Vapour Bath—Ebn Fayes—His violent threat—The Pools of Heshbon—Palace of Hircanus—Parting from Yousouf—His character—Djerash—The Valley of the Jordan—Tiberias—Acre—Observations on the Character and Customs of the Arabs—Arrival at Constantinople. 123

A JOURNAL

OF

TRAVELS IN EGYPT AND NUBIA.

CHAPTER I.

TOUR IN EGYPT AND NUBIA.

Our Party and its objects—Departure from Philæ—Our Boat's Crew—Saracenic Buildings—Supposed Boundary between Egypt and Nubia—Kalapsche—Its Temple—We are taken for Physicians—Mr. Belzoni bitten by a Water Lizard—Arrival near Koroskoff—Offidena—Arrival at Derry—Nubian Dance—Attempted impositions on the part of our Crew—Pass Ibrim—Researches of former Travellers—Abou-Simbel—The Dongola Caravan—The Mockatem Mountains—Ruins near Farras—Crocodiles—Torpedo—Camelions—Arrival at the second Cataract—Description of the Cataract—Elpha—Further troubles with our Crew—Abou-Simbel—The small Temple—Message from the Cashiefs—Arrival of the Cashiefs—We wait upon them—Presents—Offence taken by Halleel—We engage Labourers—Proceed to the large Temple—Description of the Front—Commence operations—Are abandoned by the Natives—We continue our Labours—The Darfur Caravan—Interruption from Mahommed and Ali Cashief—Arrival of a Mameluke—The Natives refuse to supply us with Provisions—We succeed in reaching the Door of the Temple.

TOWARDS the end of May, 1817, we joined company at Philæ with Messrs. Beechey and Belzoni, who were about to proceed up the Nile. The principal object of this expedition, which was undertaken at the desire of Mr. Salt, was to endeavour to open the great temple at Abou-Simbel, which Mr. Belzoni, who was that gentleman's agent, had attempted the preceding year. The whole face of the temple, as high as the heads of the statues which are in front of it, was buried in the sand which had been blown from the desert. This sand, in the course of time, had accumulated to such a degree, as not only to fill up the whole of the valley, but also to form a mountain, sloping from the front of the temple for 200 or 300 yards towards the banks of the Nile. From all external appearance it is probable this temple, which is hewn out of the solid rock, had been shut for very many centuries, perhaps for more than 2000 years; and in that case, if it had not suffered too much in the general pillage and destruction which all the sacred edifices underwent at the conquest of Egypt, by Cambyses and other subsequent princes, it was hoped that something interesting to the antiquary might be discovered.

We considered it a fortunate circumstance for us to have an opportunity of joining in so interesting an undertaking. It is advisable that travellers should be both numerous and well armed in Nubia: our party was now a tolerably strong one, as including Mr. Beechey's Greek servant, an Arab cook, and a janissary, it consisted of seven persons. We could only add one solitary musket to a pretty good stock of arms of every description which Mr. Beechey had with him. We hired a boat at a village situated on a point amidst a cluster of datetrees which bounds the view of the river from Philæ to the southward.

The crew consisted of five men, including the reis or captain, and three boys: three of the men and the reis were brothers, and the fifth was their brother-in-law. This latter was dressed in a blue shirt, from which circumstance we nick-named him the "blue devil;" his real name was Hassan; he will be by and by a conspicuous character in this narrative. The boys were sons of some one or other of the crew, and the boat they said belonged to the father of them all, an old man who wore a green turban, as a descendant of the Prophet.

In the afternoon of the 16th of June, we started with a fine fair wind, having first settled a quarrel between two of our crew, in which one of them was cut through the calf of the leg, to the bone. Our agreement with the reis was for 160 piastres per month, 4*l.* sterling; and at the end of the voyage, if they behaved well, a backsheeish or present was promised, a stipulation which always forms part of similar bargains in this country. It was expressly understood that the crew should find their own provisions. As we advanced upwards, the sand hills filling up the cavities between the black granite rocks presented a most remarkable appearance; the surface in many places was quite fine and smooth, reminding one, with the exception of the difference of colour, of some of the scenery in Switzerland, where the snow before it cracks, and after it has been drifted fine, presents just such an appearance. The mountains here close in upon the river, and we looked in vain for that rich plain which, in Egypt, is every where to be seen on the banks of the Nile. On the heights, as we proceeded, we saw several Saracenic buildings placed in most picturesque situations; they tend very much to set off this wild species of scenery; we observed also, throughout Nubia, numerous piles of stones placed on the most elevated and conspicuous parts of the mountains, to indicate the vicinity of the Nile to the caravans from the interior of Africa.

Half a day's sail from Philæ brought us to the end of the granite rocks, which now gave place to those of calcareous stone, though on the river side, in most instances, their exterior still retains a black colour and a polish. The vein of red granite, which begins below Assuan, and extends beyond Philæ, is supposed to continue in an easterly direction till it reaches the shores of the Red Sea, keeping, nearly throughout, the same breadth; the observations which we made on our trips into the desert from Assuan tended to confirm this opinion.

On the afternoon of the 17th, we came to a place where the mountains close in upon the river in a very abrupt manner, leaving no level land on the banks; the hills at the same time presented some very grand scenery. This by some travellers is termed the boundary between Egypt and Nubia, though I should be inclined to agree with the French, that the first cataract is a more natural limit to the two countries; as, immediately above Assuan, you perceive not only a country quite different from that below, but even natives of a character and colour in no way resembling the Egyptians, differently clothed, and speaking another language.

This evening we arrived at Kalapsche, and as we had to wait some time while our janissary was buying provisions, we went up to inspect the temple, though we had agreed not to visit the antiquities until we returned from the second cataract. The ruins of this edifice are large and magnificent, but it has never been finished: it consists of a large peristyle hall, (most of the columns of which have fallen, and many are unfinished,) two chambers, and a sanctuary. The exterior walls are smooth, the sculpture not having even been commenced, and in the interior it is not finished, there being in no instance either stucco or painting. There has been first a quay on the river's side, and then a flight of steps as an approach to the temple. The outer hall had several Greek inscriptions in it, some of them in tolerable perfection.

In the evening, before we stopped, we passed two crocodiles; they were on a shoal in the middle of the Nile, and retired before we got near them: they were the first we had seen since we left Philæ; indeed they are never met with near that island. On the 19th a foul wind obliged us to stop, when an old man came to beg medicine, thinking we were *hackim*, or physicians, a strange notion which all barbarous nations have respecting Europeans: we gave him some advice, though we declined any pretensions to the title he had given us. Bruce, in making himself acquainted with the rudiments of physic, showed how well he judged of the proper mode of travelling in these countries; and his narrative proves how much he benefited by this knowledge. Our denial of all knowledge of physic met with little belief among the natives; and to induce us to give them assistance, they offered us two fowls for any aid we would render to their patients. On the 20th we saw a camel swimming across the river; one man swam before with a halter in his mouth, leading the animal, another followed behind.

June 21.—We this day observed, immediately opposite Duckie, two lads crossing the river which is here tolerably wide, and pushing and towing a laden reed raft.

On the twenty-second observed the purple acacia; it bears some resemblance to a shrub, and is evidently a dwarf species of the mimosa; never attaining a height beyond a foot or fifteen inches; excepting in colour, the flower is like the yellow acacia. On the twenty-third our crew killed a snake that was basking on the river side; it was gray, with two black marks below its head. It was curious to see the precautions they used before they would surprise this reptile, which they represented as poisonous, though I did not believe it was so. We had this morning a regular wild-goose chase after an old one and four young ones; the crew jumped overboard and caught them all, though with some difficulty. I mention this merely to give some idea how expert these people are in the water; they may almost be said to be amphibious.

June 24.—This morning we were opposite Koroskoff; we purchased a sheep for nine piastres, but were obliged to send the money before they would even show the animal; we remonstrated much against this curious method of making a bargain, but nothing would induce them to change their plan. We this day saw the calibash growing wild on creepers up the acacia-trees on the river side. Our crew got three very good ones. The boys also found a sort of wild currant growing close to the water side; we tasted some, and thought them not unlike the bleaberry, though not shaped like them, being round; in size and colour they are alike.

Our custom was always to bathe morning and evening, frequently oftener. This evening, while at this recreation, Mr. Belzoni was bitten in the foot, which caused him to cry out somewhat loudly for assistance. Next morning he was bitten again, in the same place; this last bite fetched blood, taking a piece out of the toe. Mr. Belzoni plainly felt something twisting round his leg; we all agree in thinking it must have been a water lizard. The other day a man hailed us and asked "if we would buy a spyglass;" he said he was a native of Senaar. We thought it must be the property of some European who had been robbed, and therefore told him we would see it first, upon which he came into the boat, that we might carry him to the village where it was (about four hours' sail above); however, on arriving there he walked off, and we never heard again either of him or his glass—the fact is, he wanted a passage, and we gave him credit for so cunning a method of getting one.

June 25.—We this day arrived near Koroskoff, at the place where the river reaches the southernmost point, before the beginning of the second cataract; for the river here turns due north, and continues in that direction between ten and fifteen miles; after which it becomes S. W. and then west to the second cataract. The Nile here assumes a picturesque appearance, having several islands and rocks in the centre of it. In the evening our janissary shot a wild-goose; its plumage was beautiful, and its taste exceedingly good, though we had not the means of cooking it in a very savoury manner.

June 26.—Observed the Nile to have *fallen* about 1½ foot. It is now twenty-two days since it began to *rise*. It is already above the cataract of Syene (Assuan).

June 27.—We this day saw two crocodiles; our men requested us to fire some muskets to frighten them away, but were not afraid of towing the bark in the water close to the bank where we observed them. I think, from what we have noticed of these animals, that it is very seldom, if ever, they attack people. This morning a man on horseback came down to the river side, and said he was sent by Halleel Cashief with salam alicams (compliments): he, however, seemed chiefly intent upon getting something for himself; and, in a moment, enumerated several articles which he requested us to give him; such as coffee, snuff, gunpowder, salt, &c.; we told him we had none to spare, as we reserve those articles for Hassan Cashief, the chief person in this country, and whose favour it is necessary to gain by presents, in order to get permission to open the temple at Abou-Simbel. That chief has pledged his word to Mr. Belzoni, that none but the English should be allowed to work there, on condition that he, Hassan, is to have half the *gold* that was found in it: for these people have no idea that our researches for antiquities in this country have any other object than to get treasure; and they laugh when we tell them we are looking for stone statues, and slabs with inscriptions on them. They cannot conceive what motive can induce us to come such a distance, and expend three or four thousand piastres to clear away an accumulated mass of sand, for no other purpose than to find some granite figures.

We now observed the water to be exceedingly muddy, and of a reddish yellow colour. We stopped a short time at Offidena with a view of purchasing a statue; but after much prevarication, we could not even get a look at it. The natives of this place are both handsome and well made, a circumstance very rare in Nubia; their complexion, however, was unusually dark. In the evening we arrived at Derry, and sent word to Daoud and Halleel Cashief, the two sons of Hassan, (who, most unfortunately for us, was at Dongola, and by whose absence we lost the friendship and assistance of the only honest man in the country,) that we were going up to open the temple at Abou-Simbel, and would thank them to send orders for us to be permitted to work; adding, at the same time, that we would wait on them and pay our respects on our return. While waiting there we had a specimen of Nubian dancing; about twelve lads assisted; the music consisted only in clapping the hands, in the doing of which they kept very good time. I cannot say much for the elegance or gracefulness of the dance, as it was nothing more than lifting up the right foot and stamping it down again, then rising up on the left foot by the spring of the instep, and afterwards letting the feet rest on the flat sole. This was done for a backsheeish which we gave them. We also gave the reis and crew a backsheeish of ten piastres, but they said it was not enough, so we added another five. At night, when we stopped, the reis came to us to say that we were two parties, and therefore should by rights pay double the money we had agreed to give for the boat. They also complained that we had not given sufficient to the crew to eat; that Jacques (an agent of Mr. Drovetti, a Frenchman living in this country, and who hired the boat not long before us,) always gave them one-third of his coffee, meat, bread, and every think that he had; in short, they imagined that up here we were at their mercy. Now, as we had regularly fed them, and given them coffee without stint every day, we thought it time to come to an understanding, and therefore told them that the boat was at our disposal, and that it was no affair of theirs if we had two or five different parties; and with regard to food, that as they were not contented with what we had given them spontaneously, they should have nothing. We have no doubt but our janissary and the Greek servant put them up to this request, as the soldier took a poor cowardly part, and urged that as we were in a savage country, we had better temporize with them till we were on our return, thus showing of how little use these fellows are to protect travellers.

June 28.—Passed Ibrim, situated on a rude but picturesque hill of a conical shape, and of barren calcareous stone. There is not now a single inhabitant to be seen, and it presents a sad picture of ruin and desolation. Mr. Legh, in his recent publication, (a few extracts from which we have seen in the Quarterly Review for February last) says "this town was destroyed by the Mamelukes." It was the extent or limit of his voyage in Nubia. He travelled in 1813. Mr. Bankes, it appears, was the first Englishman who ever succeeded in gaining the second cataract: he travelled in 1815. I fancy he took much about the same tour in Syria that we mean to take, though we have not as yet seen his journey traced out. In 1816, Mr. Drovetti, the *ci-devant* French consul in Egypt, succeeded in reaching the second cataract, together with his two agents, Rifaud and Cailliaud; these travellers, together with Sheikh Ibrahim (a real friend of ours) and Mr. Belzoni, are the only persons that have reached thus far. Mr. Belzoni had his wife with him in man's clothes. Poor Norden, who travelled eighty years ago, could only reach Derry. His Nubian trip is interesting, though not very instructive. Denon went no higher than Philæ; and Pocock only reached that isle. On the tops of the hills near Ibrim, we remarked many conical hillocks, as marks to direct the Dongola caravans. This evening we saw a crocodile sleeping on the sand a considerable way up. We were within twenty yards of him, but as none of our muskets were loaded with ball we did not fire; we, however, made a noise to awaken him, when he rushed into the water with his mouth open, looking very savage. He was about fifteen feet long.

June 29.—We arrived at Abou-Simbel, and unfortunately found that Hassan Cashief was absent; we sent again to Derry, to Daoud and Halleel, for leave to begin to open the temple when we returned from the second cataract. The banks of the river between Ibrim and Abou-Simbel are beautifully spread over with the yellow and purple acacia, forming thick hedges, which have a very pleasing effect; a species of the tamarisk is also common here. This is the plant that produces the gum arabic, which is brought in great quantities from the interior of Africa in the vicinity of Darfur. The seeds of the acacia form also a lucrative branch of trade, being sent in the first instance to Cairo, and then shipped for Europe, where they are used for tanning. The water is now become exceedingly thick, it is not, however, unpleasant to the taste.

June 30.—While we were at Abou-Simbel, the Dongola caravan passed; it was preceded by about fifty camels, carrying provisions, &c. The conductors were armed with swords, daggers, and spears. They wore sandals to preserve the soles of their feet from the burning sand, which we now feel most sensibly, being obliged to stop every now and then to pour it out of our shoes. These sandals are much like those worn by the ancient Egyptians, and which are often found on the feet of the mummies.

The range of the Mockatem mountains terminate nearly opposite Abou-Simbel in a remarkable manner, in a considerable number of pyramidal hills rising up from the sand, and having the appearance of a gigantic camp; some of the hills are oblong, and in the form of marquees: others are so perfectly pyramidal, that it is difficult to divest one's-self of the idea that they are the work of men's hands.

July 1.—Stopped opposite the village of Farras. We here examined the site of a large Nubian city, and amongst the modern stone buildings of the Arabs found several remnants of temples, with hieroglyphics. In one was a beautiful cornice and a frieze, with the winged globe highly finished. The natives showed us some Greek and Roman ornaments, such as the spread eagle, ornamental cross, &c. Near the village are some fragments of a temple, consisting of several broken pieces of red granite pillars, also some small ones of beautiful white marble. From the appearance of these ruins, the fineness of the situation, and the rich plain of cultivated land near it, I think this must once have been a populous and flourishing city, in the time of the Greeks and Romans, as well as the Egyptians. Close to the ruins there is a natural rock standing by itself, with a doorway leading to a very small recess or chamber, in which are two Egyptian figures, in intaglio, on the wall: one is a man, the other a woman with the lotus flower in her hand. There is a double row of hieroglyphics near the inner figure, and a niche at the further end of the chamber about four feet square.

We bathed this morning opposite a village, and on a sand-bank in front of us, at not more than a musket-shot distant, we observed two crocodiles (timsah in Arabic). As soon as we went into the water they both walked into the river, to all appearance from fear, for they are certainly both shy and timid, and, I suspect, will only attack a single person; nor then, unless they can surprise him in the water, and off his guard. We saw no more of these two, but, at noon, we saw another swimming with his nose just out of the water. We also observed a pretty large water-lizard, and a small black water-snake. To-day the sand-hills have assumed a fine green appearance, being covered here and there with tamarisk. This verdure, contrasted with the dark yellow sand, forms a pleasing diversity of colour. In the evening, while towing the boat, our sailors found a torpedo on the very brink of the river, apparently asleep. It was curious to observe their caution and timidity in approaching it; they, however, succeeded in sticking one of their daggers in his head, and by that means hauled it on shore. Our Egyptian crew had done the same near Beni Hassan. We got it on board, and, though nearly dead, it sensibly affected my arm in laying hold of it. I felt a double shock up the arm near the elbow. It was about two feet long; had very small eyes. The belly and top of the back white; one dorsal fin, and the sides, were coloured dark brown with black spots; it had no scales. Our sailors in Egypt ate the one they caught, but the present crew would not touch this, even when dead, and consequently harmless, much less eat it. They all told us we avoided the shock by uttering a charm, or using some magic influence. This day one of the boys of our crew brought on board a camelion. He caught it in an acacia (called in Nubia the soont) tree, which they affect more than the date, or any other tree in this country. On coming on board, it hissed and shewed symptoms of anger, evincing at the same time a great desire to make its escape. It was then of a dirty green colour, with dark spots, and whenever it was approached it turned to a dusky brown, inflating itself at the same time. I conclude that one hue is the effect of fear, and *the other* of indifference. We had subsequently eight of these animals on board; some of them became so tame, that when the flies annoyed us we had only to take one of the camelions in our hand, and place it near the flies, and it would catch them with its long tongue in great numbers.

July 1.—In the evening we arrived at Farras, when two natives, with the men servants of Hassan Cashief, came to us, and we made a bargain with them to procure asses and camels to go above the second cataract. One of these remained in the boat, and the other promised to meet us at Elpha on the morrow with the animals. Elpha is opposite the second cataract, and is the last habitable place to which the Nubian boats ascend.

July 2.—Arrived at the second cataract, and perceiving we should have a long distance to walk to the elevated point from whence the finest view of it is obtained, we requested the reis to take us higher up the river, in order to shorten the walk, but all the boatmen persisted that it was impracticable for the boat to go higher on account of the rocks; they offered, however, to take us if we would first go over to Elpha, on the opposite side of the river, and land all our effects, and then return again. We required the reason of this odd proposition, when they said that they were apprehensive of thieves on that side of the river. We did not however like the scheme, and therefore refused to do so, urging them to advance higher up, as we plainly perceived we might go a good league farther without the least risk, but nothing would induce them to consent. In the mean time another boat arrived, and we perceived that our reis and his sailors were in league with the men of the other boat, to force us to take their bark; but we determined to walk rather than submit to this imposition, as the new comers wanted a high price, and accordingly we set out. The sand was deep and the sun very hot, so that we soon found that walking in the desert is no joke: our trip occupied us about two hours, from one o'clock to three, the hottest part of the day. On the road we found innumerable tracts of the gazelle and other animals; we saw seven of the former in one group, and three in another. They were not so timid as we expected, and stopped to gaze on us with their ears cocked up like deer in a park: their colour is brown, not much unlike the sand, and when they are in a valley it is difficult to perceive them. We were not more than two musket-shots distant from the three we first saw. When running, they are wonderfully light and nimble, and while on the rocky parts bounded with great agility.

The spot from whence we surveyed the cataract was a projecting cliff, about 200 feet high, with a perpendicular precipice down to the river side; from this place, which is on the western bank, you look down on the cataract to great advantage; it presents a fine *coup d'œil:* the river here runs E. N. E. and W. S. W. In America this would be called "a rapid," there being no direct fall, only an immense cluster of innumerable black rocks, with the Nile running in all directions with great rapidity, and much noise between them; they fill up the whole breadth of the river, which may be about two miles wide, and they extend as far as the eye can reach, altogether making a space of about ten miles of rapids: three below the rock on which we stood, and seven above. The scenery here is remarkably wild, there being no human habitation visible, excepting a fisherman's hut on one of the islands, and the village of Elpha on the opposite side of the river, in the distance; some of the rocks have beds of yellow sand on them, and most of the islands have small trees and shrubs growing in the crevices: the verdure of these, contrasted with the sand and black rocks, produces a fine effect. In front, and on both sides, the view is bounded by the desert; to the southward are the tops of two high mountains rearing their heads above the hills, and apparently seventy or eighty miles distant. The western bank of the river is richly covered with trees and shrubs, and it is curious to observe, immediately beyond this green margin, the barren desert, without the least vestige of verdure. Having bathed and dined on bread and cheese, we set out on our return to the bark, our guides urging us to be quick, lest we should be benighted; they said the serpents and other venemous reptiles always came down by night to drink, and they were apprehensive that we should tread on them; they also said we should meet robbers at night: these people have a remarkable aversion to being in the dark. I remember, when at Dendera, our servant, an Arab, hurried off and left us behind, when he thought we should be late in returning to our boat; and whenever our lights have gone out in a tomb or temple, the Arabs have always clapped their hands, and made a noise to keep their spirits up till the light returned. In the evening, after dark, we reached the boat.

July 3.—In the morning at daylight

we crossed over to Elpha, the way to which place leads through several intricate passages, amongst rocks and shoals, where the current runs with great rapidity. In one part we were obliged to pass close under a high bluff, with some ruined houses on it: it was not necessary to pass through this intricate passage, our boatmen took it when we were all asleep, and we only perceived our situation on awaking at Elpha. We here found that neither asses nor camels had arrived to take us up to the temple, the reason assigned for this was, that the price agreed on the day before, at three piastres for each animal was not enough, though the person who made the agreement was there. We now endeavoured to procure beasts of the inhabitants, but they haggled so much about the price that we could make nothing of them. While this was going on, our crew, reis and all, took their clothes, arms, and effects out of the boat, and walked off to a *sackey*,* about 20 yards' distance, on the banks of the river: here they squatted down amongst a considerable number of natives; we had not taken notice of this proceeding, as their clothes, &c. were all kept abaft, behind the end of our cabin. When we could not agree for the asses, &c., we said we did not want them, and would go back to Abou-Simbel; with this intention we called the reis, and desired him to get the bark ready to return, but received an immediate answer that "neither he nor his crew would come." When we sent to know the reason of their refusal, they replied, that we must give them more money for the boat before they would come on board: they also said that we had never fed them, nor had we given them backsheeish, and when we reminded them of what they had received at Derry, they said that was nothing.

We now threatened to go off with the boat, and for that purpose rigged the oars across, but the wind being strong against us, we did not get under weigh. When the oars were ready we sent word to the crew to come, but they replied that they would not; that we might buy the boat if we chose, but that they would not navigate her: at the same time they said that they were people who did not value their lives a pigeon, and would take ours for half a one. While all this was passing, we observed the natives assembling in every direction, armed with spears, swords, and daggers; every minute they were arriving from all quarters on asses, and always going to the rendezvous under the sackey, where our vile crew had it in their power to tell any falsehoods against us without our being able to confute them, as neither our Arab cook, the Greek servant, or janissary understood the Barbarin language. Several of the Barbarins now came to see what arms we had, and appeared to take an exact account of everything in the shape of a weapon; for seeing affairs in this posture, we had prepared for the worst, and laid out all our arms in readiness, with which, fortunately, we were well provided. After a little time a message came from the crew that they wanted money; we sent them word that they must first come and do their duty; that as soon as the boat was off from this place, they should have a backsheeish, but not one para till they had done their duty. They now sent word that we had absolutely starved them, which was no doubt what they told the natives; they also informed us, that at this very place they had beaten Jacques Rifaud during his last voyage, and that it was done in the presence of the sheikh of the place, and all the natives; and that they had made him pay fifty piastres for the stick they had broken over his head. At Derry they had talked to us about his generosity. At this moment several of the natives came down demanding backsheeish, backsheeish, in a threatening manner. We asked the reason why we should give them money? They replied, for seeing the cataract, and coming into their country. A loaded musket was now pointed at them, and they were asked if they wanted money by force

* Sackey is the Persian wheel with which they raise water from the river; it is described by Burckhardt, Norden, and other travellers.

or good means; on which they retired, saying la, la, la, no, no, no, evidently not liking the sight of fire-arms. We now told them, that if we had seen the cataract without paying, so they had seen us without giving us anything as a recompense, though we were as novel a sight to them as their cataract was to us, and therefore we were quits.

Some of the most impudent now came down, and on being refused money said we should wait where we were till the high Nile: that we should neither go upward or downward, laughing and hooting at the same time; our villanous crew all this while sitting under the sackey, and enjoying the storm they had raised against us. To all their threats we constantly replied, that we were well armed, were determined not to be robbed, and that should they come to extremities, we would certainly make good use of our fire-arms, which we took care they should all see were pretty numerous and loaded. The asses were now brought, and the people endeavoured to persuade us to go off to the temple, evidently in the hope of plundering the boat when we were gone. We saw through this trick, and positively refused to go. We also told the natives, that though we were few in number, we had the firman of the pasha, and that any violence offered to us would be sure to be well punished. Those who had brought the asses now asked some remuneration for their trouble, as we had refused to hire them. This we thought reasonable; and, to draw off their attention, (for there were about forty of them), we gave eight piastres to be divided amongst the claimants. The division of this money turned affairs very much in our favour; for they began to quarrel amongst one another immediately.

The crew now thinking that they should get nothing for themselves, sent a messenger, while the natives were disputing about the division of the eight piastres, to say they would come and prepare the boat provided they had the backsheeish. We repeated our terms, that they should have a present when they did their duty. Seeing they could not stir up the natives to any acts of violence, they returned to the boat, all armed, having their daggers fastened to the left arm above the elbow joint, the manner in which all the Nubians wear that weapon. As soon as the boat was ready, they asked for the money, when we gave them fifteen piastres. Before we were off, however, one of the Farras people came to be rewarded for endeavouring to hire the asses at that place, or rather for disappointing us. We offered him five piastres, which he indignantly refused; but seeing he could get no one to assist him in forcing us to give more (for all these people are impudent and bullying for their own interest, but never for another's), came back and said he would take the five: this we now refused; when he went off in a violent rage, uttering threats that we should hear more of him below. After this, we got off from this infamous place, and soon found what a trap they had set for us; for it was with the utmost difficulty that even the crew could get the boat through the numerous narrow passages, all of them being obliged to get out into the river, and guide her through amongst the rocks; and we were also forced to pass directly under the bluff before mentioned, where the natives, had we ourselves taken the boat off, would have annoyed us greatly, while they would have been sheltered behind the ruined village. Indeed our crew wished us above all things to take the boat off, that they might represent us to the inhabitants as robbers, stealing their bark. However, we saw through all this.

July 4.—We arrived at Abou-Simbel, and found that no message whatever had been received from the cashiefs at Derry. This was a sad disappointment to us. Our crew, now dreading the presence of the chiefs, came to beg forgiveness; saying that they had forgotten and forgiven everything, and hoped that we had. They said they would behave well in future —"that they were poor, and always made a practice to get all they could from passengers and strangers." They remarked, "that dogs, when repulsed, always made a practice of returning to get something as long as there was anything to be had." This appears to be a favourite proverb amongst them.

July 6.—We visited the small temple opposite Abou-Simbel on the south side of the river. This temple is excavated in the solid mountain; the entrance is situated on the side of a rocky precipice, which below slopes into the river: there are some remains of steps cut in the rock as an approach to it. The principal chamber is 10 paces long, by 9 wide: it is supported by four pillars, two on each side of the passage. In the centre, at the further end of the apartment, there is on each side a doorway communicating with side chambers, 9 paces by 4 each. The sanctuary at the end of the principal chamber is 6 paces by 4; this is the most common mode of construction in the Egyptian temples. At present the interior of this temple appears daubed all over with dirty plaster and Greek paintings, mostly representing men on horseback. Behind these, however, we easily discovered the Egyptian figures, hieroglyphics, &c. &c., in bas-relief on stucco. As most of the figures represent men with hawks' heads, we think this temple was dedicated to Osiris; and afterwards, perhaps, converted into a church of St. George. The sanctuary has been once ornamented, but the side apartments are plain. There is a small subterraneous chamber below the sanctuary, apparently intended for a sepulchre.

July 7.—A messenger on a dromedary arrived from Daoud Cashief to learn "if we were the same English for whom Hassan Cashief had promised to open the temple;" at the same time he sent word, that if we were the same persons he would immediately come himself; but if not, he knew what to do. The latter part of the message alluded to the French, who had used every effort to get Hassan Cashief to allow them to open the temple after Mr. Belzoni's first attempt in 1816. Mr. Belzoni, however, had fortunately, after his first effort, sent Hassan and his two sons a turban each, and some other presents, in Mr. Salt's name: this he did to bind them to their promise, and they certainly deserve credit for keeping it. It ought to be mentioned, also, that Mr. Drovetti, in the early part of 1816, on his way to the second cataract, before Mr. Belzoni's arrival in Nubia, had contracted with Hassan Cashief to open the temple, for 300 piastres, and left the money; Hassan promising that Mr. Drovetti should find it ready opened on his return from the falls: however, when he came back, his money was returned, the chief candidly telling him he could not undertake the task for so small a sum. As Mr. Drovetti would not go to a greater expense, the field now became open to any one else who chose to attempt the enterprise.

July 6.—In the morning we started early with two of the natives in search of a temple which they said was in the neighbouring mountains, about a "pipe" distant; for it is common among them to estimate a short journey by the number of pipes they can smoke during its performance. On our way we met two white gazelles; they were very timid; the belly and tail were perfectly white. After walking about an hour, we came to the mountains, where, having waited about two hours more, our conductors came and said, they could not find the temple, though the evening before they had described the size and every particular of it. In the evening we had a violent quarrel with the crew in consequence of their drawing their daggers on our servants. We told them that the first who drew his dagger should be severely punished: this threat, however, had so little effect, that one of them who had murdered his own brother at Philæ (for which reason he did not dare to go near the island, but was taken into our boat at a village above it), said he would be the first, and swore by Alla and the Prophet that he would have one of our lives; adding, that his method was not to attack people awake, but to stab them sleeping. We laughed at their threats, and told them they were more apt at talking of these matters than in doing them.

July 10.—To-day the two cashiefs, Daoud and Halleel, arrived. They did not come to us, nor send any message to apprise us of their arrival; but pitched their tents, formed of a few date sticks, the roof covered with grass, on the sand-bank at the river-side: here they waited till we should make our appearance. We accordingly set out to visit these potentates. The first tent we entered was Halleel's: he was a tall, handsome man, about thirty-six years of age, 6 ft. high, very corpulent, and had a fine expressive countenance, with dark eyes: his dress was a large, loose, white linen shirt, with long sleeves hanging down nearly 2 feet, an old turban, and slippers. He received us courteously, and immediately conducted us to the tent of his elder brother Daoud, who also gave us a very good reception. Daoud Cashief is rather taller than his brother, but not so fat. He is about forty-five years of age, and had a certain dignity and reserve in his demeanour that bespoke the chief: he wore a loose blue shirt. We were not long in bringing forward the subject of the temple, when he immediately said he would willingly give us his assistance to have it opened. Pancakes of flour and butter-milk were now brought, on which we all feasted, making use of fingers instead of spoons. Coffee was served, or rather a substitute for that beverage, which is not unpalatable; they call it gargadan: it is a small black grain, not unlike the English rape-seed; this they burn and pound like coffee, and it would puzzle those who are not connoisseurs to find out the difference.

The two chiefs dwelt much on the attempts which the French had made to induce them to consent to the temple's being opened, appearing to take great merit to themselves for having resisted all the offers that were made to them. The presents were now brought, and given in the name of Mr. Salt: to Daoud a handsome gun, which at Cairo cost 500 piastres; a turban which cost 50; and some trifles, such as gunpowder, soap, tobacco, coffee, sugar, &c. To Halleel a turban and smaller articles, equal in value to those which his brother had received. We then took our leave; but had scarce reached our boat when we heard that Halleel was highly offended because he had not received a gun as well as his brother. We immediately went back and endeavoured to appease him, explaining that we were not aware that he was a cashief, or we would certainly have brought him a gun as well as Daoud: indeed, the preceding year, when Mr. Belzoni was in Nubia, the younger brother had not assumed the title of cashief, nor was he treated as such. We promised that if he would have patience, and confide in our word, we would send him a gun exactly the same as his brother's; or, if he preferred it, we would give him one of our own; though we confessed we had none half so good as that was, and advised him to wait till we got another, as he would lose much by accepting a bad one. All was, however, in vain; he would not be appeased, but sat sulky in the corner, saying, he had better guns than ours, and that he knew what to do in his own country; meaning that we should not open the temple. This was an unexpected blow to our hopes: we began to despair; and seeing nothing would please him, we retired. A message now came from Daoud to invite us to partake of a sheep he had killed in order to regale us. We went to his tent. Halleel was not there. We noticed this, and expressed our concern at the displeasure he had evinced. Daoud said his brother was only a boy; that he was indiscreet, and did not know what he did, and that we need not mind him. We sent a message to him to say we would not eat unless he came and ate with us, but he refused. Daoud now, at our request, went to bring him; but returned unsuccessful, saying, he was only a boy, and that he pledged himself we should open the temple. However, as Halleel was evidently of a mischievous disposition, and likely to do us injury, indirectly, if not directly, we judged it the best policy to bring about a reconciliation. Mr. Belzoni accordingly went himself; and, after much difficulty, prevailed on him to come: he, however, was still sulky; and we had scarce sat down to dinner, when three strangers, apparently newly arrived, entered the tent, kneeled and kissed hands, paying their respects to Halleel before they saluted Daoud. We easily saw through this little trick, which was a concerted plan between the two brothers, to induce us to give Halleel more presents, from a supposition that his rank was equal to his brother's. The men belonged to the suite, and were disguised for the purpose.

After we had retired from dinner, we went to see if Halleel was still displeased, and found him as sulky as ever; our crew and Hassan having been with him from the first moment of his ill-humour, and doing all in their power to put him against us, for which Daoud had reprimanded them severely. Perceiving there was no pleasing him; that neither presents nor promises were of any avail, we returned to the boat; Daoud having pledged his word that we should commence our operations the following morning. Late in the evening we received a message from Halleel, requesting a gun, with some powder and shot; we immediately gave him ours, which, though good for nothing, was, nevertheless, the best-looking one we had. This prompt compliance calmed his anger; and we began to congratulate ourselves on the prospect of ultimate success. The only remaining difficulty now was to make the agreement with the workmen. The Farras man, who told us at Elpha "that we should hear of him below," now made his appearance, and endeavoured all he could to thwart our proceedings: we, however, took him to the cashiefs, and explained his conduct to them, on which they reprimanded him. After much altercation, we were glad to agree for the men to work at two piastres each per day.

July 11.—In the morning the two cashiefs came on board, and we proceeded to the temple, about a quarter of an hour's row from the village. The chiefs told us we were to have sixty men, and we paid for that number; but only fifty came. We were obliged also to give them doura, as they all complained of having nothing to eat. However, we were so anxious about the temple, that we were glad to give them anything, provided they would but work. I shall proceed to describe the object of our research, and explain where it was situated, how formed, and the manner in which the mysterious door was hidden from our view. The temple is situated on the side of the Nile, between 200 and 300 yards from its western bank; it stands upon an elevation, and its base is considerably above the level of the river. It is excavated in the mountain, and its front presents a flat surface of upwards of 60 feet in height, above the summit of the sand immediately over the door, but not so much as 40 on the north side, and a little more on the south; the breadth is 117 feet. Above 30 feet of the height of the temple, from the base, is covered by the accumulated sand in the centre, and about 50 feet on either side. The surface fronting the river is hemmed in by a mountain of sand leaning against it; and the door in the centre is buried beneath this sand, which rises on each side of it, increasing the labour and difficulty of digging in a prodigious degree: for no sooner is the sand in the centre removed, than that on either side pours down, so that to gain a foot in the centre, we had to remove the whole mass of sand which leaned against the temple; this sand also was of so fine a description, that every particle of it would go through an hour-glass. In front of the temple are four sitting colossal figures cut out of the solid mountain, chairs and all: they are, however, brought out so fully, that the backs do not touch the wall, but are full eight feet from it; and were it not for a narrow ridge of the rock which joins them to the surface, from the back part of the necks downwards, they would be wholly detached.

One of the statues has been broken off by a fracture of the mountain, from the waist upwards. There were originally twenty-two monkeys above the frieze and cornice : of these there are not now above twelve perfect. Under the arm of one of the great figures, we discovered the remains of the stucco with which they were once covered, and traces of red paint are discernible in many places. I think it very probable the whole front of the temple was once covered with stucco ; more especially as they have used that material very liberally and skilfully in the decoration of the interior. Of the cornice over the door, which was once perfect, there is not at present more than a foot in breadth remaining, just over the corner where we entered. In the progress of our labours, we discovered what had become of the rest ; and its mutilation caused us some very desponding evenings, as there was little indication of the temple being finished lower down than we could see.

July 11.—On the first day, the fifty men that came worked very badly, and we found that the burthen of the song which they sung, by way of stimulating each other, was, "that it was christian money they were working for—that christian money was very good, and that they would get as much of it as they could." This Nubian song, though cheering to them, was not much so to us. In the evening we returned to the village of Abou-Simbel; and perceiving we should never make any progress with people who, being sure of their pay whether they laboured well or ill, would only work five hours in the day, we sent to the cashiefs, and concluded a bargain with them and the natives "*to open the temple*" for 300 piastres. At this time none of us thought it would take more than four days to accomplish the undertaking; so little did we know of the real nature of our enterprise.

July 12.—In the morning, the two cashiefs and about one hundred men came and worked very well, thinking they could open the temple in one day. The chiefs requested we would not interfere in directing the labourers where to work, as it was now their own affair : they had undertaken the task, and were responsible for its execution. In the evening our boat's crew came and begged the intercession of the cashiefs to make their peace with us. They were the more anxious for an accommodation, as by the quarrel they lost the heads, skins, and offal of the sheep which we occasionally killed. We affected much reluctance, but ultimately forgave them ; the cashiefs bursting out into a violent rage against the crew, on our remarking that no European travellers would ever come into the country again, when they heard of the usage we had received. The dispute was scarcely at an end before our sailors asked for backsheeish ; this we positively refused till we arrived at Philæ, and then only on condition of very good behaviour : all came now and kissed our hands in token of reconciliation. At sun-set we returned to the village of Abou-Simbel ; when the chief of the labourers asked for 200 out of the 300 piastres, though they had consented to be paid only when the temple was opened ; we were, however, obliged to give 150, but said we would give no more till the work was finished.

July 13.—Only Halleel Cashief and about sixty men came; they worked very ill, and expressed doubts as to there being any door, though they had not yet got more than four feet down. While we were endeavouring to persuade them to persevere, one of the natives, a carpenter, with an audible voice, made a speech, the substance of which was, "that they would work the whole of that and the two successive days, and if in that time they found a door, well and good; if not, they would labour no longer." This declaration was received with tumultuous applause, in which we thought it good policy to join, as neither our approval or displeasure would have had any weight with them ; and it was possible that our appearing to be in good humour with them might induce them to do their work more cheerfully. In the evening we returned to the village, complained to the cashiefs of the badness of the work, and noticed the approach of the ramadan, when it was probable we should no longer be able to get workmen, and therefore our present efforts would be useless. Both the brothers now promised us "a host of men next morning," and that they should begin early. While we were discoursing, some Mograbins, on their way from Cairo to Dongola, were introduced: we remarked their melancholy looks, but were then ignorant of the cause. Our business being at an end, we retired to our boat, after having feasted on doura cake and dripping.

July 14.—Rose early, and sent to the cashiefs that we were ready; but, after waiting for three hours, they sent word to us to go, and they would join us by land; so busied were they in plundering the Mograbins, that we and our temple were not thought of. We accordingly went, and found only fifty men, who were doing little more than nothing; and none of the leaders or attendants were present, except old Mouchmarr, an elderly servant of the cashiefs. We asked him the reason of his master's absence, when he said "that we must not think him a Barbarin; that he was an Arab, and only lived in this country by constraint; that both the cashiefs were robbers, and were at that moment pillaging the caravan of Morocco; and that the whole tribe of natives were nothing but a gang of thieves." We could not help laughing at the remarks of the old man, which, though true enough, would have come better from another quarter, as he himself was quite as great a rogue as the rest. At noon Daoud Cashief arrived. The men still continuing to work without any energy, we remonstrated with Daoud, but only received promises of great doings on the morrow. We returned to the village in the evening, when the men asked for the remainder of the money; this was refused, and in consequence there was much discontent. Halleel Cashief came and endeavoured to persuade us to pay the money; but we persisted in refusing till they should have worked the third day, according to their own promise. We were now told that if we paid the money, they would work the next morning; but if not, that not a man of them would come. We still refused. Halleel now asked for one of Mr. Salt's handsome pipes, which the crew had told him was in the boat; having previously begged the janissary to give him his silk waistcoat, and requested of our Greek servant his Mameluke sabre. This latter article belonged to Mr. Salt: it was very valuable; and to save it, we had pretended it was the property of the Greek, not thinking the cashief would condescend to beg of our servants. He had also asked the soldier for his pistols, offering him a slave in return;—all was however refused.

Tuesday, July 15.—Both cashiefs came, and some of the chiefs; one in particular, a stranger, was highly dressed, and we were told he was a leading character, and had much influence with the natives; that nothing could be done without him. But we had now seen enough of the character of the Nubians to perceive that this was only a trick to induce us to give the new comer some presents; and we therefore affected to take no notice of him, determined for the future to give no more than we could help. In the morning the men worked with some spirit: our crew assisted them, and behaved well; but towards evening the work went on badly. We returned to the village. On the way Hassan told us we must go back to Philæ, in order to repair the boat, which he asserted to be leaky. We soon gave him to understand that we had no intention of returning till we had accomplished our work. Soon after dark, Halleel came to the boat and repeated his request for the pipe, but was again refused.

Wednesday, July 16.—First day of the moon, ramadan or Turkish fast, during which they do not eat or drink from sun-rise to sun-set. Early this morning Halleel sent us a water-melon, and shortly after made his appearance, begging the pipe again, which, being worth upwards of sixty piastres, had greatly attracted his notice. This third attempt was evaded, and he set off in a pet, without even taking leave, mounting his horse for Derry, where he intended passing the ramadan. We now went to Daoud's tent to pay him a farewell visit previous to his departure. He asked us what were our intentions respecting the temple? We told him we were determined to work ourselves, and persevere till we came to the door. He appeared much surprised at this; and said it was impossible we could succeed, recommending us to return, and come again after the month of ramadan—hoping doubtless to get more presents. To convince him of our resolution to proceed, we told him that the Nile would as soon change its course, as we our determination when once it was taken. He now asked the sailors if we had solicited their assistance; when they told him we had not mentioned the subject to them, which indeed was true. He then asked when we thought we should reach the door. We told him that was very uncertain. He said if we thought we should be only three or four days, he would remain, but if more, he must be off. We answered that we expected it would be eight or ten days before our work was over; but we promised, that whenever we should be near the door, we would give him notice, that he might be present, and *get his share of the gold.* He gave a tacit sort of consent for us to proceed, and we took our leave, thanking him for what he had done for us. Amongst the warlike instruments in his tent, we observed a shield made of a crocodile's skin: it was remarkably strong; one of the protuberances of the animal's back served for the boss or centre, and one of those of the tail for the hollow of the elbow. The natives assured us it would resist a musket ball. In general, Nubian shields are made of the skin of the hippopotamus. At twelve o'clock we sailed for the temple; and on the passage took occasion to represent to the reis and crew, that now we were about to be left together, we hoped they would continue to behave well and conduct themselves peaceably, promising on our part every indulgence they could reasonably expect, provided we had no fault to find with them. They all promised to behave themselves orderly and quietly. We dined at one; and at three o'clock set off to begin our labour, going up quietly that we might not wake the crew who were asleep on the beach; as we wished, by an apparent indifference on our part as to whether they assisted or not, to keep down their demands. We now stripped to the waist and commenced, six in number, including the Greek servant and the janissary, with a good will, and soon found that we made considerable progress. We resolved to keep to our work, and regularly to persevere from three o'clock till dark in the evenings, and from the very first dawning of the day till nine in the mornings. After we had worked about an hour, some of the crew came up. They appeared astonished to see us labouring without our shirts, and expressed surprise at the progress we had made. They now began to assist, which we appeared to take no notice of. They worked well; and at dark we left off, having done as much as (speaking within bounds) forty of the natives would have done in an entire day. Our hands certainly suffered a little from blisters: I had nine on one hand, and eight on the other. We were careful to encourage our sailors, and not to expect too much from them; as their being prohibited from eating or even drinking during the day, rendered their case very different from ours. We returned to our boat in high glee at the favourable appearance of affairs. We had scarcely supped and retired to bed, when we heard a boat approaching. It proved to be that of Daoud Cashief, who was on his way to Derry: he had given a passage to one of our sailors, who had waited behind at the village to get bread made. He sent us a kid with a civil message, and a request that we would spare him some of our small coffee-cups, which were rather handsome. We sent him two; and at the same time requested of him a ludri (a skin to contain water), which he gave us. Lastly, a message came to say that he had left several of his servants behind him at Abou-Simbel, with orders to assist us with men; to procure us supplies and provisions; and, in short, to render us any service we might require. We thanked him, and renewed our promise of apprising him when we should be near the door, that he might not think we intended to open the temple secretly during his absence; for they all believe we expect to find money. Daoud now departed. We gave our crew two piastres each man, and one to each of the boys—there were six men and two boys—and told them that if they consented to work at similar hours, and in the same manner as we did ourselves, they should daily receive the same sum. These conditions were acceded to with great apparent eagerness.

Thursday, July 17.—We started at the dawn of day and worked hard, fourteen in number, till nearly nine o'clock, when the sun being at a considerable height, and shining directly on us, the heat obliged us to desist. We had made considerable progress; and as we found that all our efforts were directed in the right way, we had reason to be well satisfied. The crew worked tolerably. Hassan was on the opposite side of the river getting bread made, and looking out for a sheep. We dined at one, and at three renewed our operations. One of the crew did not come this evening. We took no notice of it, resolving to give him only half a day's pay. The rest worked pretty well. We continued till starlight, and made great progress. At the latter part of the evening, Hassan returned, but brought nothing with him.

July 18.—In the morning, at the very first dawning of day, we again started to our work and called the crew; but, as we expected, from the moment Hassan arrived, they all refused to work, alleging that the pay was not sufficient; that it was now ramadan, and that they ought to have thirty piastres per day. Our janissary now informed us that they had spoken of this aloud in the night in order that he might tell us. Seeing them in this humour, we told them that those who did not choose to work might let it alone. At half-past eight we left off, having done nearly as much work as if they had been with us: indeed we were astonished to see what steady persevering labour would do. One of the Abou-Simbel men came this morning and worked very fairly, promising to bring ten more on the morrow: there came also a chief from the opposite side of the river with an offer of twenty men. We told him our terms of two piastres per day for each man, and that it was our intention to pay the money into the men's own hands, as we learnt that the cashiefs and chiefs had given each labourer one piastre only, and retained the other for themselves. At three, we renewed our operations. A few of the crew came, but worked very badly;—we left off at dark.

Saturday, July 19.—We commenced our labours before daylight. Only two of the crew came, and three other lads. The promised men from Abou-Simbel and the opposite side of the river not arriving, we continued working till half-past eight; when, just as we were about to leave off, Halleel Cashief and his court of bullies made their appearance in a boat; and, landing near our bark, came up to see what was doing. Immediately we saw them approaching we left off work, and, suspecting their roguish intentions, to foil them we went to bathe. The men from the opposite side of the river, about thirty in number, now arrived, but without tools: this disappointed us a little. On coming out of the water, we went to visit Halleel Cashief, as a compliment, and to keep up appearances. While so doing, a desperate dispute took place between our janissary and Hassan, who seeing the former was not armed, chased him into the boat with his drawn dagger, uttering savage imprecations. Halleel made a pretence to interfere; but soon after, while we were settling the dispute, he sneaked away in his boat with all his attendants, without taking leave: indeed he was off before we were aware, and we were very glad to be rid of him.

Our Greek servant now informed us that Halleel had asked for some coffee; and, on being told there was none, had desired the servant to say nothing to us about his having asked for it. He was very inquisitive about the stay we intended to make; and seemed desirous we should call on him at Derry on our return, no doubt in hope of getting something more. The men worked pretty well to-day. The Abou-Simbel man, who had promised to bring his nine assistants, never made his appearance. This we clearly saw was Halleel's doing. At night, when paying the men, we had a dispute with some of them, who endeavoured to impose on us by false tickets. These tickets were slips of paper on which Mr. Belzoni wrote his name, and issued them out to the workmen in the morning; and on producing them in the evening they received their pay. This day the Darfur caravan, of four thousand camels, laden with gum, ivory, ostrich-feathers, tamarinds, rhinoceros' horns, slaves, &c., passed on their way to Cairo. The mamelukes had made them pay 9000 dollars (upwards of 2000*l.*) at Dongola. Some of the jelabs who led the caravan came to see our operations. They had long hair greased with oil, and hanging down in ringlets: some had it plaited. They wore sandals, had each a long spear, and altogether were singular figures.

Sunday, July 20.—At twilight we renewed our labours, and had sixty-four men to work. The crew stimulated them by a good example, which, coupled with our own personal attendance, produced a good morning's labour. At three p.m. we recommenced our operations and got on tolerably well. This evening one of Daoud Cashief's *staff* arrived, with some aqua vitæ and a few dates as a present. He also brought Irby and me some new Nubian clothes. Two suits cost us twenty-four piastres, or twelve shillings; double what we had given for better things of the same kind at Momfalout. In the evening our cook threw a kettle of water in the face of a fellow who asked him for money in a threatening manner. This truly cook-like mode of assault unsheathed the Barbarin's sword (for the most trivial occurrence produces their drawn weapons), and it was with difficulty we could prevent some serious mischief from ensuing. At night Daoud Cashief's messenger left us, having failed in an attempt to beg a pipe for his master.

Monday, July 21.—This day no men came from the opposite side of the river, but we had about forty from Abou-Simbel. They worked tolerably well, and brought to light the bend of the right arm of the statue, to the north of the door, which was much broken. The discovery was highly satisfactory to us, as it proved that the statues were seated, and, consequently, that we should not have to dig down so deep as if they had been standing figures. In the evening, the men worked pretty well; and towards the close of the day, we uncovered a projecting part of the wall roughly chiselled, uneven in its surface, and having every appearance of unfinished work. As far as we could see down, which was not more than six or eight inches, it still continued the same. The projection was about four inches from the plane surface of the front of the temple, and it appeared to fill up the whole space between the two centre statues. This being exactly the place where we expected to find the door, the sudden change from a flat finished exterior to a coarsely-chiselled uneven surface, was precisely the circumstance most calculated to give the impression that the temple was unfinished, and that there was no door. Indeed we could not in any other way account for an appearance so extraordinary and unexpected. Discouraging as this discovery was, we nevertheless resolved to proceed with our work, and to dig down till we had ascertained, beyond all possibility of doubt, whether there was an entrance or not.

About eleven o'clock at night, a boat arrived from the opposite side. They did not make any noise; but the reis sent word that he had brought a sheep for us. The message was accompanied with the present of a water-melon.

Tuesday, July 22.—At daylight we found a great assemblage of people, the boat having brought them over in the night; and at the same time there arrived a considerable number of persons from Abou-Simbel. As these two parties amounted to treble the number we wanted, we retired to our boat to avoid disputes, leaving thirty tickets with old Mouchmarr, with instruction to employ only that number. Returning in about half an hour, we found he had only given out twenty of the tickets, keeping the other ten to himself; and so intending to pocket twenty piastres. While we were settling this with the old rogue, a violent quarrel ensued between the natives of Abou-Simbel and the party from the opposite shore, as to who should be employed; and, after much noise and confusion, hostilities having commenced in a slight degree between the parties, the whole of them, amounting to nearly two hundred, departed, shouting and hooting, the stronger party not permitting the Abou-Simbel people to work. As they retired, our crew serenaded them with repeated cries of "barout, barout," which means powder, powder, an article they are not very partial to. In the evening we renewed our labours without any assistance; but soon had the crew and about twenty volunteers, who worked very well, considering we had only three implements, the Abou-Simbel men having taken away four out of the seven we had hitherto used. The instrument was of this form, and the mode of working was to fix it perpendicularly in the sand, and then to pull it forward by a cord attached to it; one person was stationed at the handle to fix it in the sand, and another at the cord by which it was pulled forward. Instead of one, the Arabs generally employed from four to six men at the cord. This evening we came to the chair of the statue; but still there was no indication of a door; the unfinished work continuing, though the figure, drapery and all, was perfectly finished, as far as we could see down.

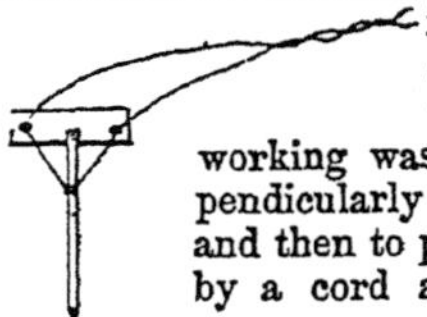

Wednesday, July 23.—It was curious to observe in the morning, on the smooth surface of the sand, drifted by the night breeze, the tracks of the snakes, lizards, and other animals, which had come down to the water's side during the night to drink; and we could plainly discern the traces of their return to their solitary haunts in the desert. Sometimes these tracts indicated the presence of reptiles of considerable size; and we now could easily account for the dread our guides expressed of walking near the water's side on the night we returned from the second cataract. We renewed our operations at the very first appearance of day, and soon had about twenty-six workmen, together with the crew. Between eight and nine o'clock, as the people were working, we perceived a boat full of men coming over from the opposite side. As soon as the Abou-Simbel people made them out, they all set off with old Mouchmarr at their head; the latter saying he knew who they were, and would go and treat with them, as they were coming to prevent our work. The old fellow, it appeared afterwards, was more intent on his own safety; as both he and his party went and hid themselves in caves in the mountains. Suspecting something, we sent for all our arms from the boat, and waited the event. The newly-arrived party now made their appearance, about forty in number, armed mostly with muskets, pistols, sabres, and pikes; they were much better dressed, and made a better figure than the attendants of Daoud and Halleel. There were two with white turbans, who appeared to be the leaders: these approached in advance of their attendants; and, after the usual salaams and ceremony of salute, seated themselves near us, and presented us with two sheep, which their men had brought with them. We now desired our janissary to ask them the intention of their visit, and to tell them we had nothing to dispose of, having given all we had to spare to the two cashiefs below. They replied that they wanted nothing; that they were in the employ of the pasha; that their office was to keep order and tranquillity in the country, and that they wished to know if any obstacles on the part of the inhabitants rendered their assistance necessary, as they were ready to be of service to us, hoping that on our return to Cairo, we should not fail to speak favourably of them to the pasha. We replied that we were going on tolerably well, and that we did not stand in need of any assistance. After sitting about half an hour, they went down to the other temple, followed by all their attendants, and soon after sent our Greek servant up with a message, "that they were at war with the other two cashiefs; that they were greater than they; that they were the governors of this country; that when the others killed one man, they could kill two; in short, that we had given a gun, shawl, soap, and tobacco, to both Daoud and Halleel, and why, they wished to know, was nothing given to them, who possessed double the authority in this country, and could prevent our labour whenever they pleased? that they must have the same, and more presents than we had already given, or that we should not open the temple." They also wished to know under what authority we acted, and desired to see our firman. We replied to these menaces by the same statement we had made on their arrival, viz. that we had already given away all we had to give; and we added, that as we had both the pasha's and Deftarda Bey's firman for doing what we were about, any violence offered to us would be sure to reach their ears. Their answer was that they cared nothing about the pasha. On seeing the firmans, they said they were good for nothing, being written in Turkish, not Arabic; that they had no Turkish interpreter; and that were the firmans even in Arabic, nothing but presents would induce them to permit us to proceed. The crew now thought it a favourable opportunity to ask for one of the sheep (for each of which we had given ten piastres), but we refused their request, saying, that they were mistaken if they thought it a proper time to ask gifts, when other people were endeavouring to plunder us; that as soon as the banditti were gone, and we were our own masters, we might give them something, but never through fear of them, or to gain their favour. Soon after, the two cashiefs and their gang proceeded to Abou-Simbel. We now learnt that they were Mahommed and Ali Cashief; that they lived a little above Derry, on the opposite side of the river; and were at war with Daoud and Halleel, in consequence of their grandfather (Hassan's father) having killed some relation of Ali's many years ago. This is what the Barbarins call the "warfare of blood for blood;" and it always lasts till an individual of one family is sacrificed to appease the other.* Sometimes this hostility exists for many ages between families; and it is for this reason that a murderer, who is one of our crew, dares not go to Philæ or the neighbourhood of Asuan, where he committed the crime.

At three P.M. we renewed our operations, and had a considerable number of assistants. It was truly ridiculous to see old Mouchmarr now make his appearance, with his matchlock in his hand, and a few of the Abou-Simbel people. He took especial care to examine both up the river and down, to be sure that the cashiefs were well out of sight; and when he found the coast clear, he came to us to relate how his people had been in the habit of making slaves and prisoners of the other party; what numbers they had bound together and thrown into the Nile, &c. We rallied him about his promising to treat with them. We found that the cashiefs had prevented many of our assistants from coming, and that they had plundered the whole country, taking two sheep from every sackey, and ten piastres from those who could not procure the animals. We also learnt that a fine of four dollars (thirty-six piastres) was to be levied on every one who came to our assistance. This evening our men worked very well; as they did not belong to Abou-Simbel, they knew they were out of the cashiefs' reach.

* "The revenger of blood himself shall slay the murderer." Numbers, xxxv. 19. "Ye shall take no satisfaction for the life of a murderer." Ibid. 31.

Thursday, July 24.—At dawn of day we went to work again; as we had broken our water-jars we asked the crew for our ludri which we had lent them; but Hassan said it was ramadan, and that as they could not drink water in the day-time, they wanted our ludri to keep it cool for them in the evening, and that they would return it when they got to Philæ. We gave them to understand that we liked cool water as well as they did, and desired the janissary to take the skin without further ceremony; asking them at the same time if that was gratitude for the sheep we gave them yesterday. Hassan answered, that the sheep was lean and good for nothing, or we should not have given it. This morning we had about twenty workmen, but neither Mouchmarr nor the Abou-Simbel men came. After we had worked about an hour, a party of about thirty came from the opposite side and volunteered to assist: as they were more than we wanted, and came late, we told them we would give them only one and a half piastre each: this they rejected at first, but afterwards accepted. An hour afterwards four other men came and solicited employ: these we refused, when one of them displaying a dirty white turban as a flag, drew the whole party off with a shout. In a quarter of an hour, however, they returned; and the work went on pretty well, the armed ruffians not making their appearance. In the evening the people worked badly, being so numerous that one skulked behind the other.

Friday, July 25.—We got up at dawn of day and found one hundred men assembled, though the night before we told them that we did not want any more assistance. We explained this to them again, adding, that at most we could not employ more than twenty. They replied, that we must employ them all or none. Seeing them in this mood, we returned to our boat, resolving to wait till they were all gone; and knowing that the heat of the sun at nine o'clock would drive them away. After much noise amongst themselves, and numerous ineffectual parleys, they all set off, taking all the implements with them, and threatening our crew that, if they assisted us, they would acquaint Daoud and Halleel Cashief of it; thus showing that these brothers had ordered that no assistance was to be rendered us. Our sailors laughed at them, saying, they cared nothing about the cashiefs or any one else. Soon after this, the whole rabble crossed the water, having a dirty white turban (the prophet's banner) hoisted. At three we renewed our work with six instruments which we had made ourselves. The crew, and also that of another bark came, and assistance was offered by a few others. We got on tolerably well.

Saturday, July 26.—At dawn of day we went up to our employment, with the same hands we had the preceding evening, in all about twenty-three persons. Our servants had another quarrel with the crew. A mameluke arrived from Dongola; he reported his countrymen in great misery at that place. We now learned that Mahommed and Ali Cashief were gone down the river again with their plunder. In the evening we renewed our operations. A man who had received money for our bread on the opposite side of the river, refused to bring it: we had a dispute in consequence, and, after much noise and confusion, half the quantity we had paid for was brought. We found the price of everything we bought had doubled since our arrival; the natives hoping by these means to force us to relinquish our work; and, with our eyes open, we were obliged to submit to the imposition.

Sunday, July 27.—At dawn of day we set to work again, and had only two assistants besides the crew, who worked remarkably well. Several volunteers came, but we rejected them on account of their laziness. One of our two assistants sang a song to cheer up the crew: this is their constant custom when working; the words were as follows: "Oh! Nubia, my country, thou smellest like a rose; when I sleep I dream of thee, and thou appearest a garden full of flowers." Our ideas of Nubia, where a flowering shrub is scarcely ever seen, were not in unison with this song; but it was a new proof of that happy disposition which nature implants in the breast of every man to love his native soil, be it what it may.

> "The naked negro, panting at the line,
> Boasts of his golden sands and palmy wine:
> Basks in the glare, or stems the tepid wave,
> And thanks his gods for all the good they gave.
> Such is the patriot's boast where'er we roam,
> His first, best country, ever is, at home."

At three o'clock we recommenced our operations. While we were working, a spy arrived from Daoud Cashief, who, after having deliberately examined us, began talking to the crew to draw them off from the work, and asked old Mouchmarr, who had just arrived from the village with some bread, how he dared assist us; adding, that the cashiefs would cut off his head for it. This news did not appear very agreeable to our friend, who now desisted from working. Our young mameluke friend, who understood the Barbarin language unknown to the crew and natives, told us of this. The spy next informed us that a firman had arrived from the Grand Signior to supersede the pasha in his government, and that new troops were now at Cairo. So paltry an attempt to alarm us was met by a hearty laugh, which made both the spy and his countrymen look very foolish; until, seeing the joke went against them, they put it off by a laugh also. In the evening old Mouchmarr came to be paid for his bread; and, on being asked to bring more, said he did not like to tell us a falsehood—that he had strict injunctions against bringing anything more, or, indeed, rendering us any further assistance. We further learned, that the whole of the natives on both sides of the river had mutually agreed that nothing was to be sold to us; but it was hinted that we might have some men to work if we chose: however, as our money was getting low, and we found that we did almost as much without as with them, we sent word that we wanted none of them: we had three days' bread, and our work had arrived at such a point that we should soon ascertain whether there was any door or not: we felt ourselves, therefore, quite independent of our troublesome neighbours. Mouchmarr now took his leave. It is but justice to the old man to say that he behaved better than any of his countrymen.

Monday, July 28.—We commenced our operations at the usual hour, with only our sailors and the mameluke, no Abou-Simbel men making their appearance. All worked pretty well. This morning no milk was brought. We affected to take no notice of this; and at breakfast were particularly careful that the crew (who came down and were watching us narrowly, to see what effect the want of this luxury would have upon us) should observe no change in our manner, that they might report to the natives the poor success of their scheme. At three we renewed our labours. While working, an Abou-Simbel man came to see what was going on. He said, that if we wished it, a certain number of people would come from each sackey to assist; and he asked us if we wanted provisions. We refused all assistance. He then asked if we could live on stones. We replied, that we had a boat, and could go and fetch whatever we wanted, and that money would always procure something. He now said we might think ourselves fortunate in having a soldier of the pasha's with us; as, were it not for fear of the consequences, in case anything should happen to him, the whole body of natives would prevent our work by force. We replied, that we were determined to proceed; and that even were the soldier not with us, we would persist in our undertaking. He now began to brag of the number of armed people they could muster from the neighbourhood: we, however, laughed at him; and he left us, having failed in all his designs. Our crew this evening worked very well; and we thought it good policy to tell them we noticed their exertions.

Tuesday, July, 29.—At dawn of day we recommenced our labours with the crew, and made considerable progress. No strangers made their appearance; the one who assisted us yesterday being deterred by the threats of the spy. In the evening, at three, we renewed our work. Towards the close of day, the sailors requested to be dismissed, that they might go to Abou-Simbel to get bread for themselves. We suspected some bad intentions on their part, but said nothing. Hassan had previously endeavoured to steal some of our doura (for bread we had none); but we were too sharp for him, and made his boy give us back what he had taken.

Wednesday, July, 30.—At twilight we went to work again; the crew coming as usual. This morning a man brought us milk again; but said he was obliged to do it clandestinely. This was a real luxury; as we found, after four hours' hard work on an empty stomach, that a limited ration of doura grain, dried dates, and water, to which we were now reduced, was not very sumptuous fare. The reis of the bark, who had before cheated us of our bread, now made his appearance with some spirituous liquors, which he said he had brought as a present from the wife of Daoud Cashief. We clearly saw that this was a trick to get a present for the bearer, which is expected to be double the value of the article given. We therefore refused it as a gift; but offered to purchase it. After some hesitation he consented. It was the spirit distilled from the date; but without the addition of aniseed, which in Egypt makes it palatable. We generally took a little before dinner as a tonic; for, without something of the kind (the average of the thermometer being 112° Fahrenheit in the shade), we found that we had no appetite. As soon as he had got his money he took himself off to the other side of the river, having evidently come to see if we yet began to complain of the want of provisions. But although we had nothing to eat but doura, and only enough of that for four days, we never once mentioned the subject to him. This evening we came to a projection, evidently a cornice, though much broken by the shock of an immense block of stone that had fallen on it Beneath the projection, we found a plane and smooth surface, and a tablet of neat hieroglyphics, highly finished, carved upon it. This strong indication of a door cheered us greatly.

At three we returned to our operations; and, by digging down and carrying away the sand in two boxes, we removed a sufficient quantity to make out about a foot of a tablet surmounted by a torus, and one end of a broken cornice above it; which, having been broken by some accident, had evidently been chiselled away subsequently, with the design of renewing it. The furrowed surface, and the marks of the tools in all directions, though rude and unfinished, prove this to be the case; and thus the mystery of the unfavourable appearances which had formerly given us so much uneasiness was cleared up. This evening Hassan asked, with more than usual impudence, for the pay of the crew, adding, that he wanted it before it was dark.

Thursday, July 31.—At twilight we resumed our task, and palisadoed the part which we supposed to be immediately over the door, by driving in piles of date trees, and pouring at the back of them mud mixed with sand, to keep the outer sand from running in between them. Just as we were going to leave off work, some armed men came from the opposite side of the river, who had been called over by Hassan: when we inquired the reason of his sending for them, he said he wanted the boat from the opposite side, to go and get some provisions for the crew. Our sailors talked freely with the strangers, who appeared very intent on what we were doing. This day the mameluke took his departure for Cairo. He went on a small reed raft which a Nubian was conducting down the river. Hassan ran with great eagerness to send some message by the Nubian: no doubt to apprise the cashiefs below of the progress of our work.

In the evening we resumed our labours, with the crew and two strangers; and towards sun-set we came to the corner of the door: it was rather broken. The sailors, on seeing it, expressed great signs of joy, uttering cries of "backsheeish, backsheeish," and immediately asked us if it was not true, that we had promised them money whenever we should find the door. We replied, that we certainly had promised them a present, and would give it when we had entered the temple. The fellows now began working hard to enlarge the entrance, appearing in high good humour, and occasionally repeating the favourite word "backsheeish," tyep, tyep—good good. At dusk we had made an aperture nearly large enough for a man's body; but we could not tell whether it would be necessary to draw up the sand from the entrance or not, which left us in great uncertainty as to the time when our labours would end; for, should the temple be much filled with sand, we might have a prodigious deal of work to do yet. When we returned to the boat, Hassan told Captain Irby and myself, it was totally impossible we could ever get into the temple by palisadoing; that the sand would fall on us as fast as we dug down, and that it was like attempting to dig into the Nile: at the same time he offered to forfeit his beard if we succeeded. All the crew joined in the same assertion. But we knew that it was the only method of getting at the door, unless we cleared it altogether, which would have taken a good month more.

We resolved to begin the next morning by moon-light, and apprised the crew of our intention, that they might not think we wanted to steal in by ourselves, and thus bring away *the gold* unknown to them. As the day's discovery had put us all in good humour, our sailors attempted to profit by it. They asked our cook for his new silk waistcoat, and begged of the Greek his new blue gown. From us they did not solicit anything further, thinking it best to wait till they got our backsheeish.

CHAPTER II.

Renewed Complaints of our Crew—We effect an Entrance into the Temple—Statues found in it—Colossal Statues in the Front—The Interior of the Temple—Paintings on the Walls—Description of the small Temple—We start on our return—The Cashiefs—Temples at Derry—At Armada—At Sabour—At Offidena—At Dekki—At Garbe Girshe—At Garbe Dendour—Unable to visit the Temple at Kalapsche—Ruins at Hindaw—Temple at Daboude—Present from our Crew—Philæ—General Observations on Nubia and its Inhabitants.

At moonlight on Friday morning, August 1st, the anniversary of the battle of the Nile, we rose and went to work. We called the crew; but, as they did not appear in any hurry to come, we went up alone with lights. While making our arrangements to begin, we heard a great noise below, plainly distinguishing Hassan's roaring voice above all the rest; and the word backsheeish frequently repeated. The Greek servant being sent down for a lamp, returned with an account that they were all abusing us; and complaining that, after having worked hard for us, they only received two piastres per day, instead of four, which they merited (although their wages from the reis are only from seven to nine piastres per month). We were called christian dogs without faith; and they said we must take all our things out of the boat immediately, as they would stay no longer, having remained till they were tired, and in a place where they could get no provisions. Mr. Belzoni now went down to find our hammer which was mislaid; but resolved to abstain from any argument with them. Immediately on seeing him they all fell down on their knees, and began praying, bowing down, and kissing the ground, according to their custom. He took no notice of them; but brought all our arms and ammunition up. The janissary also went and brought his pistols; Hassan saying in his hearing, that he must carry a soldier on his back to Derry, implying that he must murder the janissary, though it was but the day before that he came to him saying that he wished to make peace, and that what he had formerly said against him came from his warmth of temper, and not from his heart.

As soon as we had commenced working by candlelight, one of the crew came to say that we must embark immediately and depart, or land our effects and let the boat go, as they could wait no longer. We sent word that they might go whenever they pleased; but it would be to their own loss if they did, as we would pay them nothing; and that for our part we were determined to remain till our work was completed. The crew now made their appearance in a body, dressed in their turbans and gowns, as at Elpha; this being their custom when they wish to appear of consequence. They were armed with long sticks, pikes, swords, daggers, and two old rusty pistols, which would be more likely to kill the person who fired, than him who was fired at. In reply to our inquiry of what they wanted, they made long complaints of being badly paid, and of never having received any adequate recompense for having brought us provisions from the neighbouring villages, and for all their other endeavours to please us; that they had waited here till the last moment, and must now go down the river; all at the same time joining in savage imprecations, and scraping the sand with their hatchets and swords. The reis, who was the foremost of the party, in a feigned paroxysm of anger, threw the sand up in his face, where the perspiration caused it to stick.* At the same time we were accused of calling out "barout, barout," to the Abou-Simbel people, though it was themselves that first taught us the meaning of that word.

As all this farce was performed to intimidate us, and to extort a sum of money as a reward for remaining till the temple was opened, we took care that they should see by our conduct that the scheme entirely failed. Avoiding, therefore, all passionate behaviour, we replied coolly and deliberately to all their lying imputations, telling them that if they studied their own interests, they would behave very differently; that this, of all others, was the most unlikely method to obtain any thing from us; and that, as they had stayed ninety-nine days, why not remain the hundredth? At length one of the crew stepped forward, and pretended to be a peace-maker. The janissary, meantime, had squeezed himself through the whole, and entered the temple during the debate, unknown to them; till one of the strangers, having stolen behind to see what work we had done, found it out, and apprised the crew. Seeing themselves foiled in every way, they now pretended to suffer the mediator, with some reluctance, to disarm them; and then, stripping, began to work, laughing and repeating tyep, tyep — good, good, Berby tyep (berby means temple). We deemed it our best policy to suppress our feelings, and appear reconciled. Hassan had told the cook that they could murder us all if they chose; that neither law nor justice were known in this country; that they could, after committing the crime, fly to the mountains, where no one would pursue them; that they were not the *poor people* we took them for; that they had kept the French at bay four years; that they kept their own slaves, cattle, &c. &c.

We were now enabled to enter the temple; and thus ended all our doubts and anxiety. We built a wall to barricade the door: it was made of stones and mud, with a foundation of date-trees driven in to prevent the sand from giving way. A toad crept out of the temple while we were thus employed, and hid himself in the rubbish at the entrance. We brought down to the boat some statues of calcareous stone, which we found in the temple. There were two sphinxes, emblematical of Osiris (lion's body and hawk's head); a monkey similar to those over the cornice, only smaller; and a kneeling female figure, with an altar, having

* "They cried out, and cast off their clothes, and threw dust into the air."—Acts, xxii. 23.

a ram's head on it, in her lap. At three we went to work again. Two of the Abou-Simbel peasants came, and appeared astonished that we had succeeded. They said the country people had no idea we should have accomplished our undertaking. They appeared to think the temple would make a good hiding-place for their cattle, &c., whenever the Bedouins came to rob them.

Saturday, August 2.—We continued working at the wall before the door. Hassan asked for some of our money to go and purchase a sheep, stimulated, no doubt, by the expectation of the share they always had, viz. the entrails, skin, and head, none of the former of which the crew rejected: indeed, on one occasion, I saw one of them gnawing the raw head as they were skinning the animal. Having no provisions left but doura, a grain not unlike pearl-barley, we told Hassan it was to no purpose to bring us meat when we had no bread; and that unless he brought the latter, we did not wish for the former. He now took the money, promising to bring us bread also. We did not employ the sailors this evening, having finished the wall. Hassan was roaring and grumbling all day about money, in hopes that his bawling would induce us to give more. We took no notice of him, determined to give none until they had put the statues into the boat; for we perceived there was a great difficulty made about removing them. This day all the measurements of the temple were taken, both externally and internally; Captain Irby and I undertaking this task, while our companions were employed about their drawings. Towards the close of the evening, the man brought us some cakes of doura and a sheep, for which, however, he made us pay thirteen piastres, a third more than the articles were worth.

Sunday, August 3.—This morning some Abou-Simbel people brought us some butter and a lamb. We told them, however, that now they might keep their provisions to themselves. In the evening the crew, after much disputing with Hassan (who was against the measure), put the statues into the boat; this being the condition on which they were to receive the backsheeish. Soon after this we gave them a present of forty piastres amongst them. We had considerable difficulty in satisfying them; for the reis, on perceiving the money, snatched it up, saying *it was his share*. We, however, took it from him, and distributed it according to our original plan.

I shall now give some further particulars respecting the exterior of the temple, and then proceed to notice the most prominent beauties of the interior. The four colossal figures in front of the temple are all of men; they are in a sitting posture, above sixty feet high, and the two which we have partly uncovered, are sculptured in the best style of Egyptian art, and are in a much higher state of preservation than any colossal statues remaining in Egypt. They are uncovered at present only as far as the breast. Before the recent excavations one of the faces was alone partly visible, and part of the head-dress of the other remaining two. The face of the statue, No. 2, whether taken in the front view or profile, exhibits one of the most perfect specimens of beauty imaginable. It has so far resisted the effects of time, as not to have the least scratch or imperfection; and there is that placid serenity which one admires in most of the Egyptian countenances. The face of the statue, No. 3, has a more serious aspect; the nose is not so aquiline, nor is the mouth so well turned: it is not, however, without its beauties, and perhaps a connoisseur would say the features possess more character than the former. The statues are not, however, without their imperfections; the necks are short, out of all proportion, and the ears are placed considerably too high, a defect very common amongst the Egyptian figures; the bodies also seem to lean rather too much forward for the natural position of a sitting figure. However, it is scarcely fair to pass judgment on this latter defect, as, being partly uncovered, they could not be seen to proper advantage.

Little or no space appears to have been left between the figures on either side, and scarcely more in the centre than sufficient for the door. Immediately above the door, which was formerly surmounted by a cornice, now broken, is a tablet of hieroglyphics, over which is an oblong square niche enclosing a standing figure of a hawk-headed Osiris, in full relief, projecting no more than the depth of the niche itself. On the head of this figure is a globe; and below, on each side of the legs, are two symbols, which appear suspended from its hands; one is a small female figure, the other a staff surmounted with the dog's or fox's head. On either side of the niche is a female figure in intaglio, presenting an offering to the deity; and there are various hieroglyphic inscriptions, probably descriptive of the oblations. The cornice above the door presents a very curious appearance; it has been broken by a fall of part of the rock above, and the chisel has since been evidently employed to form the remaining part into some other shape, or to fashion it for the reception of a new cornice, or some other ornament of that description.

The interior of the temple is 154 feet long, by 52 broad (exclusive of the side chambers); it is comprised of fourteen separate apartments, whereof the first is the principal hall, 57 feet by 52; the second an ante-chamber, 37 feet by 25; the narrow chamber, crossing the other two, 37 ft. by 9 ft. 11 in.; after which comes the sanctuary, 23 ft. 7 in. by 12 ft. 3 in.; the rest are side apartments, placed in various directions. The interior of this temple is a work not inferior to any excavation in Egypt or Nubia, not even excepting the tombs of the kings: indeed, the effect produced on first entering it is more striking than any which those can afford: the loftiness of the ceiling; the imposing height of the square pillars, and of the erect colossal statues, full 30 ft. high, attached to them; and the dimensions of the apartments, which are on a much larger scale than any of the other excavations; all contribute to render the interior of this temple not less admirable than its splendid exterior.

The sculpture on the walls is not so well finished, nor the colouring so perfect, as in the tombs of the kings; but the composition and invention of the design, and its spirited execution, may be considered as equal to anything in Egypt. The extreme heat and closeness of the apartments, occasioned by the want of a free circulation of air, have contributed materially to injure the paint; but enough of the colouring still remains to enable the spectator to judge of what is lost, and to convince him of the original beauty of the work. The most conspicuous groups appear to represent the victories of some celebrated hero, apparently the same who is depicted at Medinet Aboo, Luxor, Carnack, and other parts of Egypt, together with the triumphant processions and consequent offerings to the deities. There is little difference in these groups from the similar sculptures in the buildings above-mentioned: the hero appears in the same manner in his car; he is of a gigantic stature, and is destroying his enemies with his arrows. The vanquished suing for mercy; the discomfiture and flight of their companions; the procession of the prisoners, and the distribution of the other parts of the groups, are likewise nearly the same. The prisoners seem to be of different nations from those represented in other places; and it is a circumstance of no little interest to see here, thus accurately painted, the costumes of the various tribes of the interior of Africa, at a date so remote that nowhere else can we expect to find any description either of their manners or their customs. How interesting would a minute copy of these groups be to travellers in the interior of Africa, who could compare them with the inhabitants of the present day! Some of the captives are perfectly black, and have all the characteristics of the tribes of the interior of Africa—such as woolly hair, thick lips, long sleek limbs, &c.; others are of a lighter hue, not unlike the present race of Nubians. The most common dress consists of the leopard's and tiger's skin, fastened round the waist, while the upper part of the body remains uncovered. The cap which they most commonly wear is of a construction which I do not recollect to have observed elsewhere, and appears to consist of the leaves of the palm-tree, dried and cut in slips; while the workmanship is a sort of neat plaiting, apparently worked with much ingenuity. Those who wear the caps have no hair, but some are distinguished by bushy hair and beards.

In one of the groups is represented the storming of a fortress, of very singular construction, which is defended by people of the race just mentioned. On the top are seen women, among whom, one in a sitting posture, wholly divested of drapery, and of a light complexion, bears no resemblance in character or attitude to those represented in other places by the Egyptians. The hero who directs the assault is, as usual, of gigantic stature. On the plain below are seen the peasants driving their cattle away from the presence of the conqueror, designed with much spirited action; some of the besieged party are also kneeling and imploring clemency. The arrows are flying from all quarters amongst the defenders; and some are seen plucking them from their foreheads, arms, and other parts of their body. Large stones hurled down from above, do not appear in any way to intimidate the attacking party. The group of twelve supplicating victims, which the hero is represented in another part as grasping with one hand by the united hair of their heads, while with the other he uplifts the axe to sacrifice them, is executed with much energy and force; and the marked difference of character in the several countenances of the various tribes they belonged to, is given in a masterly style: the expression of agony and despair in their several features is admirable.

In this temple we found several detached statues of calcareous stone; one of which, a little larger than life, is executed in a better style than is generally to be met with in Egyptian sculpture; the head and lower part of the legs are wanting, as well as one of the arms; but the remaining parts sufficiently attest the skill and good taste of the sculptor. The figure is an upright one, and seems to have represented Osiris, or the hero depicted on the walls. The surface of what remains is scarcely injured; but the substance of the stone is so decayed by time, that any attempt to remove it would probably occasion its total destruction. The statues which we brought away, and which I have already mentioned, were found in different parts of the temple.

How long this temple has been buried is a question which must ever remain unanswered. Forty feet of sand had accumulated above the top of the door, before the recent excavations, which were carried no further than 3 feet below the top of the entrance. There is reason to suppose that the temple was deserted before any sand had collected in front of it; but there is nothing either in the interior or exterior which indicates the age in which it was abandoned. Very little sand was found in the temple compared with what might have been expected: it did not reach beyond the second pilaster, and was not much broader than the door-way. This, no doubt, was partly owing to the great depth (18 ft. 11 in.) of the entrance-passage. A light black substance, which seemed to be decayed wood, was found in every apartment, in some places of the depth of 2 ft.; its substance, at the surface, was not unlike that of snow when it has been frozen over by one night's frost; it cracked under the foot, leaving the impression. Many small pieces of wood were strewed about, apparently little injured by time, but which, on being touched, crumbled into dust. The wooden pivots on which the doors traversed still remain in the upper corner of all the entrances to the different chambers; and we also found fragments of wood in many places. Some of these appeared so perfect, that we thought of bringing them away; but they mouldered at the first touch: we were, therefore, very careful in leaving what remained for the benefit of future travellers. A broken brass socket, for the pivot of a door to traverse on, was also found.

The extreme heat of the temple was such, that Mr. Beechey spoiled his drawing-book while only copying one of the groups, the perspiration having entirely soaked through it: it produces the same sensation and effects as the hottest vapour-bath. In the centre of the sanctuary is a bench with four sitting statues: the one on the right is Osiris, with the hawk's head and globe; the others are human figures: two have the crux ansata ♀ in their hand.

The eight standing figures of Osiris, 30 ft. high, which ornament the outer hall, and between which is the passage into the interior of the temple, are as well proportioned as they are highly finished: the drapery reaches nearly half-way down to the knees, and is striped like that of the figures without. The features of the countenances are perfect, and they all have the hook and scourge (the usual emblems of Osiris) in their hands, which are crossed on the breast.

I shall now describe what, speaking comparatively, we may call the small temple of Abou-Simbel. The direction of the river here is W.S.W. and E.N.E. Both the temples are situated on the left bank, at the ends of the two mountains which form the valley, through which the sand which has buried the great temple found its passage: both are cut out of the solid rock, which is of a sandy or calcareous nature. The easternmost and smallest appears to have been made before the other, as the style of the colossal statues which are sculptured in the front of it, are ruder than that of the large one, and have been cut in a less advanced state of the art. The front of the temple is not perpendicular, but sloping from the top to the bottom. Six square spaces are excavated in the surface, serving as niches to the same number of colossal figures, the remaining part being left in the form of buttresses projecting 10 ft. at the base beyond the inside of the niches. The door is in the centre, with three erect figures, one a female (Isis), with a male figure on each side of her: these latter represent Osiris. On either side, between these colossal statues, are two figures of about 6 ft. high, which reach nearly to the knees of the former: those supporting the male figures appear to represent Horus, while the others near Isis are females. The space left in the centre, and in which the door is cut, is more than twice the breadth of the other projections between the figures, and slopes on the same plane with them for about one-third from the top: it then descends somewhat more perpendicularly; and in this lower plane the door is cut, without any other projection. The points of the projecting buttresses are covered with hieroglyphics; and a single line of them extends along the top of the niches for the whole breadth of the temple, of which it forms the ornamental summit. Immediately above the door is an offering to Osiris; and on each side of it are hieroglyphics as on the other projections: a line of serpents and globes surmounts the offering, similar to what is often met with over the doors of Egyptian temples. The height of the projecting buttresses nearest the door is 34 ft. 7 in.; taken in the angle that of the others is 38 ft., their projection at the base 10 ft., that of the door only 7 ft. 6 in.; the distance between each buttress, 8 ft. 3 in.; breadth of the buttresses, 4 ft. 7 in. The height of the female figures is 24 ft. 6 in., not including the head ornament, which reaches to the top of the buttress. The male figures are 25 ft, 8 in. high, and their head-dresses 4 ft. 10 in. The height of the doorway is 11 ft. 6 in.; width, 4 ft. 10 in.; the length of the passage into the temple, 12 ft. 9 in. The whole width of the ornamented front of the temple is 88 ft., and its height, in a perpendicular line, may be about 40 ft.

The interior of the temple is composed of three principal apartments; the first and largest supported by six pilasters, three on each side, (surmounted with the head of Isis in the front,) is 36 ft. by 34; the space in the centre between the pilasters is 14 ft. 6 in., and they are 7 ft. 8 in. from the wall: the distance between the pilasters 5 ft. 9 in.; their dimensions 3 ft. 7 in. by 3 ft. 3 in. The breadth of the second chamber 8 ft. 5 in.; its length is the same as the first, taken at right angles with the line of entrance: the sanctuary is 7 ft. 10 in. by 8 ft. 9 in.: on each side of the second chamber is a small side apartment 6 ft. square.

I shall describe the decorations of the interior rather minutely, as there is more uniformity, and evident allusion to the deity to whom the temple is dedicated (Isis), than is generally met with. The interior of the porch is ornamented on each side by an offering to Isis from a human figure. Within the chamber, on each side of the entry, is a large figure having an axe in one hand, whilst with the other he grasps a bow, and holds a kneeling victim by the hair of the head. On either side are two human figures: that in front has a knife upheld, and appears to command the sacrifice; while that behind seems to preside over it with the lotus flower in her hand: the opposite side is the same, excepting that the figure commanding the sacrifice is Osiris. On the left, as you enter, the wall is embellished with, first, an offering to Isis; secondly, the initiation, by Jupiter Ammon and Osiris, of a young priest; thirdly, an offering by a female figure, of a small sistrum, surmounted by the head of Isis and the serpent, together with the lotus flower, to a male figure; fourthly, an offering to a male figure of a small sitting figure, with the crux ansata on its knees, which are raised up. On the right hand the wall is ornamented with, first, an offering of provisions to Osiris, with the scourge in his hand; secondly, an offering of the lotus flower and three water-pots, pouring water on other flowers, to Jupiter Ammon; thirdly, an offering to Isis of two small heads of that deity surmounting two short handles or staffs; fourthly, an offering to Osiris of two small water-vases. At the end, on one side of the door, is an offering to Isis of the lotus; and opposite is the same offering to a female figure. The inner chamber has offerings to Isis and Osiris, and the initiation of a priestess by two Isides; the sanctuary has a small figure, in alto-relievo, in a recess at the end.

Monday, August 4.—Early this morning we started on our return, and soon saw, on the eastern bank, Mahommed and Ali Cashief, together with the band of thieves that had attempted to plunder us. They hailed us, and asked if we had opened the temple, and how much money we had found in it. In the evening we called on Daoud Cashief, who protested his innocence of the transactions at Abou-Simbel, even before we had mentioned the subject. This was certainly not very wise in him; as nothing could tend more to prove his guilt: and, if further evidence were necessary, we saw amongst his train several of the principal spies and bullies that had annoyed us. It was, however, necessary to dissemble, and appear to credit him, as a contrary line of conduct could lead to no good; and, after receiving a present of a sheep, goat, and some bread, together with his promise to keep the temple open for Mr. Salt, we took our leave. When near Derry, we met Halleel crossing the water to be present at our interview with his brother, and thus get his share of anything else that could be squeezed out of us: he was, however, too late.

In the evening we arrived at Derry, and went to see the temple with candles. This temple is situated about a quarter of a mile from the town: it is cut in the solid rock, but is so much ruined that nothing perfect is to be seen. There has been a middling-sized hall, with eight square pilasters and four terms, with standing figures in alto-relievo. The latter seem to form a sort of portico to the principal chamber. The eight outer pilasters have fallen; but those of the portico are perfect, with the exception of the terms, which have all been broken off. Within is the principal chamber, 17 paces by 16, supported on each side of the centre by three pilasters; this latter leads to the sanctuary, on each side of which is a small chamber surrounded with benches. At the further end of the sanctuary are the marks of four sitting statues which have been chiselled off: they appear to have resembled those of the large temple of Abou-Simbel. In this temple the stucco and paint is imperfect, and the whole has a black and dismal appearance; but, to judge from the size and execution of the figures, &c., in intaglio, on the walls, it may once have been handsome. The dedication appears to have been to Osiris. There are boats, battles, sacrifices, &c., like those at Abou-Simbel.

We had just gone to bed this evening, when Halleel arrived. He sent us a present of some aqua vitæ, and a miserable sheep. All these presents are paid for at the rate of double their value.

Tuesday, August 5.—Early this morning Halleel came on board; when we told him, as we had his brother, that we had nothing left to bestow upon him, having given away everything we had to spare. All this while he was whispering to one of our sailors, asking, no doubt, if we had anything left, and whether it was true, that we had given nothing to his brother. He now examined attentively everything in the cabin; but as nothing was forthcoming, he took his leave, and we started also, glad to get rid of him and Derry too. It was here that poor Norden, eighty years ago, met with the treatment from Baram Cashief, which prevented his going farther up the river. This morning we visited the temple at Armada, and saw two gazelles near it. This temple is built in the desert (at least it is a desert now), not far from the river, on the opposite side from Derry, and about one quarter of the way between the latter place and Koroskoff. It consists of a hall, supported by twelve pilasters and four pillars, in four rows of four each; but as a wall of intercolumniation surrounds it, the detached pilasters and pillars within the hall are only six in number. Beyond the hall is a small cross chamber, 9 paces by 3, and within that is the sanctuary, which is 8 paces by 3. The interior of the latter is daubed over with plaster, and modern Greek paintings of the twelve apostles, saints, &c. Underneath this plaster, however, the ancient Egyptian figures and hieroglyphics, &c., in bas-relief, appear: they have been executed in a very superior style; and the colouring has been rich beyond description. There is a small chamber on each side of the sanctuary. The dedication is to Osiris. The sand has drifted into and nearly filled up the hall. Some modern sun-burnt brick ruins attached to the temple have probably been additions by the Greeks.

At noon we arrived at Sabour, and proceeded to inspect its temple, situated on the western bank, about 100 yards from the river side. It is built of calcareous stone, in a plain at the foot of the mountain, at present covered with sand. The approach to it is by an avenue of sphinxes, with two statues in a standing position at the end nearest the Nile, all of calcareous stone. At the further end of the avenue is a pylon, with two fragments of ill-carved statues, which have been thrown down: they are all full-length figures, and much dilapidated. On each side of the entrance within is a peristyle space, with four terms on either side; these appear to form the hall of the temple, which, being filled with sand, cannot be entered. The masonry is here much ruined; and there is not one perfect figure to be found. We observed that the hieroglyphics on the back of the two statues, nearest the temple, were the same as those on the frieze of the large temple at Abou-Simbel, with the difference only of being written vertically instead of horizontally. These hieroglyphics occur on either side of the crux ansata, which occupies the centre of the frieze: on one side they are written from right to left, and on the other from left to right. The hieroglyphics on the upper part of Cleopatra's needles at Alexandria, are exactly the same; and we noticed similar characters on the two great obelisks at Luxor.

Towards the close of the evening we had another quarrel with Hassan, who drew his dagger on Mr. Belzoni, uttering savage imprecations, and saying, that all who disbelieved in the prophet were dogs. We made a great effort to get him out of the boat; but the reis and crew adhered together so much, that we could not succeed. In this country it is difficult to chastise an insult; for should a traveller so far forget himself as to use a weapon against a Nubian, he would be sure to be sacrificed, as the whole country would rise against him, and escape would be impossible.* A pistol went off twice by accident in the boat during these unpleasant disputes; but, fortunately, did no harm; and Captain Irby had his hand much cut in wresting a dagger from Hassan, who, foaming with rage, was in the act of stabbing Mr. Belzoni. It is not a year ago, since a Russian was murdered a little above Derry: he was in company with another who escaped to Assuan; they were unfortunately unarmed. Our reis and one of the sailors quitted the boat in consequence of our last quarrel.

Wednesday, August 6.—We started at dawn on our voyage. About seven the reis returned. He now wanted to land the statues and leave them behind. This we told him he should not do; and advised him to beware what tricks he played us, as we would bring him to an account at Assuan, where, at least, there is some sort of government. Our young mameluke joined us this morning, having been robbed of his money and the reed-raft which he had purchased. About noon we inspected the small temple at Offidena, which has been left in so unfinished a state, that it is difficult to make much out of it. All that is at present to be seen is a small peristyle hall, with fourteen pillars; but neither the columns, their capitals, nor the sides of the hall, are finished. The Greek Christians had converted this temple into a chapel. On the ruined wall of a detached building, there are three figures, evidently not Egyptian. They are in intaglio, and are either of ancient Greek or Roman workmanship. They appear to represent an Egyptian, and a Grecian priest and priestess. In the same tablet is a figure of Isis, with Horus presenting her an offering.

The people came and crowded round us here, asking for backsheeish. As they demanded it in a very impertinent manner, we did not give them anything till we had explained to them that a more quiet mode of begging would have got them more money. We endeavoured here to purchase a statue, the same that we had attempted to buy on going up; but, after being detained about two hours, we were obliged to give it up.

In the evening we visited the temple at Dekki. The exterior and part of the interior of this temple have not been finished; but the basso-relievo in the interior bears every mark of having been executed by a skilful artist. Only one chamber, however, has been completed with stucco and painting. The whole building is on a small scale, but the plan is very neat; it is approached by a pylon, beyond which is a portico of two columns in front. Within this are three small but distinct chambers: the centre apartment is narrow, with a smaller one on each side. One of these has steps by which you may ascend to the top of the temple. The width of the building is narrower than that of the pylon, and a wall from the exterior of the latter surrounded it. The entrance of the pylon is covered with Greek inscriptions; amongst which, several commemorate the homage paid to the god Mercury, by Greek and Roman visitors; the latter under the reign of Tiberius Cæsar. This temple, like some others in Nubia, has been subsequently used as a Greek chapel, as appears by their daubed paintings. Other ruins are scattered about near the temple: probably those of some small town.

Thursday, August 7.—We started at dawn, and visited the temple of Garbe Girshe. The natives here have a very bad character. Last year they murdered a soldier of the pasha's, and not having been punished for it, have become remarkably insolent.

* This part of the country has, however, been since garrisoned and taken possession of by Mahommed Ali.

Seeing us all armed, and not being numerous themselves, they asked for backsheeish in a quiet manner, and we gave them some. This temple is principally an excavation in the rock, but has been fronted by a built portico or peristyle hall; of which four terms on each side, and two pillars in front, remain in a mutilated state. But there have been many more of the latter; and probably it was approached by a flight of steps preceded by an avenue of sphinxes, fragments of which still remain. The excavated chambers have a black and dismal appearance, and the interior ones have become the habitation of bats. In plan it is not dissimilar to the great temple at Abou-Simbel, but much smaller; and the sculpture is unusually bad and heavy. The first chamber is 19 paces by 18, and is supported by six terms, three on each side of the centre, with alto-relievo figures of Osiris in an erect posture; but, instead of the arms being across the breast, with the scourge in one hand and the hook in the other, as at Abou-Simbel, both the insignia are here in the right hand, which is uplifted, while the left hangs down: these are executed in a most heavy and unsightly manner. On either side of this chamber are four niches, in each of which are four alto-relievo figures. The second chamber is smaller, supported by two pilasters, one on each side of the centre. Beyond this is the sanctuary, which is small; the altar remains in it, and four sitting statues at the further end. There is a small chamber on each side of the sanctuary; and side apartments leading from the second chamber.

Towards sun-set we inspected the temple of Garbe Dendour. This is a small unfinished edifice. It is built with a small portico of two columns in front, and has two small chambers within it. The sanctuary at the back is an excavation in the rock, before which the temple is built. Before the building is a portal and a square space walled in, probably intended as a quay to protect the edifice from the river near which it stands—Garbe Merie. We passed this place without stopping, there being nothing but the broken wall of a temple with hieroglyphics on it.

In the evening we landed at Kalapsche, and went up to see the temple. Here we found all the natives collected together, armed with their daggers, to dispute the entrance. We demanded the reason of their being assembled in such numbers, and what they wanted: they said they must be paid before we entered the temple. We asked the speaker if he meant that he himself was to be paid, or who it was that we were to give money to. They all cried out, that we must pay every one of them. Now, as there were about sixty, and others were arriving, we thought it a bad speculation, and explained to them that we cared very little about going into the temple, as we had already inspected it; but that, if they chose to let us enter, we would give them a reasonable present when we came out. While we were settling this, our janissary thought fit to pick a quarrel with the natives, abusing them all, calling them thieves, and saying we would enter the temple by force. In consequence of this, they all rushed on him with their drawn daggers, and had nearly wrenched his musket from him, when, thinking it high time, we flew to his rescue, and, after much struggling, succeeded in regaining him his arms. We were now glad to get to the boat, being well hooted as we went down; and, on our shoving off, they pelted us with stones. We fired a musket over their heads, to show them that we had ammunition. Our Greek servant told us, that, while we were absent, one villain had entered the boat with a drawn sword, and was proceeding to plunder it, when, conceiving that this was carrying things a little too far, he pointed a loaded gun at the fellow's head, with a threat that he would lay him dead on the spot unless he desisted. This timely firmness caused him to quit the bark; the crew all the while not interfering or saying a word. We commended the Greek for his presence of mind; but had not so much reason to be satisfied with the janissary, whose unseasonable rashness alone prevented our seeing the temple; this was the more provoking, as higher up the river such a fit of valour might occasionally have been of use.

It is a great inconvenience to a traveller in this region that both servants and interpreters always think themselves wiser than their masters; and, therefore, when they are desired to say or do anything, always act according to the dictates of their own judgment, never letting their employer's wishes influence them. When interpreting they never tell you half what is said, and frequently when you explain something which you are anxious should be interpreted, they answer, "Yes, yes, I know it;" never thinking of telling the other party, but taking it for granted you are speaking for their information, not for the purpose of their explaining your words to others.

This evening we repassed the gates of Nubia. As the Nile was now high, and the river at this point is much contracted by the approach of the mountains on both sides, the rocks jutting down perpendicularly into the water, our crew, in the hope of obtaining backsheeish, made a great merit of taking the boat through the rapids; but, though noticing all that was going forward, we took care, by an assumed carelessness, to make them think that we were regardless of the whole proceeding, and thus escaped an additional tax.

This evening the current drove us past the two small temples of Teffa. Mr. Belzoni, who has seen them, says that only one of them is finished; it is dedicated to Isis, and is about 20 ft. square; it is in a dirty state, being used as a cow-house—not a bad application for a temple of Isis, to whom the cow was peculiarly sacred. The other, which is of the same size, and situated near the former (both being on the western bank of the river and near the water's edge), has never been completed.

Just before dark we went to visit Hindaw. The ruins in this quarter are very extensive, but nothing can be distinctly made out as to the nature of the buildings, which, whatever they may have been intended for, have never been finished. Beginning from the southward, the first object is a great square, situated on a bed of rock surrounded by an unfinished wall, built of immense blocks of calcareous stone. On the north side, in the middle, there is a portal similar to those by which the Egyptian temples are generally approached: the top of the door-way is ornamented with the winged globe, and a figure of Isis, in basso-relievo, appears half finished on the side of it. It is not improbable that this wall (which incloses a space about half-a-mile square) may have been intended to surround several temples; its extent being too great for us to suppose that only one was intended to be constructed within it. Further north is an extensive quarry, from which, it is probable, the stone for these buildings was obtained. Within this quarry we perceived a doorway carved in the Egyptian style; and on each side of it a convexity, as if it had been intended to carve out pillars. There is also a niche, with a bust of Roman execution on each side, and forty-two very perfect Greek inscriptions, written in the time of the Romans, to commemorate the visits of various generals, and other persons of distinction, who had come here to pay their vows. Mr. Bankes copied all these. To the northward of the quarry, on an eminence, is a small unfinished portico, of two pillars on each side, and two in the front; the capitals are finely executed: those of the former combine the lotus flower with the vine, date, and doura grain; the latter have a quadruple head of Isis.

Friday, August 8.—At noon we inspected the temple at Daboude; it is situated about two hundred yards from the river side, and is altogether unfinished. The approach is by three portals. The temple consists of a portico, composed of four columns in front, and a wall of intercolumniation reaching half way up the pillars. Within, there are two chambers and a sanctuary: the latter contains two handsome monolithe cages of red granite, between 6 and 7 feet high, and about 4 broad; these are the only objects of interest which the temple contains. Towards the river side, on the banks, are the remains of a quay. To-day the murderer quitted the bark, not daring to show himself near Philæ: he did not appear ashamed of the crime which he had committed.

In the evening our crew stopped at their village, and brought a scabby, half-starved lamb as a present to us. We could not forbear from laughing, as it was really the most pitiful animal we had seen in the country; and it must have put them to no small trouble to find such a specimen. We refused the present most stoutly, but it was all in vain; they forced it into the boat. At three we arrived at Philæ, called by Hamilton and Burckhardt, Giesiret el Berbe el Ghassir, or Giesiret Anas el Wodjoud. The first of these names means the Island of ruined Temples—not an inapt denomination. Philæ is the easternmost of a group of islands and rocks which compose the first cataract. It is about half-a-mile long, rather high, and, being entirely covered with magnificent ruins, has a grand and imposing appearance: the lofty pylons are seen at a great distance, and produce a fine effect. The island divides the Nile into two streams, and the water, finding so great an impediment in its course, rushes by with considerable velocity. The principal edifices are approached by an avenue formed on each side by a gallery supported by columns, the capitals of all which are different. There are thirty of these pillars on the left, and on the right only sixteen, with cells (probably the habitation of the priests) within them; the greater part of these last-mentioned columns are finished, but there are some incomplete. These show that the columns were first constructed and erected in the rough, and that the sculpture was finished afterwards. The rough outlines which we found traced were very curious; and, neatly as all the capitals are sculptured, the artist who finished them had but a rough and coarse pattern to guide him. The difference in the number of columns in the two galleries is occasioned by a small temple having been situated at each end of the one on the right: these temples are now entirely ruined. At the end of the avenue is a large pylon, formed by two moles. The entrance in the centre has had two lions, and two small obelisks of red granite, ornamented with hieroglyphics, before it. It is on the pedestal of one of these latter that Mr. Bankes discovered the Greek inscription; and it is on the doorway of this pylon that the inscription was written, announcing that this island was the boundary of the French conquests in Egypt, and consequently of their progress up the Nile. The following is a verbatim copy of it:—

"République Françoise, An 6, Le 13 Messidor. Une Armée Françoise commandée par Bonaparte est descendue à Alexandrie. L'Armée ayant mis, vingt jours après, les Mamlouks en fuite aux Pyramides, Dessaix, commandant la première Division, les a poursuivis au-delà, jusqu' aux Cataracts, où il est arrivé le 13 Ventose, 3 Mars. Les Généraux de Brigade." Here follow the names.

"An 7 de la République, de Jes. Chr. 1799."

It was in the portico of this temple that we noticed the elephant as an hieroglyphic. This is the only instance of our finding this symbol in the country. The portico leads through the left end of the great pylon, after which there is a handsome court or hall, and then you enter the temple.

We here first noticed a singular imperfection or peculiarity in the sculpture of the large figure of Isis in the great pylon—she has two *left* hands. We have since observed the same singularity in other places. The French work has given some of them. In all parts of the island, on the sides of the temples, are Greek inscriptions, commemorating the worship of Greek and Roman generals who have come to pay their vows to Isis and Serapis. Philæ is said to have been the spot where Isis was appeased of her wrath for the violence offered by Typhon to her husband; and hence we find no less than four temples dedicated to her in so small a compass.

Before I quit Nubia, I will add a few observations on the country and its inhabitants. At present only two English travellers have been in this country. Mr. Hamilton, Colonel Leake, and Captain Hayes, visited Daboude, but were prevented from advancing further by the united efforts of the cashiefs, and the mameluke bey, Elfi. Mr. Hamilton's book contains the result of the mission into Upper Egypt. The French had penetrated only as far as Philæ, where they left the inscription just given. Several years elapsed before any European travellers entered Nubia, when Burckhardt led the way, and was followed by Mr. Legh and Mr. Bankes:—the former has published.

Immediately after passing the first cataract, the traveller observes that the Mockatem and Lybian chains of mountains close in upon the Nile: this remark is applicable, with few exceptions, throughout Nubia, at least as far as we went; there is, consequently, only a narrow strip of cultivated land on either bank of the river. The ancients, to preserve the soil and prevent the rapid stream from washing away the land, constructed immense walls, or, more properly speaking, piers, built of huge masses of stone piled one on the other, and reaching into the river from the foot of the mountain, or rather the limit of the Nile's rising, to the point of the water's lowest ebb. These piers are invariably built at right angles with the stream, and are generally about 15 ft. wide. As they are very numerous, and as the labour and expense of their construction must have been prodigious, some idea may be formed of the importance that was attached to them. From the number of temples, and from the fine plains of loamy soil, now generally covered with a surface of sand a foot thick, which makes them look like the rest of the desert, there is every reason to suppose that this country was once both populous and flourishing. At the time of the height of Egyptian power, it was considered as an integral part of the state; this is evident from the figures and devices in the temples resembling in every respect those of Egypt. Of the land in Nubia which might be cultivated, I do not suppose one-fourth is made use of; this indifference to agricultural pursuits proceeds from the despotic nature of the government, where the authorities think of nothing but making the most of their situations whilst they hold them, consequently their sole aim is to get money, no matter how it is procured. A licentious soldiery are ever ready to contribute to the oppression of the inhabitants, more especially when the funds from whence they derive their own pay and emoluments are drawn from this source. This observation applies to Egypt as well as to Nubia, only that the fact is more easily perceived in the latter country. The consequence is, that the date palm, the fruit of which ripens without cultivation, and which pays no duty, is here more encouraged than any other production, and the date may safely be called the staple of the country. The doura, which is the Holcus arundinaceus of Linnæus, is the only grain to be met with; it makes very good bread, but they grow barely sufficient for their own subsistence: indeed, it is so prized, that they frequently prefer it to money in payment for the articles we purchased. The miri, or land-tax, is paid at the rate of ten dollars per sackey, consequently every sackey which the Nubians build becomes an additional inducement to the Turks to come into their country; and it is only the scantiness of the produce which deters the pasha from quartering his troops on them; this the crafty natives are well aware of, and take care to put no temptation in his way. The present mode of collecting the miri in Nubia, is by sending thither annually about two hundred Turkish soldiers in boats, and the money they get hardly defrays the expenses of the expedition. The duty is not paid in cash, but in doura, which they purchase back from the Turks; but they generally contrive that the soldiers do not return very full-handed. These soldiers usually make Derry their head-quarters, and remain about six weeks in the country, during which time the cashiefs retire into the mountains, and the natives conceal their arms, which are always taken from them whenever they are found. In several parts of Nubia we noticed the sites of ancient towns, indicated, as in Egypt, by mounds of rubbish.

As we resided longer in the country, and had more dealings with the natives than any other Europeans have ever had, I shall subjoin a few remarks regarding them. The Nubians are a very distinct race of people from the Arabs. Their dress is commonly a loose white shirt and a turban; sometimes they are uncovered, except a cloth round the waist. They are very superstitious, most of them wearing charms to keep off "the evil eye," or other apprehended ills. These charms consist of some words written on a scrap of paper, and sewn up in leather; they are worn mostly on the right arm over the elbow, and sometimes round the neck. All the cashiefs we saw had them, and one Nubian dandy had nine of these appendages. These people pride themselves on their cunning schemes to deceive strangers. Few of them smoke, instead of which they use salt and tobacco mixed, enveloped in wool, and kept between the under lip and gum; the boys commence this practice when quite young. They are all rogues, but being bred up such, do not think there is any harm in being so; the opprobrious terms, harame, cadab, (thief, liar,) are not considered abusive with them, as they have no notion of honesty, and cannot possibly keep from pilfering anything within their reach; we detected our sailors at this work almost daily, but they always made a joke of it. The several districts differ much in regard to dress, and particularly in the manner of wearing the hair: some have it curled, "à la Brutus," others plaited and hanging down with great uniformity, in ringlets, to the shoulders, where it is cut off square at the bottom, and looks exactly like a mop. These latter grease their locks plentifully with oil; the former have generally a skewer sticking in their hair in readiness to disturb any animalcule which may bite too hard. There is great difference in the features and make of the several Nubian tribes: the natives of Elpha are tall and good-looking; the people of Derry ugly and deformed; the tribe at Armada are small, but handsome, and well made; all of them are considerably darker than the Arabs. Nubians are frugal in their mode of living, subsisting principally on doura, made into flat cakes, and baked on a heated stone, and on sour milk and dates. It is usual to see a man set out on a journey of several days with no other provision than a small bag of dates. They eat the offal of all the beasts they kill, not rejecting any part; and when we were at the village to which the crew belonged, the women came down eagerly to dispute for some fowls, which, having died, had been thrown on shore. They are great boasters, but do not appear to have any firmness; and they have an especial aversion to fire-arms. They evince much outward show of religion, praying four or five times a day; and to display their piety, they leave the sand on their foreheads, which sticks there while they are performing their devotions. They are respectful to their cashiefs, to whom they refer all their quarrels and disputes. They are invariably armed, and appear very proud of their weapons; most of them carry a dagger on the left arm, a long pike and a sword slung across the back. The boys, when young, have weapons given them; this, they imagine, shows their independence, and they acknowledge no government. They are exceedingly passionate with each other, but are soon reconciled, even after the most inveterate abuse. They adhere together, and no bribes can separate them; we never saw an instance in which we had any of them on our side, or where they revealed anything to us. Ear-rings are common amongst the men; they usually have but one, and it is immaterial in which ear it is worn. They eat the locusts grilled, and affirm that they are good. Necessity has led them to the only manufacture which they possess. It consists of neat close-grained platters, made of the date-tree, to contain their milk and food. No earthenware is made in the country; their water-jars are brought from Egypt.

The women do not cover their faces so scrupulously as the Arabs; they are not ill-looking, are generally well made, and have good figures. They wear a brown garment reaching down to the ankles; it is thrown over the right shoulder, comes close under the left arm, the shoulder of which is bare, and has not an ungraceful appearance; they are very partial to rings and bracelets; the former are frequently worn at the nose, the latter are made of one piece of brown glass, which, not yielding and being forced on as small as possible, often causes much pain: they always go bare-footed. Young girls have a covering round their loins made of strips of leather, hanging down and ornamented with cowry-shells and beads. The hair of the women is plaited somewhat like the men's, and greased with oil. The Barabras, from their frugal mode of life, are subject to few diseases. They are all marked with one, and sometimes two, scars on the spine of the back, where they have been burnt for the cure of an endemial disease, which attacks them when young. This mode of treatment draws all the humours to one spot, and keeps the discharge open till the patient is recovering; experience has doubtless shown it to be often successful. A boy, while we were at Abou-Simbel, was in a state of cure, and accidentally injured the part, which caused it to bleed; the father immediately applied a remedy, of which there is no scarcity in the country. He threw some sand upon the wound, which soon appeased the boy's cries and pain.

CHAPTER III.

Descent of the first Cataract—Ancient Quarries at Assuan—Visit from the Aga—Elephantina—Koum Ombo—Mountains of the Chain—Temple at Edfoo—Fine Ruins at El Cab—Esneh—Luxor—Tombs of Gourna—Mummy Pits—Magnificent Tomb—The Tombs of the Kings—View from the Summits of the Lybian Chain—Observations on Thebes—Tentyra—Singular Use of the Mummy Cases—Ruins at the Foot of the Mockatem—Arrival at Cairo—Visit to the Pyramids—Observations on Cairo—Massacre of the Mamelukes—Appearance of the Country—The Nile—Travellers in Egypt—Expenses.

Tuesday, August 12.—After about four hours' disputing and bargaining with the crew, we persuaded them to take us down the cataract in the boat, for the sum of fifty piastres; but they would not start unless we paid them every para of the money beforehand. We tried to induce them to take half the cash at first, and the other half on our arrival; but, no, they must have it all. It was of course the same to us, whether we paid them before or after; but knowing their character, we were afraid that when they once got the money, they would turn our things out of the boat and take themselves off, especially as there was a great crowd assembled who would have aided them in any of their pranks. We could not help laughing when we found that, however unfavourable an opinion we had formed of them, they were equally suspicious of us. Having at length given them the money, they prepared to depart. A pilot and eight additional hands came on board to conduct us down. Just before putting off, Hassan sneaked off and disappeared, dreading, no doubt, the report we should make of him to the Aga. We were about two hours on our passage, which was amongst all the windings and turnings of the innumerable islands which form the rapids, for cataract there is none. The scenery was wild, barren, and romantic. Sometimes the bark was carried away pretty sharply by the stream, and occasionally, when she was roughly handled in the vortex of the current, the sailors cried out, "tyep,

tyep," (good, good,) and asked us whether they were not bold fellows for undertaking what they had done. At times they made such a violent noise, all speaking and bawling at once, that a person not used to Nubian manners would have thought the whole concern was going to the bottom. The boat only struck once, but it gave her a prodigious shock, and made us fully sensible of the hardness of granite rocks. The sailors immediately began to sound the well, expecting that she was bilged, but she did not make much water, and we soon got off. At the commencement of the rapid, and while near Philæ, we observed oyster-shells incrusted on the granite rocks, bordering on the river; some of them were very perfect and large. We reached Assuan (the ancient Syene) in the evening. Mr. Ruppell, a German traveller who was at Thebes with us, discovered on one of the barren and uninhabited islands which compose the fall, a fine tablet of red granite, with a perfect Greek inscription on it, of great interest. This stone Mr. Ruppell takes with him to Frankfort, to be presented to the musuem of that town.

On our arrival at Assuan, we proceeded to visit the ancient granite quarries in the neighbourhood. Our principal object was to examine the column which is there, and which has a Latin inscription upon it of some interest. At first our guide lost his way, and took us to another part of the quarry, where we found an immense granite basin, 17 ft. long, by 7 wide, and 3 deep. It is hewn out in the rough, and is narrower at the bottom than the top. We were at a loss to imagine for what purpose such an immense vessel could be intended, unless for a bath. The whole of this quarry was highly interesting. Here we had an opportunity of noticing the manner in which the ancients used to cut the prodigious masses which one meets with throughout Egypt. It appears, that, when they wanted to detach a mass, they cut niches in a right line throughout the piece they intended removing: these niches were about 2 ft. apart, 5 or 6 in. long, and about 3 deep, by 2½ broad. As soon as they were finished, the block was separated by some violent blow or concussion. We met in all directions specimens of the progress of their work; some masses were but half detached, others wholly separated; here we saw an obelisk in the rough, and there a column. The whole was a most interesting sight. The ancient road, regularly paved with granite, is still plainly to be seen, though the sand covers a great part: in the vacancies between the hills are causeways, some of considerable length, to connect the elevated parts one with the other, and thus keep a communication open with the several quarries. All these roads lead to two principal ones which conduct to Assuan. We now searched for the column with the inscription, and at last found it. The pillar is small, not being more than 10 ft. in length, by about 3 ft. in diameter; the inscription is tolerably perfect. An Arab, acquainted with Mr. Belzoni, told him of it, and that no traveller had seen it until last year. As Mr. Belzoni had copied the writing, we did not think it worth while to do so. Its purport is as follows:—"To Jupiter Ammon, Kneephis Bona (the Good Spirit), and to Juno the Queen, under whose protection is this mountain, in which were discovered nine quarries near Philæ, during the happy age of the Roman Empire, under the most pious Emperors, Severus and Caracalla, and ———, and Julia Domna, his august mother; and a vast number of statues and large columns were taken out of these quarries by Aquila, prefect of Egypt. 'Curæ Magna Opera,'" which Mr. Salt interprets, "under his directions, Aurelius Heliogabalus ordered this stone to be erected in the calends of March." The vacant space before Julia Domna, the mother, is where the name of "Geta," the other brother was erased. Caracalla, having murdered him, ordered his name to be blotted out of every inscription where it was inserted. Mr. Salt tells us, that there is one instance of this at Rome, and that he has met another on an inscription, discovered at the late excavation of the sphinx. As the inscription says, that the Romans *discovered* the nine quarries, *not that they made them*, one must infer that they were first worked by the Egyptians; and as they were so numerous, and of such magnitude, they must have been of great consequence, and are doubtless of the most remote antiquity. It is difficult to understand how the Egyptians could have cut, hollowed out, and polished, such immense blocks of the hardest stone without the use of iron, a metal which they are said to have been wholly ignorant of. The niches above mentioned may probably have been cut with brass. We examined the construction of numerous mummy cases, and boxes containing the sacred emblems of the Egyptians; they were invariably fastened with wooden pegs, no nail of any description being visible. Some of the cases were of beautiful workmanship. Mr. Ruppell has two legs of a chair elegantly worked in the form of a lion's feet and paws. These specimens of cabinet-making bespeak great taste and judgment; and it is difficult to conceive that they could have been carved with brazen tools. The negroes in the South Sea at this day certainly cut hard woods shaped as clubs, and ornament them in the most exquisite style; but I doubt much if they could with their flints make cases and boxes.

Syene was the place to which Juvenal was banished by the Emperor Domitian, being sent there with the title of "Governor of the Frontier of Egypt:" he returned to Rome at eighty years of age. Assuan has nothing to interest the traveller; an immense heap of rubbish lies behind the town, which is a dirty, ill-built place.

Wednesday, August 13.—This morning the Aga came to pay us a visit: he was asleep all yesterday, for as the ramadan prevents them from eating and drinking during the day, the great people invert the order of things by sleeping during that time, and sitting up and feasting all night. We complained to him of the treatment we had experienced from our crew. He told us that they were a notorious set of rascals; that no one would employ their boat, their character being so bad, that people were afraid to trust their goods in their hands. Our friends had not waited to be catechised for their conduct, but took themselves off the day before, after having made great efforts to persuade us to give them some more backsheeish. We visited Elephantina, so glowingly described by Denon. It certainly has a pleasing, flourishing appearance, the north end being richly covered with fine crops of doura; and there are also a few palm-trees. The south end of the island is high, and here are situated the ruins of the ancient town, together with the temples, only one of which, dedicated to the serpent Kneephis, is in any degree perfect; it is small, with an ante-chamber and sanctuary. There are the remains of several others, but so mutilated that nothing can be made out. A high quay leads directly down to the Nile at the S. E. end. At eleven o'clock we started on our return, having hired a boat to take us to Thebes for 120 piastres.

Thursday, August 14.—We inspected Koum Ombo, the ancient Ombos. Here are the remains of two temples situated on a promontory of the Nile's eastern bank; the large one, dedicated to the crocodile (as appears by the principal offerings being presented to a deity having the head of that animal), is situated at a short distance from the river, which it fronts. The smaller one, to Isis, is close to the river side; and not far distant from the other, to the S. W., and close to the river side, is a building which appears to be part of an unfinished pylon. There is a whimsical irregularity in this edifice: the base is built of small blocks of stone, which gradually increase in size till you come to the top, where are the largest masses of all. The large temple consists of a portico of three rows of columns, five in each row: the column at each of the outer angles has fallen. The cornice, only parts of which are perfect, is ornamented with four winged globes.

The frieze consists of a double border of large hieroglyphics. The columns are of great dimensions, and have dissimilar capitals surmounted by a plinth. There are two entrances, one on each side of the centre pillars; this is occasioned by the unusual circumstance of there being an odd number of columns in front: these entrances conduct to another ruined apartment, originally supported by ten pillars in two rows of five each; beyond which are three other apartments; the communication from the one to the other is by two large doors, one on either side, instead of a centre one usual in most Egyptian temples. The cornice over the entrance, on the left, from the second to the third apartment, has an inscription in Greek, stating that it was written by direction of Ptolemy and Cleopatra, and that the temple was dedicated to Apollo, &c. The decorations of this edifice are in basso-relievo, highly finished, and in a good style. Amongst the figures, we noticed the lion with the hawk's head, similar to the statues we found at Abou-Simbel—a union we had not elsewhere noticed. The small temple of Isis points to the south; it consists of a small portico of four columns, surmounted by the usual quadruple head of the deity, with the passage in the centre; and beyond the portico are two chambers and a sanctuary; but all the western side of the temple has fallen into the river, and with it the chief part of the flooring of the chambers, together with a large plain altar of black basalt, which had evidently been in the sanctuary. The want of hieroglyphical inscriptions on this altar is probably the only cause why travellers have not removed it. The ornamental parts of this temple are in no way inferior to those of the larger edifice; we did not, however, notice any representations that we had not before seen. In consequence of the elevation of Koum Ombo, the view is extensive, but the country to the north and east presents nothing but a barren, sandy desert; to the S. E. there is a small portion of land cultivated. Opposite to the temple, in the middle of the Nile, is the large island of the Mansouria, which is highly cultivated, and a smaller island to the south, the soil of which is also good. Exclusive of the temples, the promontory of Koum Ombo has several Saracenic ruins of both baked and sunburnt brick; and the ruins of the ancient town are marked by the rubbish of the former material.

We visited Djibel Selsilis. This name, which means "mountains of the chain," has been given from a tradition that a chain was here drawn across the river, to prevent the irruption of any hostile parties from above. The principal objects of interest are several small temples hollowed out of the rock, which is of calcareous stone. The northernmost consists of a portico and sanctuary, with three recesses in the latter, containing statues in alto-relievo; the walls have been stuccoed and painted, but at present are so much disfigured that little or nothing can be made out. To the southward are two other small temples, each consisting of one single niche or hollow in the rock. The fronts of both have two handsome columns, together with a cornice and frieze, executed with considerable taste. The colouring must have been extremely rich. There are numerous other niches with statues, &c. The quarries near this spot are very extensive; and one large detached block, of considerable height, would seem to be the mass of stone where the chain which secured the river was fastened. On the opposite side of the river the quarries are also numerous; the vicinity of the Nile, so favourable for embarking and transporting the stone, was no doubt the principal inducement to the Egyptians to establish these extensive works.

On *Friday, August* 15, we reached Edfoo, the ancient "Apollinopolis Magna." It is situated in a fertile plain, at a short distance from the western bank of the Nile. The large temple appears to have been one of the most magnificent of any in Egypt; though in beauty it must yield to Tentyra and some few others. It consists of a remarkably high pylon, the exterior wall of which is sculptured with a large figure on each side, sacrificing a number of human victims; and above these are two rows of figures presenting offerings to Osiris and Isis. The inside of the pylon is decorated similarly; the cornice is imperfect as far as the torus, or astragal moulding, which at present forms the summit of the pylon. Within is a large and magnificent peristyle court, forming an oblong square, with a covered gallery supported by columns on each side; beyond this is the portico of the temple, presenting a front of six pillars, behind which are two other rows, making eighteen pillars in all; those in front have had a wall of intercolumniation reaching up half their height. These pillars appeared to be of very large dimensions, but on measuring them we found the upper part of the shaft to be only 6 feet 4 inches in diameter, while those at Carnack are 11 feet 6 inches at the base of the column. This portico is filled with rubbish more than two-thirds up to the roof. The frieze in front of the portico is ornamented with a row of standing figures of monkeys, in basso-relievo, and the architraves within have rows of figures of Isis sitting on a chair. The chambers of the temple are inaccessible, as the rubbish which fills the portico blocks up the door. The whole of the large peristyle court, and the top of the portico, and other parts of the temple, are covered with the mud-built huts of the modern town of Edfoo. The temple is surrounded by a wall, about 8 feet thick, which is continued in a line from the outer part of the gallery of the peristyle, leaving a passage between the sides of the temple and the wall. The extèrior of the edifice, and both sides of the wall, are ornamented with offerings and hieroglyphics; we remarked nothing novel in the symbolic representations, excepting the horse, an animal we had not before seen in this character. The ruins of the ancient Apollinopolis Magna are high, but not extensive. The paltry modern town of Edfoo presents a striking contrast to the magnificence of the ancient buildings; seen from the top of the lofty pylon, the huts at its foot, and in the peristyle court, do not look like human dwellings. You here enjoy a fine view of the river, and an extensive fertile plain. To the S.W. of the great temple there is a smaller one, which is nearly buried. An interesting discovery was made a few weeks ago near this place. A Frenchman, named Cailliaud, who understands mineralogy, has lately been employed by the pasha to examine the Mockatem and Lybian chain in search of coal mines. His last trip was to inspect the ancient emerald mines, which are south of Cossur, at five hours' journey from the Red Sea. On his way from the point opposite to Edfoo, where he quitted the Nile, he crossed a road at two days' journey from that place, which appears to be the ancient Egyptian road from Koptos to Berenice; and he also found there the ruins of a temple. The road is paved with granite, and in some places is cut or hollowed out of the solid rock. He observed several tablets, with hieroglyphic characters and inscriptions, but he could not spare time to examine them. We have seen some of the specimens from the emerald mine which Mr. Cailliaud brought with him. Our friend Ruppell, who is a good mineralogist, and who has made a valuable collection, tells us that these specimens are composed of black mica; it is of a softish, scaly nature, and may easily be separated into laminæ. The emeralds which we saw were very small, and ran in narrow layers through the other substance.

This evening, *August* 15, we stopped at El Cab, the ancient Eleethias. The ruins are situated on the eastern bank of the Nile, not far from the river. This city has been inclosed by a wall of sun-burnt brick, 37 feet thick; the inclosed space is about a mile square. Within the great wall is another inclosure surrounding the ruins of a small temple, and other buildings much dilapidated, and consequently uninteresting. At the back of the ruins, in the side of the Mockatem, are several sepulchral grottoes, two of which are well worthy of notice; the one is remarkable for a highly finished tablet of hieroglyphics, in intaglio; the other is a very interesting chamber. Some of the groups have great originality of design, and are executed with good taste. On the left, as you enter, the first object of interest is a man writing on a tablet, which he holds on his left arm; fronting him are various men driving asses, cattle, pigs, goats, &c.; near to these are several hillocks of corn, and people in the act of reaping and sheafing, with gleaners, &c., following behind them. After this are three distinct rows of agricultural proceedings; the upper one begins with two men bearing on their shoulders, by means of a long pole, as brewers carry a cask, a sort of net basket shaped thus  filled with wheat in the ear; next to them are two other men, one bringing on his shoulder an empty basket, while his companion carries the pole; next is a man in an inclosed space, with six head of cattle, treading the corn, their mode of threshing. Behind these are four people winnowing the grain, by holding it up over their heads, and pouring it down for the wind to blow through it; near these is a man seated on the top of a high hillock of grain, and writing down an account of the quantity; and there are four men piling it up. This group terminates with two men depositing the corn in a square inclosure, which was doubtless the granary. The next group is a ploughing scene. There are two ploughs, each drawn by two oxen; a man walks opposite the animals, sowing grain as they advance; this he takes from a basket suspended from the yoke across the horns of the beasts. Behind him is a person driving a wheel harrow; the ploughs are preceded by four men, using a sort of pick-axe in the shape of the Greek letter alpha; this was probably to break the clods of earth. Further on are four men working another plough. Below this scene is a pair of scales; at one end is a man writing an account, while another is weighing some small articles shaped thus , and which we think may probably represent their loaves, as bread is at present sometimes made in that form in Egypt. Four of these are in one scale, and many others on the shelves at the side of the wall; the weight in the other scale is in the form of a cow couchant. Next to this are persons carrying the weighed articles into a boat, by means of a gang-board, and near to this boat are three other boats already laden, with men poling them. The cargo is placed in a square magazine, built in the centre of a boat, not unlike the cabin of the Thamesis. Below is a boat under sail; the sail is square, with a yard at the head and foot. It is trimmed by means of a wheel, which is attached to the foot-yard, acting the part of a roller, and working on a pivot on the top of the square magazine or cabin, which is nearly half the height of the mast. There is a door and window to the cabin, and seven men are rowing on each side: the helms-man steers with an oar. The next group represents fishermen drawing their net, with two men carrying the fish away in baskets, and another splitting them and hanging them up to dry. Beneath this is another party catching geese with a net; after which are others employed plucking and trussing them, while one man is putting them in jars. Above are men plucking grapes, while two are carrying them away in baskets; six others are pressing them, and others filling jars with the wine. Among numerous other groups of figures, we noticed a female, standing and playing a harp with ten strings. The instrument is rudely shaped, and badly finished. Another plays on a wind-instrument not unlike a clarionet, with this difference, that the end is not shaped like a trumpet's mouth, but plain. As most of the other groups are met with in other places, I do not deem it necessary to describe them. We visited a small temple situated in the plain, at a short distance to the N.W. The serpent Kneephis is said, by the French, to have been worshipped in this temple, though we could not make out any more marked allusion to a serpent than is usual in the sculpture of other temples.

On *Saturday, August* 16, we reached Esneh, situate on the site of the ancient Latopolis. In the centre of the town, near the market-place, is an Egyptian temple, which must have been magnificent, but the whole of it is now completely buried, and built over with modern houses, except the portico or ante-chamber. This is supported by twenty-four columns, in four rows of six each; the outer row in front having a semi-wall of intercolumniation like that at Tentyra. The sculpture, in basso-relievo, is executed in an indifferent style: the signs of the zodiac are represented on both ends of the ceiling, but they are much inferior to those of Tentyra. The chief beauty of this portico consists in the elegant proportions of the shafts of the columns. The capitals, all of which are different, are well executed, representing the fruit and leaves of the date, vine, lotus, &c. &c. Three miles north of Esneh there is a small temple in ruins, supposed to be situated on the site of the ancient Aphroditopolis, and on the opposite side of the river there is another on the site of Contra Latopolis. We visited neither of them, as they were reported unworthy the trouble, and time was growing precious. As we had inspected the ruins at Erment, the ancient Hermontis, on our passage up the Nile in May, we did not again visit them. The city appears to have been extensive and compact. There are the remains of four temples, but only one at present is in such a state as to indicate what they once were. This temple has but seven columns standing, each of which has a capital of a different pattern from the others, the whole being composed of representations of the palm leaf in various forms. There are two sanctuaries in the temple, both ornamented with various symbolic representations, in basso-relievo, stuccoed and painted. Some of the groups are peculiar. In the larger sanctuary are sixteen hippopotami, in two processions, walking upright; also a hippopotamus presenting an offering to Horus, who is sitting on the lotus flower; several crocodiles, with hawks' heads, on square cases, either altars or sarcophagi; two rows of three monkeys, and two of four cats; a human figure, with the Ibis's head, presenting offerings to a cat; a man bearing a globe on his shoulders; an oblong-square case ornamented all over with flowers; above it appear twelve human heads, in four groups of three each, and below are their feet with sandals; (these last are probably men carrying a sarcophagus;) a small human figure (Horus), with a hawk's head, riding between the horns of a cow (Isis). In the inner sanctuary are two cows, with a child sucking each, the animals with their heads turned round and looking at the infants—probably Isis and her son Horus. On the ceiling are two rams with wings—a taurus and a scorpio; twelve figures in three rows of four each, with a circular head ornament, and a star in the centre, probably have some allusion to the signs of the zodiac. All the ornaments of these two sanctuaries are highly finished. Near the temple, on the east side, are the ruins of an ancient basin, in the centre of which Denon mentions, on the authority of Aristides, there was a Nilometer, but the column on which it was graduated no longer exists; the remains of a flight of steps, from the basin up to the temple, are still to be seen.

Sunday, August 17.—Early this morning we arrived at Luxor, part of the ancient Thebes, and took up our quarters in one of the temples. Having established our household, we devoted the day to a careful re-examination of both Luxor and Carnack. At the former place we carefully inspected the sculpture on the exterior of the great pylon. We also clearly made out that, with the exception of being written vertically instead of horizontally, eight or ten of the upper hieroglyphics on the magnificent obelisks are the same as the first characters of the frieze at Abou-Simbel, and the same also as the upper hieroglyphics in what are termed Cleopatra's Needles at Alexandria.

Monday, August 18.—We devoted this day to visiting the tombs of Gourna; and Messrs. Beechey and Belzoni having been employed for months, by Mr.

Salt, in digging and making excavations in various directions among the rubbish of ancient Thebes, and particularly at Gourna, were the best guides we could possibly have. It is customary with the natives to deceive travellers, and tell them that they have seen all, before they have inspected half; and it was precisely this trick they played on Mr. Irby and myself on our former visit. They have not been unmindful of the eagerness with which travellers inquire after objects of antiquity; especially the papyri, which are generally found under the arms or between the legs of the mummies, and the demand for which has been so great of late, in consequence of an opposition between the French party, employed by Mr. Drovetti, and the English, employed by Mr. Salt, that they now sell for thirty, forty, and fifty piastres each, whereas, formerly, you could get them for eight or ten. About a dozen of the leading characters of Gourna, that is, the greatest rogues in the place, have headed their comrades, and formed them into two distinct digging parties, or resurrection men, designating them the French and the English party; these are constantly occupied in searching for new tombs, stripping the mummies, and collecting antiquities. The directors have about three-fourths of the money, and the rest is given to the inferior labourers. They dread lest strangers should see these tombs, which to them are so many mines of wealth, and should commence digging speculations of their own—hence the care of the Gourna people in concealing them. It would be endless to describe all the intrigues which are carried on; or the presents given to the Defterdar Bey, the Agas, and the Cashiefs, to attach them to the one or the other party. Lately, Mr. Drovetti obtained an order from the Defterdar Bey, that the natives should neither sell nor work for the English party, and a cashief was most severely bastinadoed by the bey's orders, and in his presence at Gourna, for having done so. At present, things are on a better footing. Mr. Drovetti is not an amateur, but collects to sell; he offered his museum to Mr. Salt, on his arrival, for seven thousand pounds, but most persons seem to think he will never get this price. He is now gone into Upper Egypt in search of a temple and Egyptian road, which are said to have been seen by the jelabs, at one day's journey, in the desert, from Madfuni, the ancient Abydus.

The tombs of Gourna are situated in a valley to the S. W. of the Memnonium. Those which we first inspected are considered the best, and consist of two square courts cut in a bed of calcareous stone. There are excavations on three sides of the square, and the fourth, or south side, is that by which they are entered. The principal excavations are on the north side; these are very extensive, and we were at a loss which most to admire, the beauty of the sculpture on the walls, or the grandeur and extent of the excavations. The figures are cut on the smooth stone, which is very close-grained, resembling the finest chalk, but without cracks or flaws, and rather harder; the colour is of so pure a white, and admits of so fine a polish, that stucco has been quite unnecessary. There is a harmony throughout the decorations of these tombs that we have no where else noticed; the sculpture, which is in intaglio, will bear the minutest inspection. The plan of the excavation is extremely singular, sometimes abruptly turning either to the right or left, without any apparent cause. At the further end there is a fine quadrangular court, having the solid rock in the centre. You here meet with some very rich groups; and there are innumerable remains of fine statues, in alto-relievo, leaning against the wall in all directions; we could not, however, distinguish one that was perfect. The art and precision with which the decorations of these sepulchres are finished, exhibiting an endless variety of symbolic representations, in the most elaborate and highly finished style, are truly astonishing. In some places the roofs are arched, in others they are flat; here you meet with a deep well in a corner; shortly afterwards you descend a flight of steps. Some of the hieroglyphics are painted blue on a pale red ground; blue is much used, the colour of the stone itself serving occasionally for a fine white field. Amongst the figures, in basso-relievo, there were many quite perfect, and so minutely cut, that the eye-brows and ears, the hair, nose, lips, and the hands and nails, would bear the closest inspection; in short, throughout the whole of this mausoleum, the work of most skilful artists is observable. The examination of the principal tomb occupied us two hours.

We afterwards went to see the mummy pits. It is impossible to conceive a more singular and astonishing sight than this. Imagine a cave of considerable magnitude filled up with heaps of dead bodies in all directions, and in the most whimsical attitudes; some with extended arms, others holding out a right hand, and apparently in the attitude of addressing you; some prostrate, others with their heels sticking up in the air; at every step you thrust your foot through a body or crush a head. Most of the mummies are enveloped with linen, coated with gum, &c., for their better preservation. Some of the linen is of a texture remarkably fine, far surpassing what is made in Egypt at the present day, and proving that their manufactures must have arrived at a great degree of excellence. Many of the bodies, probably those of the lower orders, are simply dried, without any envelopment. Innumerable fragments of small idols are scattered about; they are mostly human figures of Osiris, about two inches long, with the hook and scourge in either hand; some are of stone, some of baked earthenware, and others of blue pottery. Except as being so odd and extraordinary an exhibition, few of the common tombs, which were most likely for the poorer class of natives, are worth seeing, as none of them are ornamented in any way whatever; the bodies are stowed away in compact masses, tier on tier, always crossing each other. In some instances we found the hair quite perfect. It was in a tomb of this description that some of the diggers found a beautiful net-work, composed of long blue hollow beads, with threads passed through them; the parts of the net hanging down over the shoulders, and all emanating from a scarabæus Thebaicus, which was on the crown of the head. It was found on the head of a female mummy.

At the commencement of this year the diggers also found two remarkably fine Egyptian vases of brass, covered with hieroglyphics; they are nearly two feet high, and are the most valuable remains of antiquity which have been discovered for some years, being quite perfect. Mr. Belzoni was fortunate enough to get them for Mr. Salt, for one hundred and seventy piastres—4*l.* 5*s.*

We now went to inspect a newly discovered tomb, that well recompensed us for the trouble. Having crawled in by a small hole barely sufficient for the body to be squeezed through, we entered a small sepulchral ante-chamber adjoining to a tomb filled with mummies. From the finished style of the decorations of this chamber, we concluded that it must have been the tomb of some noble family; the paintings are all in fresco, and so wonderfully well preserved, that not the least scratch or stain is visible; the pure white ground of the wall not being even tinged with yellow. Amongst the groups we noticed an interesting troop of six female musicians, dressed in white robes reaching down to their ankles; over this they have a sort of black, loose woollen net hanging over the shoulders, and reaching down to the waist. Their hair is jet black, plaitted in ringlets, reaching down from the outer part of the eye-lids all round the head, and has, at first sight, the appearance of a veil. They are walking in procession and playing at the same time: the leader has a harp with fourteen strings; then comes a girl with a guitar, which is not unlike that now in use; then one with a lute, handsomely shaped; after which comes another girl clapping her hands, apparently keeping time; then another with a sort of double pipe: this instrument is played on like a clarionet, and is long and slender; both the tubes are of equal length. The procession closes with a female beating on a tambourine, which is in this shape  . The gestures of these musicians, with their uplifted eyes, would lead one to suppose they were playing some impassioned air. The preservation of this painting is astonishing, the colours being perfectly fresh, and no part whatever in the least defaced. What would not the French have given for such a specimen to put in their splendid work? There is nothing throughout Egypt to be compared to it. In this apartment there are figures of two male harpers; both are squatted down, and playing on smaller instruments than that just described, having only nine strings each: one is playing alone, the other is accompanied by a man playing on a guitar. These last-mentioned musicians are bare-headed, and have bare feet; they are apparently elderly men. There are many other groups. The sacred Bull (Apis) is here most magnificently ornamented, and is a handsomer animal than it generally is. The ceiling of the apartment is divided into four compartments, each of which is painted with a different device. Adjoining the chamber, and connected by means of a small well, is a tomb filled with mummies, amongst which are the fragments of a mummy-case, richly painted and glazed. Some of the bodies are covered with canvas, over which is a coat of plaster painted. We found concealed in the envelope of the corpses, some of the small ornaments of earthenware, called Nilometers.

The valley of Gourna ends at the foot of the Lybian mountains, where their sides present a perpendicular precipice. Here are some interesting antiquities—a granite portal, discovered this year by digging; an arch, the only one of Egyptian masonry to be seen in the country. It is well known that the Egyptians were ignorant of the scientific mode of building an arch; and it is this circumstance which enables us frequently, in this country, to distinguish the works of the Greeks and Romans from those of their predecessors. The Egyptians built their arches in this form  ; the Romans thus  All the temples are roofed over with blocks of stone, frequently 30 ft. long; but as this was the utmost extent to which they could carry their system of building, you never meet with a space between a row of columns wider than that. Their staircases, whether circular or straight, are built on the same principle as their arches, being merely blocks of stone firmly inserted in the side of the wall, the workmen taking care to leave stone enough within the wall to support the weight. A painted chamber and a granite slab appear to be the other objects of interest near to this spot. The chamber seems to have been a sepulchre rather than a temple, and was approached by two or more avenues. It was discovered by digging, at Mr. Salt's expense, this year; but the Defterdar Bey, or governor of Upper Egypt, made the men desist from their researches.

We next proceeded to visit a small temple dedicated to Isis, which is situated to the N. W. of Medinet Aboo. Its position is seen from Memnonium, but being surrounded by a Saracenic wall of sun-burnt brick, nothing but one portal is visible. This constitutes the approach to the edifice, and through it you arrive at a small portico, the pillars having capitals of the head of Isis. There is, besides the portico, a cross ante-chamber, a sanctuary, and two wings: it is altogether a neat little temple. In the evening, after examining the statues and temple at Memnonium, we returned to Luxor.

Tuesday, August 19.—Early this morning we crossed the water with our janissary to pay a farewell visit to the Tombs of the Kings. One of the chief diggers accompanied us to show us two new tombs discovered by Mr. Belzoni this year. We found them quite unworthy of notice. They are situated in a small valley adjoining the great one. We afterwards again explored the other tombs. In the small chamber where Bruce made the drawing of the harp which he gave to Mr. Burney (for his History of Music), we saw that traveller's name scratched over the very harp. This is, we think, strong presumptive evidence that he made the sketch upon the spot, though he has been accused of drawing it afterwards from memory: he is, however, in error as to the number of strings. In other respects, he has given the form of the instrument correctly, but the musician is very indifferently copied. This evening, we found some scorpions, which our guide took up in his hand with great indifference: we remarked, however, that he took good care always to seize the reptiles by the tail.

We returned on foot, by the way of Memnonium, ascending to the top of the Lybian chain, which on one side gave us a fine view of the valley and Tombs of the Kings, while on the other side we looked down on the plain, which contains the whole of the ancient Thebes, together with the Nile, both seen to great advantage, and forming a splendid specimen of Egyptian scenery. As we descended, we counted on one spot upwards of fifty mummy-pits, discernible by their open mouths or entrances, on the sides of the hills, exclusive of an innumerable quantity of doors of grottoes, sepulchral chambers, &c., &c., cut out of the sides of the mountains. We now returned to Luxor, and having seen everything, began to think of returning. I cannot, however, quit Thebes without adverting to Homer's description of it. He says—

> "Not all proud Thebes' unrivalled walls contain,
> The world's great Empress on th' Egyptian plain;
> That spreads her conquests o'er a thousand states,
> And pours her heroes through a hundred gates,
> Two hundred horsemen and two hundred cars,
> From each wide portal issuing to the wars."

In our researches throughout the whole of the Theban ruins we did not meet with any remains of either walls or gates, unless the term is applied to the pylons, and other buildings, which constituted the approaches to the sacred edifices. Now, if Thebes had been a city with a hundred gates, there must surely have been a wall through which to construct them; and it is not unreasonable to suppose that the wall of so extensive and magnificent a city would have been built with stone, or at least that the frames or portals of the gates would have been of that material. Still no vestige of either gate or wall is to be seen; and as so many ruins of temples and their porticoes remain to this day, how is it that not one solitary gate, nor even fragment of the wall, is left? Under these circumstances, I do not think it an improbable conjecture, that it was the numerous porticos, pylons, &c., of the Theban temples, that obtained for her the boasted reputation of a hundred gates. That she vanquished and subdued many states, and that her inhabitants were proud of their warlike achievements, appears from the battles so frequently traced on the walls; but we nowhere observed Egyptian horsemen, the horsemen being always of the enemy's party in the act of flight, and looking back with dismay on the conquering Egyptians, who are invariably in chariots. Numerous as have been the researches amongst the ruins of Thebes, I suspect that many treasures of art still remain concealed: and if the English party are not prevented from digging, it is probable we shall be continually hearing of some new discoveries.

Friday, August 21.—We started early this morning for Cairo, having bargained with the reis to take us down for thirty piastres—fifteen shillings. The boat was laden with lentils for the pasha. We placed a few mats over-head for a shade, and found the cargo a good soft foundation whereon to put our beds; the sailors, in the boat, helping us in our cooking operations, we found we did as well without as with a servant.

Saturday, August 22.—This morning we stopped at Tentyra, and, as our reis said he should not start for an hour, we determined to revisit the temple of Isis.* We accordingly started on foot for that purpose. When we had got two-thirds of our way, we found the canal was filled, and that we must either swim over it or return. As we were dressed in our Arab costume, the former alternative was not difficult; we therefore threw our clothes over and plunged in. We examined the temple, and did not forget the little chamber, in which we had before noticed the circular astronomical table on the cieling as being a monument of the same kind as the Isiac table which we had seen at Turin. It was in the ceiling of the other half of this chamber that Mr. Ruppell discovered a complete lunar system, which had totally escaped Denon and all the other French savans. Mr. Ruppell took an exact copy of this interesting tablet. It clearly contains twelve moons and a bit of another, which no doubt was meant for the odd five days, as the twelve make 360. As this throws an additional light on the Egyptian mode of calculating the year, it is a matter of no small interest, and reflects the more credit on Mr. Ruppell, as so many travellers have examined this chamber, without the circumstance having occurred to them. In the great French work they have put down fourteen or fifteen moons, never having taken the trouble to count them.

Tuesday, August 25.—We stopped at Siout, and went up to pay our respects to the hospitable doctor, Marouky—found him as friendly as ever;—stopped two hours, and then pushed on.

Wednesday 26.—Visited Mr. Brine, a grateful remembrance of whose kindess also induced us to pay our respects to him. We here took charge of the heads of two Egyptian mummy-cases, and other antiquities dug up for Mr. Salt from a spot supposed to be the burial place of Hermopolis, near the Lybian chain.

Thursday, August 27.—We stopped at Houarti. As this was the village where our crew live, we were obliged to reconcile our minds to stop for three days, while they made merry with their friends and relations. We had scarcely been here an hour, when our reis came to ask us to lend him the two mummy-cases which we had on board. He said he should like to have them up at the village for an hour. We lent them immediately; but it was not until the following day that we found out his reason for borrowing them. Numbers of women came down to us and asked permission to walk three times round them, crossing over them each time. This we found was to procure them families. The women were constantly arriving, young and old, and all going through the same ceremony. They were all very serious during the performance of this mystery, and seemed to think it odd that we laughed so much. Our sailors informed us there were some antiquities at the foot of the Mockatem, about one hour and a half's distance. They mentioned temples and catacombs. We did not much believe them, but were glad of any excuse for a trip to pass away the time, and accordingly started with one of the reis's brothers as our guide. He took us to the site of a very extensive and finely-situated city, which, from the state of the rubbish, must have been of some consequence. It stands at the mouth of a valley in the Mock-

* The inscription on the listel of the cornice, in front of this temple, speaks of it as dedicated to Venus, which agrees with Strabo, who says "The Tentirites worship Venus. Behind the temple of Venus is a sanctuary (ἱερὸν) of Isis." The latter still exists; it is a small temple without columns. It is curious that the French savans did not copy this inscription: either they did not see it, or, stranger still, none of them knew Greek enough to be able to copy the letters, which are considerably broken and erased. It was first copied by Colonel Leake and Mr. Hamilton. It is not surprising that the French, having failed as to the inscription of Tentyra, should have omitted others more difficult, or that they should have occupied Alexandria for three years without having been able to decipher a single word of the inscription on the column of Diocletian. Colonel Leake was the first to discover the legibility of this inscription, by making out the words ΑΛΕΞΑΝΔΡΕΙΑΣ and ΕΠΑΡΧΟΣ ΑΙΓΥΠΤΟΥ. The joint efforts of himself and Mr. Hamilton, and Colonel Squires during several days afterwards, deciphered all that is at all legible of the remainder. See *Classical Journal.*

atem, on an elevated spot, at the edge of the cultivated plains, of which it commands a fine view. The modern village of Tehene is close to it. The ruins have been much dug up by the Arabs in search of antiquities. We only found one capital approaching to the Corinthian order, most likely of Roman workmanship. Immediately above the rubbish is a considerable range of catacombs and ancient temples hollowed out of the rock. One small temple of Isis is well worthy of notice, the decorations in basso-relievo being finished in a good style. At about a quarter of an hour's walk along the side of the mountain, to the southward, we saw a large excavated space, and on the top a frieze with a Greek inscription, the letters of which are remarkably large. It is about three fathoms long, and its size (the letters being nearly one foot high) led us to believe it must be generally known; we therefore did not copy it. We clearly made out the word ΠΤΟΛΕΜΑΙΟΣ. We have since found that no travellers have noticed this inscription. We have therefore given the particulars to Mr. Salt. A very old map of Danville's, on a small scale, has the site of an ancient town, under the name of Cynopolis, placed nearly in a parallel of latitude with this place.

We continued our voyage, and arrived at Cairo on the first day of September.

Wednesday, September 2. — Our first care now was to shave our beards, which we had allowed to grow from our first departure from Philæ, and we resumed our European costume. We felt as awkward at first at this change of dress, as we did when we first assumed the Arab costume. Mr. Salt received us very civilly. We found that great discoveries had been made during our absence; and the first thing that drew our attention was Mr. Salt's explanatory plan of the pyramids, the sphinx, and all their interesting environs. We found, at Mr. Salt's house, Colonel Stratton, of the Enniskillen dragoons, and Mr. Fuller. These two travellers had just made the tour of Palestine, having arrived by land from Yaffa and Gaza. They embarked at Constantinople, after having completed the tour of Greece. As they had not yet been to the pyramids, we gladly arranged to accompany them.

Friday, September 4.—We set off early in the morning, and Mr. Salt having lent us a copy of his newly made plan, we regularly went over the whole of the ground, place after place, according to it. To our disappointment we found there was nothing new for us to see, excepting a few of the upper steps fronting the sphinx; as, unfortunately for us and all future travellers, they have filled up all the excavations around the sphinx, so that there is not so much to be seen now as there was previous to our departure, the base having been perfectly cleared on one side before we started for Upper Egypt. From the several drawings and plans which we have seen, as well as from what we have heard, it appears that the indefatigable Captain Caviglia continued his operations till he had cleared all the breast of the animal; that he afterwards pursued his labours till he reached the paws, at fifty feet distance from the body: and here it was, between the two paws, that he discovered the temple. I imagine that this small edifice is composed of three large, flat stones, like a similar shrine in the possession of Mr. Salt, and that the door was filled up by two smaller pieces of stone on each side of it; the sides have some fine specimens of basso-relievo: a man is depicted as presenting an offering to the sphinx. Some of the inscriptions also are interesting, and one of Caracalla has the name of Geta, his brother, erased, as in the Latin inscription at Syene. The lions which were found, together with the tablets, in basso-relievo, have been sent home to the British Museum, as well as the great head of Memnon. There are still at Thebes the remains of thirty-seven statues, of equal, or larger dimensions. Beyond the small temple is an altar. At some distance from the paws is a flight of steps, which lead some depth below them to the base of the temple. Mr. Salt is of opinion that this descent by steps was meant to impress the beholder (after having first viewed the sphinx at a distance, on a level,) with a more imposing idea of its grandeur, when he views the breast in its full magnitude from below. A wall of sun-burnt brick was on each side of the steps, to prevent the sand from filling up the space. We afterwards went all over the great pyramid, again descending to the lower chamber, which Captain Caviglia discovered, and also reinspected the well, &c. We could not go into Colonel Davidson's chamber, as the Arabs had stolen the rope ladder which was left there. We slept at the entrance of the great pyramid, and in the morning returned to Cairo; the excursion occupied us two days. When we were last at Cairo, a trip to the sphinx used to take two hours; we were now five hours going there, the inundation of the Nile forcing us to go more than double the distance round the edge of the canals. As we are now about to leave Egypt, I shall add a few remarks on Cairo. All Turkish towns impress Europeans with very unfavourable ideas; the streets are invariably narrow, and the fronts of the houses look like so many barn doors. Cairo is particularly ill-built, and a stranger, after having heard so much of "Grand Cairo," can scarcely believe his own eyes when he enters; and this is the more striking, as, at a short distance, the lofty minarets give it a grand appearance. Miserable narrow streets, the square bow-windows meeting over the head, and built with unpainted deal wood; no pavement to be seen; gratings substituted for panes of glass; a dirty ill-dressed populace, and women covered up like so many ghosts, all conspire to render it disagreeable in the extreme. The various classes of inhabitants, such as Turks, Arabs, Copts, Jews, Franks, &c., have their respective quarters where they reside in detached societies; each quarter has its gate and porter to attend it; all are shut at eight o'clock in the evening; after which time it is customary to fee the porter to get admittance. In case of tumults, when the troops go about robbing and plundering all they meet with, these gates become of great service. The citadel of Cairo is built on a commanding eminence; here the pasha resides. Great merit is due to Mahomed Ali for the tranquillity which exists at present throughout Egypt, and could such an atrocious crime as the murder of the mamelukes be overlooked, he might be considered as a great man. This barbarous act was committed about six years ago: the unsuspecting victims, about two thousand in number, were invited to the castle to be present at the presentation of the Pelisse to the pasha's son, Toussein, and his investiture with the command of Jidda, including the government of the sacred city of Mecca. During the ceremony, the walls and tops of the houses, the castle, &c., were lined with troops, and, on a signal given, as the mamelukes were quitting the palace, the soldiers opened their fire on them, and nearly all of them were slain.

Egypt at present presents a very different appearance to what it did when we took our departure from Cairo, in March; the Nile having overflowed, all the villages are insulated, and the date palm-trees, which invariably surrounded them, partly conceal the mud-huts, and give a pleasing and lively appearance to the face of the country. The river, also, in some places, appears of prodigious width, the plains being overflowed for many miles. We have been fortunate, in having seen Egypt throughout, with the Nile at its lowest ebb, and also at its greatest elevation. There is no freehold property in this country, all the land being let out by the pasha, who afterwards forces the peasants to sell their property to him only, and *at his own price*. Soldiers are quartered in all the principal villages to enforce a due observance of this law. All the boats are likewise monopolised by him, and gun-boats are stationed at the narrow parts of the river, to prevent the passage of any barks unless laden for the pasha. The Arabs, Copts, and others, who become rich in spite of this oppressive system, are allowed but little enjoyment of their wealth. It is not at all an unusual occurrence when any one of them has built a handsome house, that he should be desired to turn out, and give it up to some Greek, Turk, or perhaps to an European consul, and should he not immediately obey, his head is the forfeit.

It is a curious fact, that no water-plants or weeds grow on the banks of the Nile; a sedgy margin is never to be met with in this country. The lotus, affecting fens and marshy places, can only flourish during the most propitious part of the year, when the overflowing of the Nile promotes its growth: hence it was so favourite a plant with the ancients; and is so generally coupled with all symbolic allusions to the river. This year the Nile has risen 17 pics or 34 ft.; this is called a good Nile. Last year it rose 18 pics, which produced a very plentiful crop. We went to the island of Rhoda to see the Mekias, but the column of graduation was wholly covered by the water; so that we might have spared ourselves the trouble. The appearance of the island, however, now a complete carpet of verdure, with splendid sycamore trees (ficus sycamorus of Linnæus), was beautiful. There are no barns in Egypt: the peasant being sure of fair weather at harvest-home, the corn is immediately threshed, and the grain is piled up in immense hills, encircled by a wall. The birds are then freely allowed their share, though, during the time it is ripening, their claims are disputed by children, who are placed on elevated mud-hillocks, scattered in all directions throughout the plains; bawling, and flinging stones by means of a sling, to drive away the feathered robbers. The other day we went to Boulack, situated on the banks of the Nile. It is, properly speaking, the port of Cairo, and the busy scene it presents at this time of the year is not exceeded by any of our quays in Europe. The large dgerms, some of 40 and 50 tons, bring their owners immense profits during the overflowing of the Nile. The stream brings them down with great rapidity, and the strong north breeze takes them up again with equal speed. It is said these boats sometimes clear half their original cost the first season; a great part of the year, when the Nile is in its bed, they are laid up in ordinary, as their great draught of water prevents their moving. Throughout Egypt we never met with the remains of anything like a pavement in their cities, with the exception of Antinoe, where we clearly made out that the streets had been paved in many places.

English travellers are now beginning to make their appearance in Egypt. A few days ago Captain Bennet, of the dragoons, and Mr. Jolliffe arrived from making the tour of Palestine. The former is gone up as high as Assuan, with Colonel Stratton and Mr. Fuller; the latter is obliged to return immediately to England. We start in a few days for the tour of Syria. Sheikh Ibrahim, who travels for the African Association, and who is mentioned in Mr. Legh's publication, has been of great assistance to us with his advice in tracing out our route, &c. This he also did for both the travellers mentioned above. Mr. Salt is very kind and attentive to us; we dine with him every day, and he has allowed us to copy his map of Syria. We intend to cross the desert on camels to Gaza; to visit the whole sea-coast up to Latachia; from thence to cross over the mountains by Antioch to Aleppo; to go to Palmyra or Damascus, according to circumstances, and from Damascus to Jerusalem, visiting in our way all the objects of interest in the neighbourhood of our route. We calculate that the tour will occupy us till the middle of January, when we mean to embark at Alexandria for Smyrna and Constantinople. By the time we start for Syria (which will be in a few days), we shall have been fourteen months absent. We have supplied ourselves with provisions, clothes, and arms (viz., two muskets and a brace of pistols), and have, up to the present time, spent only one hundred and ninety pounds each, including our share of the boat-hire from Philæ up to the second cataract and back to Thebes, and also of the expenses at Abou-Simbel, excepting the payment of the labourers and the presents to the cashiefs. Mr. Salt furnishes us with letters of introduction to Lady Hester Stanhope, Mr. Barker, the consul at Aleppo, and all the English agents in Syria. Lord and Lady Belmore arrived at Alexandria in their yacht on the eighth instant, and embarked for Cairo on the seventeenth ; we expect them daily.

We have been so fortunate as to discover an interesting tomb opposite to Mr. Brine's at Radimore ; the sides are covered with paintings, amongst which are two groups, of a description very rarely, if ever, to be met with ; one of them represents the removal of a colossus between 30 and 40 ft. high, seated on a chair ; upwards of a hundred labourers are employed to move it. The other drawing represents an Egyptian garden, with exotics in flower-pots arranged on a terrace, near to which is an arbour, bee-hives, &c., &c. Mr. Bankes and Mr. Beechey are the only travellers who have visited this tomb since we discovered it : the former has made accurate drawings of all its contents.

CHAPTER IV.

TOUR IN SYRIA.

Departure from Cairo—Route to Jaffa—El Arish—Haneunis—Gaza—Ancient Khan at Asdoud—Ruins of a Roman Bridge—Jaffa—Singular appearance of the British Consul—Liberality of the Aga—Cesarea—Ruins at Athlite—Convent on Mount Carmel—Acre—Zib—Value of Medical Knowledge—Tyre—Sidon—Lady Hester Stanhope—Bayruth—Tripoli—The Cedars of Lebanon—Baalbec—Arab Village—Latachia—Picturesque Scenery on the Orontes—Heavy Rains—Antioch—Aleppo—Mr. Barker—His Hospitality and Kindness—Abundance of Game—Proposed Route—Observations on Aleppo.

On the 1st of October, at 8 A.M., we were without the walls of Cairo. We had made a bargain with an Arab to provide us with three camels, and to conduct us to Jaffa, for thirty dollars. About eleven, we passed, on our left, the obelisk of Mataria, the site of the ancient Heliopolis ; and shortly afterwards we passed close to the ruins of another ancient city on the skirts of the desert, where the only object of interest was a statue in a sitting posture, mutilated, but originally well executed. Our road was in the desert, but close to the cultivated plains, which extend no further from the Nile than where the soil is benefited by the overflowings of the river, either by natural or artificial means. This causes a distinct line of separation between the barren sand and irrigated land, having the appearance of a sea beach. We had left Cairo with only one camel and three asses ; the other two camels were to meet us at a village in the evening. We had enlisted in our service a Maltese interpreter, who mounted the third ass, while the camel carried our baggage. Arriving in the evening at the village before mentioned, we parted with the asses, and, at eleven at night, set out again on the three camels, with their owner and his black slave. We heard the howling of wild beasts during the night, resembling the cries of human beings in distress.

October 2.—This morning we were joined by a man with a laden camel, who, seeing we were armed, was anxious to have our protection. As the Tarabeen Arabs of the desert through which we were to pass are notorious robbers, we were not sorry to see our number thus increased ; the stranger was bound to a village near Gaza. To-day we passed occasionally through the skirts of the desert, as well as of the cultivated plains ; the latter are rich beyond description ; the crops of doura were the finest we had seen. The soil being saturated with water, and receiving at the same time the heat of an ardent sun, produces a very rapid vegetation. We slept this night in the desert; and on the following morning we halted at Selahieh, the last village on our road, which is situated on the borders of the cultivated plains of Egypt. We remained here a few hours to lay in a stock of water and provisions. On leaving the village at 2 P.M., we were astonished at the picturesque appearance of the desert, which was covered with wild shrubs. The occasional hill and dale give a pleasing variety to the scene, very different from what we had been accustomed to in Nubia, where the desert deserves that appellation in the strictest sense, being nothing but a barren expanse of sand and rock, totally destitute of every sign of verdure or vegetation. This difference is to be attributed to the nightly dews in this more northern climate. Wells of brackish water are occasionally met with, which serve to sustain the numerous gazelles which we constantly see feeding in the distance. We frequently met with birds; and in some places the quail and partridge were in considerable numbers. We found that, although the camels are capable when grazing, and not in work, of going five, six, and even seven days without drinking, it is necessary that, when travelling, they should drink at least every third day; and our driver, whenever he met with water, even if they had drunk the day before, never failed to let them drink again, which always appeared to refresh them; for the heavy sand fatigues these animals greatly. They perspire but very little, which tends much to the retention of that moisture so necessary for their support: they were constantly feeding as they went along, the length of their necks allowing them easily to do so. We could not but notice the provident bounty of nature in planting the desert with vegetables of a succulent and nutritious kind. It is undoubtedly to the want of verdure in the Nubian desert, as well as throughout the interior of that of Lybia, that we are to ascribe the difficulty of exploring those parts of Africa, as every camel there must have another to carry provender. Our road, or rather our track, was tolerably good. At Selahieh we had been joined by several persons—a man with asses, an Arab without a nose, a free negro, and six Muggrabins, one of whom was from Morocco, another from Algiers, and a third from Tunis, all bound on their pilgrimage to Mecca. By keeping with us they secured for themselves a supply of water, of which we had a good stock. They had separated from the great caravan from Morocco, consisting of 10,000 camels, which we met on our last expedition to the pyramids, when we learnt that the two sons of the emperor of Morocco were among the pilgrims. At the time we met it, this immense assemblage had been five months on its journey.

October 4.—We passed, on our left, the great lake, which is situated to the east of Damietta, and were obliged to cross several rivers and pools of salt water, sometimes up to the bellies of the camels, the Arabs and asses swimming across. In the afternoon we saw, on our left, the ruins of Pelusium, but they were too far distant for us to visit them, and too many pools and lakes lay between. In the evening the desert became more hilly, with occasional clumps of palm-trees in the valleys. In one of these we remained for the night, near a well of brackish water.

October 5.—To-day we had much the same country; the palm-trees, however, had disappeared. We saw many carcases and detached bones of camels and asses, which had probably dropped with thirst and fatigue. We also passed a few wells of indifferent water. This evening, Mahomet, our camel-driver, made some bread. He kneaded the dough in a leathern napkin, and, mixing a good deal of salt with it, made a flat round cake about half an inch thick, and baked it on dried camel's dung. It was very good.

October 6.—In the morning we came near a bay on the sea-coast. On the right we saw some Bedouins. The sand now became heavier, and the shrubs less plentiful: we, however, occasionally passed through some long damp plains between the sand-hills. We met a small caravan laden with tobacco; the attendants were armed,

They asked backsheeish of us in a very rude manner, but we refused to give it, and determined to make the best possible display of our fire-arms for the future. I have little doubt that these people use their arms to commit robberies when opportunity offers, as much as to protect themselves. We still find the road strewed with bleached carcases of camels and asses. In the course of the day we were surprised to see a very fine hare.

October 7.—We passed over a plain of about four miles in length, covered with thick, hard salt, resembling in appearance sheets of firmly frozen snow.* The surface bore the weight of our animals without giving way. Whilst we were at breakfast, a man on horseback came and talked to the camel-driver a good deal, saying, he wished to know who we were; that he was a guard, and had orders to stop all Europeans travelling without a soldier of the pasha of Egypt. He also asked for backsheeish, but did not address himself to us. We took care to let him see our arms, and when he found that we took no notice of him, he retired. The road was now level, which relieved the poor animals a good deal, and we soon reached the sea beach. At three in the afternoon we arrived at El Arish. About an hour before we reached it, we stopped at some wells of fresh water, where we found a great assemblage of camels and many Tarabeen Arabs, who appeared to stop all passengers. They entered into a violent dispute with our conductors, which we did not understand, but they took no notice of us. They presently levied a contribution on the Arabs who had joined us; and certainly we should have shared the same fate had it not been for the appearance of our arms, as the chief followed us all the way to El Arish, surveying our baggage with the most thievish inquisitiveness. We were also passed by the horseman who had visited us at breakfast, but observing that we kept our muskets in our hands, he said that it was not against us that he meditated hostilities, and galloped on. At El Arish are some Roman ruins: we noticed several marble columns. The village, which has a very fine well of good water, is situated on a slight eminence about half a mile from the sea, from which it is hidden by sand hills and clumps of palms. The principal part is inclosed within a high wall of considerable thickness, having loop-holes all round for musketry. There is an octagon battery for cannon at each angle. Some ruined guns and old French ammunition boxes are all the warlike stores it contains. This place is remarkable for the treaty made between Sir Sidney Smith and the French army, for the evacuation of Egypt, which his superiors would not ratify. The land about El Arish is quite barren.

October 8.—Soon after midnight we left this place. The morning was cold and foggy till sunrise, about an hour after which we stopped to breakfast. We begged our camel-drivers to halt in a vale at some distance from the road, that our Tarabeen neighbours might not discover us. We had, however, scarcely unladen the camels, when one of them came and seated himself in the midst of us. We could not help being surprised at the way in which this fellow stuck to us, as we were now nine hours from the place where we had first met him. We requested he would take himself off, as he could have no business with us. He walked away, apparently disappointed at not meeting some of his companions to assist him in plundering us. The desert was now much the same as at first, the number of shrubs increasing. In the forenoon we passed an extensive plain, where there are wells of tolerable water, a sheikh's tomb, and a Mahommedan burial-place. In the afternoon we had occasional views of the sea. We met many flocks of sheep and goats, peasants, and several laden camels. The attendants were usually armed, and eyed our baggage with a scrutinising look, but the sight of the muskets has always a tranquillising effect on them. We saw some par-

* "He shall inhabit the parched places in the wilderness, in a salt land and not inhabited." Jeremiah, xvii. 6.

tridges, and a good many gerba, a sort of rat which jumps like the kangaroo. About four we passed a temple of considerable magnitude. Two pillars of grey granite are standing, with several prostrate fragments; and there is a large wall, constructed of antique remains. At sun-set we reached the village of Haneunis. It has a long square fortification, inclosing a mosque. The approach to this place is picturesque: it is seated in a valley, and its environs are prettily laid out with gardens, trees, &c. There is but little land turned to agricultural purposes. We remarked both the houses and inhabitants to be cleaner and handsomer than those of Egypt. There are many marble fragments of columns, &c., which mark the site of a Roman town. We had often, before we left Cairo, inquired about the cheer we were likely to meet with in crossing the desert, and were always told of the hardships we should experience; such as want of water, the fatiguing motion of the camels, and the total privation of every accommodation. Bruce's narrative had also led us to expect very indifferent fare. With these unfavourable impressions, we were not a little surprised to find our journey a most pleasant one. The pace of the camels, though tedious, being little more than two miles an hour, we found very agreeable. The open air was the best sleeping-place during the night, and even then it was rather too warm; and as for water and provision, as we had taken care to lay in a good stock of both, we fared remarkably well. Indeed, if I except the heat, which about noon is certainly a fraction more than is agreeable (the skin of our noses being blistered off by it), I can truly say, I never made a more pleasant trip in my life.

October 9.—At daylight we proceeded, the road leading through a barren country resembling a heath. In two hours we came to the village of Esdier, prettily situated, with a view of the sea. There is here some land well cultivated and artificially watered, with the sackey, as in Egypt. The principal produce is tobacco. Beyond the village, scattered about over an uncultivated plain, are some beautiful sycamore trees, similar to those in Egypt. We remained four hours under one of these trees for the purpose of drying all our things, which had been wetted by the salt water some days before, but we had not discovered it until now. While we were thus employed, a woman came hastily forth from the village, and seating herself on the ground, under a tree near us, bewailed most bitterly, throwing the sand over her head with frantic gesticulations which lasted about twenty minutes, when her husband, with whom we heard she had quarrelled, came, and with difficulty took her away.

There are some marble remains of antiquity at Esdier. We thought we perceived a decided change in the climate; the dews for some nights past had been very heavy. This morning the N.E. wind blew keenly, but the sky was fine and clear. From Esdier to Gaza, which latter place we reached at 4 P. M., there are fine extensive plains prettily cultivated; and the neighbourhood of Gaza itself is richly wooded with the olive, sycamore, mulberry, cedar, fig, and other trees. The country is inclosed by hedges of prickly pears, the hills gently rising to the view beyond each other, and the whole has a beautiful appearance. Excepting the less perishable materials, with which the houses are constructed—stone being substituted for mud—the town partakes of the wretched appearance of those in Egypt. The rains in winter have forced the natives to roof their houses, whereas in Upper Egypt they merely lay some canvas across to shade them from the sun, that being the only inconvenience they have to guard against. We remarked that the inhabitants here were better looking and cleaner, the women being dressed in a white or blue shirt, and a white shawl thrown loosely over the head, with which those who have no other veil occasionally cover their faces. Being tired, and having nine days' beard, we did not visit the town; we were further discouraged by our servant having been scoffed at on account of his religion. This was the frontier town of the land of Canaan.*

October 10.—At 4 A.M. we left Gaza; the road for two hours was through beautiful groves of olive trees. Then entering an open country, partly cultivated, we passed some villages on each side of us, and the dry torrent of the Escol over a bridge of two high arches. About noon we had on our left Majudal, a large village with a mosque, situated in a valley, surrounded by groves of olives. At three in the afternoon we arrived at Asdoud, the site of the Roman Azotus; near it is an antique building in the form of an open square, which we at first took to be Roman, but as the Turkish khans for the accommodation of caravans and travellers are built much in the same manner, we are rather inclined to believe that it is one of them of very ancient date. Its inclosed court is entered by an arched passage, within which, on each side, are piazzas formed of five arches, two on each side of a larger one in the centre. On each side of the south entrance are chambers, with steps to ascend to the top of the building. The chamber on the left has evidently been used as a primitive Christian chapel, as appears by an altar and a cross; and there is an inscription in some Eastern language over the door. There are other arches in ruins, and partly buried, closer to the village, amongst which is a marble fragment, which would appear to have once formed the capital of a Corinthian column. The natives of this place flocked round us in numbers, looking at us, and everything belonging to us, with wonder and astonishment. After we thought they had sufficiently surveyed us, we begged them to retire. They showed no incivility, but said they merely came to look at us. Some women came also, with a sick young man, apparently in a consumption, asking medical advice. We assured them we were not hackim, which they did not believe, and we luckily recollected that our Maltese interpreter had some "balsam of Mecca," which the friars say is an antidote for all distempers. We gave them some, which appeared to excite much gratitude. They, however, soon returned to beg some of our hair, saying that the smoke of Christian hair, burnt while the medicine was warming, would ensure a cure of the disorder.* We could not help laughing at their superstition, but they continued to entreat us. For my part I had little to spare, and Irby did not seem inclined to give away any of his. They at length retired without the desired remedy, and brought us some honey and bread by way of return. This we offered to pay for, but they would not accept anything. We had been advised by Sheikh Ibrahim to go from Gaza to Jáffa, by the way of Ascalon or Ashkelon, but our camel conductor could not be prevailed upon to go through that place, as it is not on the direct road, and he would be liable to a penalty if he deviated from the common route of the camels—a regulation intended, we suppose, to prevent smuggling, as Ascalon is on the sea-coast. At that place we should have seen part of a Roman amphitheatre, and some excavations made by Lady Hester Stanhope, in search of supposed treasure, which failed of success; but what we saw at Azotus in some measure recompensed us, and this we should have missed had we gone by the other route. It was at Ashkelon that Samson slew thirty men (Judges, xiv. v. 19). Asdoud is called Ashdod in the Old Testament (see Isaiah, xx.; Jeremiah, xxv.; Amos, i., ib. iii.; Zechariah, xix.; and Zephaniah, ii.). It is called Azotus in the Acts of the Apostles, and by the Romans. Palmyra, built by Solomon by the name of Tedmor, or Tadmor, is another instance, among many in Syria, of places having regained their original names. The Arabs in that neighbourhood know nothing of Palmyra, always calling it Tedmor.

October 11.—Before daylight, we quitted Asdoud; the country is open

* Genesis, x. 19.

* Mungo Park, at Dingyee, was requested by a foulah to give him a lock of his hair to make a saphie.

and little cultivated, though the soil is very rich. In the afternoon we passed some ruins, probably Roman; they appear to have been an aqueduct to convey water to the road-side, which is to the eastward of the tract we traversed. We also passed a well which our conductor told us contained poisonous water; on our right was Yabne, the ancient Jamnia, situated on a small eminence. About noon we crossed the nahr (or river) El Rubin, close to the ruins of a Roman bridge, one arch of which, and a part of another, are all that remain. They are overgrown with bushes and weeds, which have a pretty effect; and certainly, to an amateur of the picturesque, the ruins of Syria must have a decided advantage over those of Egypt, where an arid climate totally prevents there being the least spot of verdure on a ruined fabric, be it ever so old. The traveller is, however, recompensed for this deficiency, by the comparatively high state of preservation in which he finds the Egyptian monuments, notwithstanding their superior antiquity; and I think that he who has once seen Egypt, will never feel equally interested in any other country. It is this feeling that has brought Mr. Bankes back to the Nile, after having explored Greece, Asia Minor, and the Archipelago; and he is now gone a second time to Thebes. The river El Rubin, above the bridge, is nearly dry, and filled with wild flowers and rushes. Below it there is a handsome winding sheet of water, the banks of which are likewise covered with various water-flowers, and many black water-fowl were swimming on its surface; the water is bad, but not salt. On the opposite side of this river, on a small eminence, is Sheikh Rubin's tomb, surrounded by a square wall, inclosing some trees. There are in Syria and Egypt numbers of these tombs, which the Arabs erect to the memory of any man who they think has led a holy life, for the title of sheikh is not only given to their chiefs, but also to their saints. These tombs are generally placed in some conspicuous spot, frequently on the top of a mount. The sepulchre consists of a small apartment with a cupola over it, white-washed externally;* within are deposited a mat and a jar of water, for the ablution of such as retire there for devotion. Sheikh Rubin, who lived many years since, appears to have been much respected, and the people still go to pay vows at his shrine; they also bring provisions and celebrate festivals there; the river no doubt receives its appellation from this sheikh. Leaving the neighbourhood of the nahr El Rubin, we crossed the sand hills and came to the sea beach, four or five miles south of Jaffa, and continued coasting till we came to the back of the hill, on the opposite side of which stands the town; here we crossed over between the most beautiful gardens, filled with vines and fig-trees, the prickly pear, &c., though the soil is a deep sand. We arrived at Jaffa, the ancient Joppa, about 5 P.M. On our right we saw Ramla and Loudd, the ancient Arimathea, and Lydda; the former is in the road to Jerusalem. There being no inns or khans in the sea-port towns for the accommodation of travellers, we were obliged to repair to the residence of the English consul. We found the representative of Great Britain sitting at the door of his house; he was a man apparently about sixty years of age, dressed in the Turkish mode, excepting an old brown cocked hat covered with grease, and put square on his head. His beard might be of some seven or eight days' growth, and his back was ornamented with a plaited pig-tail, reaching down to his middle. It was difficult to refrain from laughing at the sight of so odd a figure, for his dress was all soiled with fat and the drippings of soup. He received us with a dignified reserve, and, uttering several "favoriscas," showed us into the apartment, which performed the office of a saloon. This room was filled with water-melons; some English prints decorated the walls, and an old dirty sofa, without a

* "Ye are like unto whited sepulchres, which, indeed, appear beautiful outward, but are within full of dead men's bones." Matt. xxiii. v. 27.

covering, and well stocked with fleas, constituted the furniture, whilst numerous holes in the floor gave free access and egress to the rats. In the evening, when supper was announced, we were in hopes of a splendid repast, and as we had not tasted anything since our early breakfast of dried fruit, we entered the room with our appetites very sharp set. Great was our disappointment when we found nothing but rice and cabbage, our host observing that it was "Giorno della Penitenza." We slept in the *saloon*, and got unmercifully bitten by the fleas. Next day we received some scraps of meat, but the old consul took care first to fill us so full of rice, that we could hardly find room for the better part of his feast. Jaffa, situated on the sea-coast, is a small fortified town; the defences were in a very ruinous state, but the Aga was busily employed in repairing them. Vessels were arriving from the northward daily, with stones, &c., and he himself superintended the operations constantly. The Christian and Mahommedan inhabitants were obliged to work alternate days, the parties being changed every morning at sunrise by the sound of the drum. We saw the place where the French entered the town on their advance into Syria, and the hospital where Buonaparte poisoned his sick, on his retreat, to prevent their falling into the hands of the Turks. This place is now the Armenian convent, and one of the priests, who was in the town at the time, says there were *only* thirty-five men thus poisoned. About a mile without the town the French army was encamped, and it was here that Napoleon inhumanly massacred the inhabitants in cool blood, after the town was fully in his possession. The number thus slain is uncertain, but many people now in Jaffa attest the truth of the story. Our camel-driver being bound to Jerusalem, we sent the heaviest part of our baggage to that place by him, and endeavoured to purchase horses to continue our route in Syria. As we found great difficulty in procuring them, we sent to request the Aga would lend us a soldier to assist us, as old Damiani, the consul, was of more harm than good in the business. Instead of doing so, the Aga very kindly said he would lend us government horses for nothing, as he had also done to Colonel Stratton, and that we might keep them as long as we pleased: he added, that an Englishman, to whom he had granted the same favour, had three years afterwards sent him a spy-glass in return. This observation savoured a little of self-interest, but he was a kind-hearted man, as the following incident shows. Our Maltese interpreter, twenty years ago. had been in a better situation of life, and, whilst trading in a small way in cotton, became acquainted with this Aga; on some occasion he had given him a watch as a present; they never again met till the other day, when the Maltese, travelling as interpreter to Colonel Stratton, was recognised, at Jaffa, by the Aga, who, seeing him in reduced circumstances, forced him to receive a sum of money, saying, it was now *his turn* to give a present. The Maltese, who is an honest man, declined accepting the cash, but the other forced him to take it. This is one, amongst other instances we have met with of the disinterested generosity of the higher class of Turks. Jaffa is the ancient Joppa: Hiram, king of Tyre, sent Lebanon cedars by sea to Joppa, for the building of Solomon's temple; and the latter had them removed by land to Jerusalem (see 2 Chronicles, c. ii. v. 16). The scene of St. Peter's vision was near Joppa (Acts, x.).

October 15.—At 9 A.M. we left Jaffa. We had not slept in a house, or under any cover since we departed from Cairo; as yet we had found no inconvenience from this; but as we were going to the northward, and the winter was fast coming on, we thought it advisable to equip ourselves in a thick Arab garment, made of a sort of coarse wool or sackcloth; it was very heavy, and, although of the best quality, cost only ten piastres, little more than five shillings; a pair of coarse white Turkish breeches, and red worsted turban completed our costume. The sun in the desert had browned us to a good standard colour, which according well with our dress, we thus avoided the curiosity of the natives, who before used to flock round to gaze at us as if we had been wild beasts. For five piastres we purchased a woollen mat to do duty as a bed; and thus furnished, and with four good hack horses, we felt quite independent. As to provisions, we always had a staple of bread, cheese, and onions, which served for breakfast, dinner, and supper, unless we were fortunate enough to meet with a fowl. Our road led along the sea-beach, and we shortly crossed the nahr El Petras. In the afternoon we passed through a wild but pretty country, and crossed the nahr Arsouf, leaving the village of that name (the ancient Apollonia) on our left. The following morning we set out very early, and crossing the nahr El Kasab arrived at Cesarea. Here we stopped two hours, examining the antiquities. A small part of these are inclosed within the ruins of an old wall and ditch, which appeared to be Saracenic; and on a promontory which bounds this extremity on the south side, are the remains of a large edifice, constructed apparently upon the ruins of a Roman temple. Many fragments of immense pillars of granite have been used to form a landing-place on the north point of a small bay. The Roman remains extend far beyond the limits of the walls before-mentioned, and to the north of them. Above, and parallel with the sea-beach, are the ruins of some arches, and of a wall, which appears to lead to the hills, which now begin to approach closer to the sea, and to the nahr Zerka, where the water is fresh; this circumstance, and the wells of the town having bad water, led us to suppose that these arches had once been part of an aqueduct. There are also wells on the promontory, but they are now dry. Without the Saracenic walls, to the south, we found a column of marble, with a Roman inscription of the Emperor Septimius Severus, but too much buried for us to take a copy of it. About noon we arrived at Tortura, the ancient Dora (see Judges, i. 27). There are extensive ruins here, but they possess nothing of interest. We left this place at two, and at four reached Athlite, where we remained for the night. Between Tortura and Athlite are numerous stone quarries. The village of Athlite is situated on a peninsular-shaped promontory, and has apparently been constructed from the ruins of an ancient city. It is of small extent, and would seem from its elevated situation, and the old wall which surrounds it, to have been a citadel. There are the ruins of two other walls, one of which incloses a square space, the farther or southernmost end of which juts into the sea. There are three entrances through this wall, two on the east, and one on the south side, and steps in various places to ascend to the top of it. The other wall approaches near to that of the citadel; but the outer one, which we may suppose to have included the remainder of the ancient town, incloses a considerable space of ground now uninhabited. There is a small bay to the south of the promontory, which may have occasioned the construction of a town on this site, as it makes a tolerable haven for small vessels. The most interesting thing within the citadel, is the ruin of a great building, which we were puzzled to make out; the half of the circumference, which is still standing, has six sides. On the exterior, below the cornice, in alto-relievo, are heads of men, lions, and sheep. The exterior walls of this edifice have a double line of arches in the Gothic style; the lower row larger than the upper one; the architecture is light and elegant. There does not appear to be any ancient name to this place, and from all the information that we could obtain, the ruins are no older than the time of the crusades, when the town went by the name of Castel Pelegrino. From the commodiousness of the bay, the extent of the quarries in the neighbourhood, the fine rich plains near it, which now are only partially cultivated, it would seem that this place was formerly of much importance, and that the neighbourhood, though now very thinly inhabited, was once populous.

October 17.—At day-light we departed through the northernmost of the two passages in the eastern wall. Here the rock has been cut away to form the road, and various circumstances combined, induced us to form an opinion that Athlite is of much greater antiquity than is represented. Passing by the part of the coast formed by the foot of Mount Carmel, we entered the bay of Acre, and in less than three hours from Athlite we were at Caiffa (the ancient Hepha). Here we found the only friar at present belonging to the convent of Mount Carmel, an intelligent man (a Maltese), who, after supplying us with breakfast, attended us to the summit of Carmel, where the convent is situated. This building was formerly fitted up with beds, and every accommodation. It was pillaged and destroyed by the Arabs after the retreat of the French army from the siege of Acre; the latter having used it as a hospital for their sick and wounded, while their operations were carrying on; and in the places where the poor fellows were laid, the numbers by which they were arranged are still visible on the walls. The friar shewed us a cave cut in the natural rock where the prophet Elijah had his altar (see 1 Kings, xviii. 17, and following verses). In front of this are the remains of a handsome church in the Gothic style, built by the Empress Helena at the time she made her pilgrimage to Jerusalem. From Mount Carmel there is a beautiful view of the bay of Acre, the mountains inland, and the Mediterranean. Near the convent are some prostrate columns. We found an immense scorpion amongst the rubbish in the court. There is a well of excellent water. The mount is of very inconsiderable height, and quite barren, though at the north-eastern foot of it are some pretty olive-yards. On mentioning to the friar our suspicions of the ruins of Athlite being partly Roman, he suggested the idea that it might have been called Athla, as the present name Athlite resembles that word much in sound. We returned from Mount Carmel, and leaving Caiffa at three in the afternoon, followed the coast of the bay of Acre, and shortly passed over to the right of the brook Kishon, where Elijah slew the worshippers of Baal after he had proved to them the existence of the true God, by the miracle he had wrought on Mount Carmel. We soon after crossed the mouth of the river Kishon, and subsequently the river Belus, and reaching Acre at sunset, were shown to the house of Signor Malagamba, the British agent. All the rivulets we have hitherto passed in Syria are fordable in the Autumn, close to their junction with the sea, where the counteraction of the rapid streams of the rivers, and the surf, form sand-banks or bars. The water is generally fresh close to their junction with the ocean.

October 13.—We found Signor Malagamba more useful to us than Damiani: but as he had no room to lodge us in, we took up our quarters in the convent, where we were kindly received by the "Padre Superiore." We ate our meals with the worthy consul, whose house is in the same khan as the convent. Acre is a strong fortified town. Since the French siege, in 1799, the Turks have doubled the walls which inclose the town. We were shewn the breach made by the French army, now entirely repaired, except the spent shot-holes. The situation of Acre is delightful. The principal objects of interest in the town are the mosque, the pasha's seraglio, the granary, and the arsenal. A great religious festival was solemnised by the Turks while we were here. The mosques were brilliantly illuminated at night. The next day we went to see the pasha's finest horses: they were splendidly caparisoned with gaudy trappings of leopards' skins embroidered with gold and silver; but the animals themselves were ill made and good for little, the whole affair being more for show than use. Acre was the Accho of the Old Testament, which, together with Achzib, Dor, Sidon, and some other places of the sea-coast of Syria, were never completely subdued by the Israelites (see

Judges, i. 31). Gaza, Ekron, and Ascalon, further to the southward, were subjugated (same chap. i. v. 18). We here procured a firman from the pasha, having travelled thus far without any authority from the Syrian governments. This firman was worded very strongly in our favour; it was addressed to all the Agas in the pashalic of Acre, and our horses were ordered to be furnished with fodder, &c. free of expense wherever we might go.

October 20.—At one in the afternoon we quitted Acre. Our route lay across the plain of that name, in which there was nothing remarkable to be seen except the extensive aqueduct by which the town is supplied with water. We stopped at Zib, the ancient Achzib (see Judges, i. 31). The inhabitants were dressed for the Mahommedan feast, and crowded round us, and all their sick came for medical aid, but we had nothing to give them but the balsam of Mecca, which had been so useful at Ashdoud. Amongst our patients was the sheikh's son, who had burnt his hand most terribly. He evinced much gratitude for the assistance we rendered to him and the rest of the villagers. He offered our interpreter a considerable sum of money, which he refused. A small medicine chest, with Reece's or some other book on the subject, would be a truly valuable article in the trunk of a traveller in these countries, and would be the surest means of conciliating the natives.

October 21.—We were mounted and on our route at daylight, and in about an hour's time reached Cape Blanco. The descent on the north side reminded us, in its numerous windings, of the mountain roads of Switzerland; and the sea dashing against the rocks below us had a fine effect. The road was execrable. About three hours before we reached Tsour, the ancient Tyre, we stopped to visit some ruins on a small eminence on our right; they consisted of the remains of a large city, and the ruins of a temple in a most dilapidated state. Only two columns are standing. In the lower part of the capital of one we distinguished the Echinus moulding. The material used in these buildings is the natural stone of the country, which is calcareous and very porous. Beyond these ruins we distinctly traced the remains of the ancient paved way towards Tyre, and we afterwards ascended what is called the ladder of the Tyrians; it is a picturesque spot, the road being cut in the side of the perpendicular cliff on the sea-shore, to the height of several hundred feet above the level of the water. This, according to Maundrell (page 52), was the work of Alexander the Great. After descending from this elevated spot, we passed the ruinous heaps of another ancient city and some picturesque rivulets, and arrived at Tsour at one in the afternoon. Here we put up at the house of an Arab, who called himself a Christian archbishop; he was not at home, and, at first, his wife, daunted by our rough Arab attire, was unwilling to receive us, but our conductor assuring her that we were Englishmen travelling for pleasure, she treated us with great civility and attention. The establishment was a very humble one, as might be expected in so mean a place. The prophecies of the fall of Tyre in Isaiah, Jeremiah, and Ezekiel, seem to be fulfilled in the present appearance of Tsour, there being no vestige remaining, but mere rubbish, of the ancient city (so called from Tiras the son of Japheth). The city, formerly built on an island, is now on a peninsula; the isthmus, which Alexander caused to be made for the prosecution of his attack on the city, has now the appearance of natural ground. The walls and castle are visible, but I should strongly suspect they are not the same which existed at the time when Tyre was in its glory, and the port is much choked up with mud.

October 22.—At sun-rise we proceeded on our journey. We saw the remains of the ancient aqueduct, and crossed the mouth of the Kasmia; the banks of this winding river, which proceeds from an extensive valley between the mountains, are very picturesque. There is a bridge with one arch over it, a little below which is a small island. We continued our route through a country nearly barren, very thinly populated, and very uninteresting, with mountains on our right, destitute of either beauty or vegetation. We passed through the ruins of five or six large cities, now mere rubbish, and only distinguishable as sites of towns, by numerous stones much dilapidated, but still showing marks of having been cut square with the chisel, with mortar adhering to them, and here and there were fragments of columns. The only place marked in the map in this quarter is the ancient Sarepta or Zarephath, remarkable by the miracles wrought there by Elijah (see 1 Kings, xvii.) In the afternoon we crossed the dry beds of several torrents, and a river by a bridge of five arches; the banks of all these streams were covered with wild-flowers, amongst which was the oleander, in full bloom and beauty. As we approached Saida we observed that the sides of the hills were covered with vineyards, but their appearance is not at all picturesque. Half an hour before we arrived, we passed the ruins of another ancient city; also a fragment of a granite column, and a Roman mile-stone, like that near Cesarea, and having upon it an inscription of the time of Septimius Severus. The immediate neighbourhood of Saida (the ancient Sidon) is pretty. The place derived its name from Sidon, the first-born of Canaan (see Genesis, x. 15). The plain at the foot of the hills is entirely appropriated to extensive and shady groves and gardens, with narrow and pretty lanes between them. There is no English consul or agent at Saida, we therefore went to the convent, but found no friars there, and the church was shut up. The French consul had entire possession of all the apartments; he was now on a tour to the Holy Land. We had seen him at Acre; he was then with his wife going to Nazareth. We had some difficulty in obtaining a room in this convent, but at last we got one belonging to one of the absent servants. We were now in the neighbourhood of Lady Hester Stanhope, and as we were entrusted with a letter from Mr. Salt, a packet of English letters from Acre, and a book from Jaffa, we deemed it our duty to wait on her, and therefore set out for her usual residence, an old deserted convent in the mountain, about one hour and half distance from Saida, called Mar Elias Alza; but her ladyship had removed from thence on account of the heat to a more elevated spot in the mountains, called Castle Jeba: we therefore forwarded the letters, &c., together with a note, requesting permission to wait on her. The following morning we received a letter, saying, that she had made her mind up not to receive any more Englishmen, with the exception of officers of the army and navy, "all fine fellows," as she was pleased to express herself; at the same time she strongly dissuaded us from undertaking the trip to Palmyra, and recommended us to make a short tour of fifteen or twenty days round the vicinity of Saida, and then to return and pass twenty days with her in her convent. This, at the present season of the year, with the winter and rainy season fast approaching, would have been the most impolitic plan we could have pursued, and therefore we returned a polite answer declining her civilities with as good a grace as we could. She is always dressed in the Turkish costume as a man; her generosity we heard spoken of in all directions. Saida possesses as few relics of its ancient magnificence as Tyre. The port, although it may once have been extensive, is now small, and nearly filled up with mud. The castle, connected to the main land by a bridge, is an old building, but the same remark which I made on the ancient edifices at Tyre is applicable to those of Sidon, viz., that they are more recent than the time when the city was in its splendour.

October—25. At 9 A.M., we left Saida by a wretched rugged road, and through an uninteresting country. We met occasionally with the remains of the ancient paved way. In the afternoon we passed the ruins of an ancient town and burial-ground; here are many stone sarcophagi, some never opened; their lids are high and massy, and terminate in an angle. A little beyond them are two arches in the mountain's side, the ruins either of a bridge or an aqueduct. Shortly afterwards we quitted the sea-coast and passed over the hills which form the promontory of Bayruth; here we had a fine view of the plain, covered with groves of olives, and of several villages on the mountain's side. Descending, we passed through plantations of figs, and of young mulberry trees for the silk-worm, and from thence through gardens neatly inclosed by walls, where we met occasionally with fragments of antiquity. It was dusk before we entered Bayruth, the ancient Berytus. It stands well, and like all the other towns of Syria that we have seen, has pretty environs and rich gardens at the back of it; but these beauties are always confined to particular spots, and an hour's ride usually conducts you again into an uninteresting and rocky country. There is a fine view of the sea from the marina, and the jetty is built on foundations of antique granite columns. There is also an ancient bath within the town. We were at the house of Mr. Laurella, the English agent, a very good fellow.

October 26.—At two in the afternoon we left Bayruth, the road being for a short time very pretty, with gardens on each side of us. We soon crossed the nahr El-Sazib below the junction of the nahr El-Leban, or River of Milk, so called from its foaming when overcharged with water. It is a pretty rivulet; the bridge has six arches. From hence the road led along the sea-beach until we came to a rocky promontory, the ascent of which reminded us of the ladder of the Tyrians, though it is neither so high nor so picturesque; on reaching the summit, we saw below us on the other side the nahr El-Kelb, or River of the Dog, running beautifully through a deep chasm in the mountains, and a very good bridge over it, which Maundrell describes as being a bow-shot from the sea. The banks are planted with vines and mulberries. There is a Roman inscription on a tablet carved out of the rock on the side of the road we descended; this was copied by Maundrell, 120 years ago, and appears to record the construction of the road by the Emperor Antoninus. Near the bridge is also another inscription in the Arabic language. We passed the night at the mouth of the river, and at daylight the following morning proceeded along the sea-shore. In an hour's time we ascended a rocky point of a small bay inhabited by fishermen. At the foot of this promontory, close to the sea, are the remains of a chapel cut out of the rock, which we were informed was the sepulchre of St. George. The old fishermen, whose cottage is situated on the promontory above the chapel, were so superstitious as to believe, and endeavoured to persuade us, that the water of the sea near this spot is a cure for all distempers, and that numerous people came hither for the purpose of being healed by it. We had here a good view of the grand convents of Harissa Soummaar, romantically situated on the summit of the mountain. The valley at the end of this bay is cultivated and studded with cottages. Proceeding along the sea-beach we passed a Roman arch constructed with large stones over the bed of a torrent; from hence the road led over rugged rocks, till we came to a handsome bridge of a single arch, over the nahr Ibrahim, the ancient Adonis, which, like the nahr El-Kelb, proceeds from a deep chasm between the mountains, but the level land is more extensive than that near nahr El-Kelb. We now proceeded by the sea-coast to Gebail. On our way we crossed over one of those *natural bridges*, over a torrent now dry. This is one of many places where the water meeting with inclined beds, has undermined the intermediate earth, and formed caverns, or natural arches. We reached Gebail, or Gibyle, at two in the afternoon, and stopped at the convent of Maronites, a poor miserable set of people who make a merit of never eating meat, &c. At Gebail, without the town, there are many Roman ruins, and a bridge with several granite columns; within the town, the castle and some other modern edifices are constructed upon ancient foundations. The Roman name of Gebail is marked in the map as Byblus, but in Ezekiel, xxvii. 9, it is called Gebal, and is mentioned as furnishing the fleets of Tyre with caulkers.

October 28.—We went from Gebail to Tripoli, which we did not reach till dusk, though we started at daylight. We saw nothing of interest except the remains of a Roman temple, and we passed over a very rugged and bad road until we reached Batroun, the ancient Botrys. Here the road turned to the right through a fine valley between the mountains, in which we noticed an old picturesque castle standing on a high rock; it is called Temseida, and was probably constructed to defend this pass. The hills on the south of the vale are covered with shrubs, and by the roadside are plantations of mulberries, vines, &c. A small river, which we occasionally crossed by bridges, takes its winding course through the valley. Leaving it, we passed to the north over the mountains by rugged paths, bordered by the myrtle and other wild shrubs, until we again came down upon the coast. At sun-set we reached Tripoli, and not being aware that there was an English consul in the town, took up our quarters in the convent with Padra Hermenigildo. This is the best town we have seen in Syria, the houses being all well built of stone, and neatly constructed within. It is seated at the foot of the mountains, at some distance from the sea-shore, and is surrounded by luxuriant gardens, producing innumerable oranges and lemons. The town is commanded by two old castles on the heights, built in the time of the crusades; the port is near an hour's distance, on a low point of the sea-coast, it is but an indifferent one, being an open anchorage, only a little sheltered by the Pigeon Islands. Three cities formerly stood here, one subject to Aradus, a second to Tyre, and the third to Sidon; hence the origin of the name Tripoli. There are square towers, apparently of the time of the crusades, all the way from the port towards Tripoli. On the second day of our arrival we received a message from the English consul, expressive of his regret that we had not come to his house; we immediately waited on him, and explained the circumstance to his satisfaction. He was a fine old man, nearly eighty years of age, and remembered Bruce, who stayed some days at his house; we were delighted with the affable and sensible conversation of this veteran.

On Thursday, at four in the morning, we left Tripoli, for the purpose of visiting the cedars of Lebanon and Baalbec. Signor Giuseppe Mazolière, the son of a French merchant, accompanied us, at the request of the padre of the convent. The ascent from Tripoli is gradual; the first object of interest is the aqueduct and bridge over the nahr Kavdas, or Abouli river. These structures are overgrown with bushes and weeds, and the river runs picturesquely under them in two channels. At first the road is good, and passes through cultivated plains, groves of olives, and beautiful valleys watered by branches of the river. Afterwards it becomes very rugged, steep, and irregular, and continues so the whole way to the village of Eden, passing between two conspicuous points of the mountain. Eden is delightfully situated by the side of a rich and highly cultivated valley; it contains between four and five hundred families, who, on the approach of winter, descend to another village only an hour's distance from Tripoli; the families were in the act of removing to their winter habitations when we arrived; and on our return from Baalbec, all those who had not previously quitted their summer quarters descended with us. They have an Arab catholic bishop, a church, and several priests; there is another Christian village, lower down in the vale. We arrived at Eden about two o'clock, which, including stoppages, makes it ten hours from Tripoli. Here Signor Mazolèire's relations received us most hospitably. The wine was delightful;

that of Lebanon has always been esteemed.*

Early on Friday morning, we set out by moonlight for the cedars, and arrived a little after daybreak. The ascent from Eden to the cedars is not considerable, the distance, allowing for the windings of the road, which is very rugged and hilly, may be about five miles. On the right, higher up the mountain, is a larger and deeper vale than that of Eden, with the village of Beshiri in the bottom; this valley is very rich and picturesque. It is surrounded by lofty mountains, and is watered by a winding stream. It reminded us of the vale of the Dive in Savoy, and its "Pont de Chèvres." The famous cedars of Lebanon are situated on a small eminence, in a valley at the foot of the highest part of the mountain. The land on the mountain's side has a sterile aspect, and the trees are the more remarkable as they stand altogether in one clump, and are the only trees to be seen in this part of Lebanon. There may be about fifty of them, but their present appearance ill corresponds with the character given of them in scripture. There was not one of them at all remarkable for its dimensions or beauty; the largest amongst them is formed by the junction of four or five trunks into one tree; according to Maundrell this is 12 yards in girt; but we are much more inclined to agree with Volney than with Maundrell, in the description which they have respectively given of the cedars of Lebanon. Numerous names carved on the trunk of the larger trees, some with dates as far back as 1640, record the visits of individuals to this interesting spot, which is nearly surrounded by the barren chain of Lebanon, in the form of an amphitheatre of about thirty miles circuit, the opening being towards the sea. We thought the *tout-ensemble* more resembled the Apennines at the back of Genoa, than any other mountain scenery we had ever seen. Mount Lebanon and its cedars are frequently alluded to in scripture. The words, "All the trees of Eden, the choice and best of Lebanon," Ezekiel, xxxi. v. 16, would seem to imply that the boasted cedars were always near the place in which the few remaining ones now are, as they are not more than five miles distant from the modern village of Eden. In the 2nd Chronicles, ii. 8, the words, "Send me also cedar-trees, fir-trees, and algum-trees, out of Lebanon," clearly prove that formerly other kinds of wood grew on this mountain, none of which are now to be found here, unless the walnut tree of the present day, which is in very high perfection at Eden, is the algum-tree of the ancients. By the first book of Kings, chap. vi. and vii., it appears that much cedar was used in the construction of Solomon's temple. With respect to the village of Eden it appears to stand where of old was the garden of God, so called throughout the whole of the xxxi. chap. of Ezekiel, particularly in the 8th and 9th verse; but by reference to Genesis ii. verse 8, the position of the garden of Eden, where Adam and Eve were placed, seems very uncertain, for from the 10th to the 14th verses you observe, "A river went out of Eden to water the garden, and from thence it was parted and became into four heads:" the river of Ethiopia (the Nile) appears to be one of the four, and the Euphrates another. Maundrell gives no extracts from scripture concerning Lebanon; probably because he thought it would be useless, as it is mentioned in so many different places. Volney is also silent on the subject, I mean as far as respects quotations. Eden is called Aden by the natives at this day.

We hired a guide to conduct us across Lebanon into the valley of Bekaa Mathooalis, in which Baalbec is situated. Leaving the cedars about an hour after sun-rise, we ascended to the crest of Lebanon, where we had an extensive view over the hills at its S. E. foot into the valley, with Baalbec in the distance. We beheld also to the westward a considerable extent of sea. Altogether it was a fine view, but scarcely deserving the commendations

* "The scent thereof shall be as the wine of Lebanon." *Hosea*, xiv. v. 7.

which Volney bestows on it. Lebanon, in the Syriac language, signifies white, which this mountain is, both in summer and winter; in the former season, on account of the natural colour of the barren rock, and in the latter by reason of the snow.

The valley of Baalbec, or of the Kasmia, or Bekaa Mathooalis, has an excessively rich soil, but is very little cultivated, and has no trees except in the immediate neighbourhood of Baalbec itself, and those are chiefly the fig and walnut. The valley is bounded on the N. W. side by Lebanon, and on its S. E. by Anti-Lebanon; its breadth may be about ten miles, while its length from N. E. to S. W. extends as far as the eye can reach. The Kasmia has its source to the north of Baalbec, and running through the plain, discharges itself into the sea a little to the north of Tyre. How deplorable that so luxuriant a spot, with so fine a soil, should lay waste and desolate! and what ideas of former wealth and magnificence do the splendid ruins of Baalbec call to the mind. The inhabitants of the mountain are nearly all of the church of Rome; but those of the Bekaa Mathooalis are a particular sect of Mahomedans, differing from the Turks in general; they are more hostile to the Christians than any other of the natives of Syria.

In descending from the summit of Lebanon the road was excessively steep and rugged; we dismounted and walked our horses down it; the sides of the mountain abound in red-legged partridges, and other game. At the S. E. foot of this part of Lebanon, is the source of a fine clear rivulet, which finally unites with the Kasmia. From hence we proceeded over some rugged hills covered with various shrubs; among which a species of oak, the myrtle, and the almond-tree, were remarkable. Mr. Mazolière told us they have a tradition that there were formerly gardens here, and the almond and pear-trees seem to confirm it. Crossing these hills, you come, near the plain, to the first village, after leaving the cedars. Late in the evening we arrived at Yead, a village about an hour's distance from Baalbec; the horses had been without any food for fifteen hours. We blamed our guide much for this, as we would have brought fodder with us from Aden, had we known how uninhabited the country was through which we had to pass. When we heard of the distance to Baalbec from the cedars, we threatened to return to Tripoli. But the guide, intent only on his own interest, and fearing to lose his money for the trip, declared there were several villages in the way where we could refresh the horses.

Saturday, November 1.—Early this morning we arrived at Baalbec, and employed the whole day in visiting the antiquities. Yesterday had been excessively fine, the sky being perfectly clear; but this evening they collected much on Lebanon and on the tops of the other hills, and the natives announced to us the approach of bad weather. We measured every part of the ruins; but as Wood and Dawkins, as well as Volney, have given correct descriptions, it would be superfluous for me to enter into minute detail. The imposing grandeur of one part of the building, of which six pillars are standing, particularly struck us. It is the remnant of a colonnade standing. Their beauty and elegance are surprising. Their diameter is 7 ft., and we estimated their altitude at between 50 and 60 ft., exclusive of the epistylia which is 20 ft. deep, and composed of immense blocks of stone, in two layers of 10 ft. each in depth, the whole of which is most elaborately ornamented with rich carved work in various devices. We imagine these pillars to have been the remains of an avenue of twenty columns on each side, forming an approach to the temple. The space originally included by them was 104 paces long, by 58 broad. We were much pleased with the architecture and sculpture of every part of the ruins, although they have been much disfigured by having been formerly converted into a fortress. Remarkably large stones have been used in the construction of the various edifices, and in the S.W. part of the elevated walls on which they stand, we measured a single stone of 66 ft. in length, and 12 in breadth and thickness. In the construction of the pyramids and temples in Egypt, we never noticed a single stone of more than 30 ft. in length, and these were most of calcareous or sand stone, excepting some few of granite. The whole of these buildings, together with the walls, are of coarse marble, excessively hard. The inhabitants of Baalbec, although much prejudiced against Christians, treated us civilly, and seemed less curious and inquisitive than the natives living near any of the other objects of interest which we had visited. We left Baalbec on Sunday at mid-day, but the afternoon turning out very rainy, we stopped for the night at a small village beyond the opposite side of the plain. We observed that considerable quantities of snow had fallen on the mountains, which may give some idea of the great height of Lebanon; indeed, when we crossed the mountain the preceding Friday, we found several patches of last year's snow, and we were told that it remains in some places, near the summit, throughout the year.

November 3.—Monday, the morning was foggy but calm; and the sun breaking out at times, we hoped the haze would clear away and that we should have fine weather. We accordingly proceeded on our return to Tripoli, but had not gone far when we met some peasants returning to their village, after having made an ineffectual attempt to cross Lebanon, where they said that much snow had fallen. In fact, an exceedingly cold N.E. wind began to blow with violence, accompanied by such heavy showers of sleet, snow, and rain, that we were obliged to take shelter in a cave at the foot of the mountain. We found here many peasants, who had made ineffectual attempts to cross; but as we had a difficulty in getting room for our horses, the cave being small and nearly filled before we arrived, we removed to a larger, though more exposed one, being little more than a cleft of the rock, where we got ourselves and our horses also under a roof, and made a large fire for the night. The next morning being fine, we began the ascent. The peasants with their cattle were unwilling to make the first trial, as they knew it would be difficult to find the road on account of the depth of snow; and they were aware also that the second party could profit by the mistakes of the first. We therefore led the van and met with no difficulty until we came nearly to the top: when, losing the road, the snow being very deep, and the sides of the mountain steep, our horses all fell with us, and were partly buried under the snow. We were obliged to dismount, and had considerable trouble in reaching the summit. The cold was excessive; and having on loose linen Turkish breeches, and shoes without any stockings, we felt it the more severely. In descending the opposite side, the snow was also very deep, and we found it advisable to push on lest we should be caught in a fog, which the appearance of the weather seemed to threaten. Shortly after we began to descend, it became thick and hazy, but we reached Eden in safety about two in the afternoon. We were informed at Eden that the bishop had publicly offered up prayers for our safety. We were told that people are prohibited from crossing Lebanon after the first of November; but I much doubt the truth of this. None of us received any injury from the weather, except Mr. Mazoière's servant, whose legs were much chapped and cracked by the cold. The poor fellow had never been among the snow before.

On *Wednesday, November* 5, the weather was fine, and we returned to Tripoli; the natives of Aden with their wives, children, and baggage, descending at the same time. The first part of the descent was in some places so steep and difficult, that we observed the peasants held on by the tails of their horses to prevent them from falling. On our arrival, we learnt that on the coast they also had experienced very bad weather. Wet weather detained us at Tripoli, where we were treated with the greatest kindness by the Padre Hermenigildo, until the afternoon of the 9th of November, when we set out and proceeded as far as the nahr El-Bered, or Cold River; where we passed the night in a khan, a place appropriated to the use of travellers, which Maundrell very well describes in the first and second pages of his book. The map places a village here named Orthosa, the site of the ancient Orthosia; but there is nothing except the khan now to be seen. There is a difficulty, in some instances, in distinguishing Roman buildings from these khans, as both the Romans and the Turks alike employed the arch.

The next day we went as far as Tortosa, nearly opposite the island of Ruad, where stood the famous city of Aradus. There are Roman remains at each of these places. The walls of Tortosa are constructed on the ancient foundation cut in the rock; and the remains of the castle within the gates are ancient. There are some old sepulchral caves by the road side. They serve to show that the Romans, as well as the Egyptians, had burial-places of this description. But the climate, so different here from what it is in Egypt, has destroyed all remains of stucco or painting, if ever they were thus decorated, which we have reason to believe they were, as Mr. Bankes told us he saw a Roman cave with fresco painting in it near Saida. The island of Ruad, according to Maundrell, is the Arvad, Arpad, or Arphad of scripture. Arvad was one of the places which supplied the fleets of Tyre with seamen.*

November 11.—To-day we went as far as the nahr El-Mulk, which we crossed by a bridge, and stopped for the night at a village about half an hour's distance from the river, the huts of which appeared to be temporary habitations, being constructed of reeds and straw. There are Roman ruins at the mouth of the nahr El-Mulk. We had hitherto been in the habit of sleeping in the open air, when we arrived at an Arab village; but now, the month of November being far advanced, we disliked the idea of doing so, and accordingly asked for shelter, which was refused, unless each of us, we were four in number, would consent to sleep in a separate habitation. This we knew was the place where Monsr. Boutin, the French traveller, was killed; and not being pleased with the proposition, we bivouacked in the open air as usual, the weather being fine and clear. In the night a man came to endeavour to persuade us not to lie where we were, saying that the wolves would destroy us. We, however, had more apprehension of the two-legged wolves stealing some of our things, and told our informer we had our fire-arms ready, and should keep a good look-out for those or any other mischievous animals. In the morning our bread and part of a ham which Padre Hermenigildo had given us were missing; but we suspected that, as far as related to the latter article, the dogs, with which all Arab villages abound, were the thieves, for pork is an abomination to the Turks.

November 12.—Just as we were starting, we found out that a hut close to which we had slept was empty and uninhabited. It appeared to have done duty as a barn; and the people, if they had had any civility, might have offered it to us. In the afternoon we reached Latachia. Two hours from where we slept is Jebilee, the ancient Gabala, where are Roman ruins, the principal of which is the remains of a fine theatre at the north side of the town. The whole journey from Tripoli, with one exception in the neighbourhood of Markab, a village inclosed in ancient fortifications, and seated on the top of a square mountain, near which the coast is rocky, is along a vast rich plain at the foot of the Ansanar mountains. These hills are of no considerable height, and are said to be inhabited by Pagan tribes. The plain is watered by many rivers, and there are also several channels of torrents now dry. Most of the rivers are pretty, their banks being covered with myrtle, oleander, wild vine, fig, &c. Though the soil is rich, it is very partially cultivated and thinly peopled.

* Ezekiel, xxvii. v. 8.

The principal produce near Jebilee is cotton, which the natives were gathering in as we passed. The city of Latachia was founded by Seleucus Nicator, under the name of Laodicea, in honour of his mother. He also built three other cities in this neighbourhood, viz. Seleucia, now Suadeah; Antioch; and Apameia, now Famiah. Latachia is seated on the N.W. side of Cape Ziaret, an elevated projection of the coast. In the neighbourhood are gardens planted with olives, figs, &c. in the manner of all the towns of Syria. The port, which is half an hour's distance from the town, is very small, but better sheltered than any we have seen on this coast. There is a fine old castle at the point of a bed of rocks projecting into the sea. The Marina is built upon foundations of ancient columns. There are, in the town of Latachia, an old gate-way and other antiquities. There are also sepulchral caves in the neighbourhood, but as they have no paintings, we did not think it worth while to visit them. Mount Lebanon was in sight the whole way from Tripoli, and was the only mountain on which we could see snow. Mount Cassius was before us. The Christian natives of Latachia and of all the pashalic of Aleppo to the north of Latachia are mostly of the Greek church; they speak the Arabic language. We lodged at the house of the English agent, Signor Moses Elias, a very excellent man. We were detained here till the 15th, by the intrigues of the Arab conductor, who affected to be unwell, and who had previously at Acre, Bayruth, and other places, tried all in his power to oblige us to send him and the horses back to Jaffa. This occasioned us a good deal of trouble and inconvenience.

November 16.—The road was along a fine plain, until we came near the village of Candele; when crossing some hills we descended into the valley of that name. The village is seated amongst the sand hills to the west of the vale, and we had some difficulty in finding it. The next day we were continually passing over hills richly wooded, with numerous narrow intricate roads, amongst which we lost our way several times. The night had set in, without our finding the village of Lourdee, whither we were bound; and we were on the point of giving up the search, and bivouacking in the wood, when luckily the barking of some dogs indicated to us the vicinity of the place, which is in an elevated situation and immediately by the side of the highest pinnacle of Mount Cassius.

November 18.—We descended the north side of these mountains, the scenery still continuing wild and woody. This day, also, we lost our way several times. In the afternoon we reached the banks of the Orontes, at the place where the picturesque part of the river commences, and immediately below the spot which is marked upon the chart as the site of the "city and groves of Daphne." Mr. Barker has visited the spot; and from him we learn that there are still to be seen the grand sources of water which composed the celebrated fountain. He states that, in some instances the water boils up in a column as thick as a man's body; and *jets-d'eau* of that thickness, and upwards of 50 feet high, might be formed here. We now followed the banks of the river, and were astonished at the beauty of the scenery, far surpassing anything we had expected to see in Syria, and, indeed, anything we had witnessed even in Switzerland. The river, from the time we began to trace its banks, ran between two high hills, winding and turning incessantly; at times the road led along precipices, looking down perpendicularly on the river. The luxuriant variety of foliage was prodigious; and the rich green myrtle, which was very plentiful, contrasted with the dark-red gravel of the road, made us imagine we were riding through pleasure-grounds. The laurel, laurustinus, bay-tree, fig-tree, wild vine, plane-tree, English sycamore, arbutus, both common and andrachne, dwarf oak, &c., were scattered in all directions. At times the road was overhung with rocks covered with ivy; the mouths of several caverns gave a wildness to the scene; and the perpendicular cliffs, upwards of 300 feet high, jutted into the river, forming points round which the waters ran in a most romantic manner. On one occasion the road wound round a deep bay, so that, on perceiving ourselves immediately opposite the spot we had so recently passed, it appeared as if we had crossed the river. We descended at times into plains cultivated with mulberry plantations and vines, and prettily studded with picturesque cottages. The occasional shallows of the river, roaring over its rocky bed, completed the beauty of this delightful scene, which continued for several miles. In the plain of Suadeah the river becomes of a greater breadth, and runs in as straight a line as a canal. By the time we entered the plain, night had closed in, and we had difficulty in finding Suadeah. There is no bridge ; but a peasant at last showed us a place where the river was just fordable. Suadeah is a straggling village, consisting of unconnected cottages, and situated in a plain chiefly inclosed with mulberry and lemon plantations. We put up at a house appropriated for the use of travellers, and found it the best halting-place we had yet met with. The soubash of the village, a sort of petty governor, was in the house, and treated us with much civility, ordering us a good supper, feeding our horses, and refusing to let us pay a single para. All he asked for was a little gunpowder. Unfortunately we had given nearly our whole stock to young Mazolière at Tripoli, but we gave him all that we could spare. Whatever may be the generally received character of the Turks, it is certain that we have always met with the greatest civility and attention from them.

November 19.—In the morning, being pressed for time, and understanding that the ruins of the ancient Seleucia, which are near the sea, and half an hour's distance from Suadeah, possess no particular interest, we pursued our journey towards Antioch. It rained heavily ; and after we had been on the road about three hours, being still two hours' distance from Antioch, we perceived some cottages ; and, being thoroughly wet through, we requested shelter. In the two first cottages we found only women; and, as their husbands were absent, they did not dare to receive us. At the third, the men were willing to admit us, but the women would not hear of it, and expressed their refusal in a violent and ill-natured manner. During the time we were thus soliciting shelter, even that of a cow-house, the rain was pouring in torrents, and we made a pitiable appearance, being perfectly soaked through. Seeing that no entreaty availed, we gave them the *kat-ack-harack*, the Arab expression of thanks, and tried another cottage, where we were admitted without the least hesitation. These cottages consist of a single long room ; the cattle occupy one end, and the family the other. The inhabitants have extensive plantations of young mulberries for the silk-worms, and looms for manufacturing their produce. The occupants of the hut, who consisted of the proprietor, his mother, wife, brother, and children, were of that tribe of Mahommedans which Volney designates as Turkomans: they were extremely kind, placing us near a large fire, giving us good beds and coverlids, and making us share with them their humble supper of doura and wheat boiled. It rained during the whole night ; and we were detained till noon on the following day, when we proceeded to Antioch, after giving our host eleven piastres, and his wife a double gold Napoleon, as an ornament, besides paying for the horses, corn, &c. The women in this country ornament themselves with pieces of money, varying in value, according to their circumstances ; the poorer class with paras, and the higher orders with sequins and gold roubees. We gave the gold coin, not merely to reward our host and his wife for their kindness, but to vex the fair ladies in the other cottage, and make them ashamed of themselves. We also thought that a few extra piastres thus laid out might benefit other travellers.

Antioch is beautifully situated on

the left bank of the Orontes, at the foot of a hill. There is a handsome bridge over the river, and some of the heights are picturesque. The present town is a miserable one, and does not occupy more than one-eighth of the space inclosed within the old walls, which have a fine, venerable appearance, having square towers every hundred yards, with occasional watch turrets: these are the works of the Roman and Greek emperors. Antioch is said to have once contained between eight and nine hundred thousand inhabitants. The plain on which it stands is considerably elevated above that of Suadeah. We were annoyed at not having been able to visit the ruins of the city and groves of Daphne, but it was impossible to do so without a guide, and there was no procuring one. The houses of Antioch, Suadeah, Lourdee, and their neighbourhood, unlike those in most of the towns of Syria, are roofed and tiled, and without terraces. In the side of the hill at the back of Antioch, there are many sepulchral caves. This town is celebrated in the Acts of the Apostles.

November 21.—To-day we went as far as Gesir Adid, four hours' distance, near a bridge over the Orontes. Our road was across a barren plain, bounded to the north by mountains, at the foot of which is the lake of Aggi Dengis. Rain prevented our leaving this place till noon of the 22nd, when we reached Bourkee, the site of a Roman town of considerable size, and where the ancient sepulchral caves cut in the side of the mountains, serve the present natives for habitations. We took up our abode in a deserted and ruinous water-mill.

November 23.—We travelled over some rocky hills into the plain of Alaks, supposed to be that in which Aurelian conquered Zenobia. We passed many sites of ancient towns, castles, tanks, temples, &c., all of the lower empire, and very uninteresting. On one occasion we counted the vestiges of eleven towns, in a rich plain, with a fine loamy soil; all of them now desolate and uninhabited. So much for the Turkish government, and its encouragement of agriculture, the arts, &c.! The eastern part, however, of the plain of Alaks, which is nearest Aleppo, has a few villages, the inhabitants of which we saw in considerable numbers, engaged in collecting their cotton. We stopped at Tourneen, the easternmost of these villages.

November 25.—About 3, P. M. we arrived at Aleppo, passing through an open country, with a thin surface of soil, well tilled in most parts, but monotonous and destitute of trees, as, indeed, is the case all the way from Antioch. We had been recommended by our friend and adviser Sheikh Ibrahim to take the route to the northward of Aggi Dengis, as it would conduct us to the mountains and ruins of St. Simon, which latter, however, are of the date of the lower empire, and, as we have since learnt, totally uninteresting. We have reason to rejoice in having taken the route we did, as the Curds who inhabit the mountains were in rebellion against the pasha, who had sent a military force to quell them shortly before our arrival. We have since heard that the chiefs escaped; but an example was made by the death of about twenty of the prisoners. Some of those executed are supposed to have been innocent; and the pasha is said to have been much affected on hearing this, and recalled his troops, saying, that as the chiefs had escaped, and the natives had submitted, he did not wish any further severity to be shown.

On arriving at the house of Mr. Barker, the consul-general, we found Mr. Bankes there. He was on his way to revisit Egypt and Nubia; and intended to penetrate from the second cataract into Abyssinia. We mutually gave each other all the information we possessed; Mr. Bankes on Asia Minor and Greece; and we on Egypt and Nubia.

December 22.—We have been detained at Aleppo nearly a month, waiting for the arrival of the caravan which brings kali from Sukne to this place, a journey of five days. Palmyra is seven days journey from Aleppo. The kindness we have experienced in Mr. Barker's hospitable mansion merits our sincere gratitude. I fear we shall be a little spoiled when we turn out for Palmyra; for here, independent of the society of Mr. Barker and his amiable family, we have had every comfort and luxury we could imagine. Our amusements have been most agreeably varied; sometimes we went out shooting in the gardens near Aleppo, which abound in woodcocks, &c. We coursed the gazelle and hare alternately, the greyhounds in this country being very swift and strong. One day we were indulged with a hawking scene. The cheapness and abundance of game are astonishing; woodcocks, partridges, wild-geese, ducks, teal, the bustard, wild turkey, joli notes, &c. We thought the flesh of the gazelle well-flavoured, although Bruce abuses it. The white species is supposed to be the best. We have frequently had the porcupine at table; it forms a delicious dish, somewhat resembling in appearance and taste both the pig and the hare. The porcupines inhabit holes in the rocks, and they are so quick of hearing that it is very difficult to shoot them, as they never quit their holes till dark, and even then with the greatest circumspection. The people wait patiently in the cold for hours, near the holes, till the animal makes its appearance. They commit much mischief in the gardens near the city. We had thought of visiting Bagdad, for the purpose of seeing the ruins of Babylon; but as Mr. Massick, the Dutch consul here, had recently received a letter from a friend, stating that there is nothing whatever to be seen there, we gave up the idea. Mr. Barker has resided nineteen years as consul-general in this place, and we find his advice and assistance of the greatest use. As we came into this country with only one hundred and fifty pounds, which Mr. Salt supplied us on our bills, we had made up our minds to return to Cairo, to replenish our funds for Asia Minor, Greece, &c.; but Mr. Barker, divining that some such motive was the cause of our intended return to Egypt, most kindly anticipated our wishes on this point, and insisted on supplying us with whatever money or letters of credit we wanted. This will prevent the necessity of our going to Egypt again, and will assist us much. We are anxious to complete our travels in the Mahommedan countries, and again to enjoy the comforts of Switzerland and Italy. There is a great sameness in all Turkish towns; and the absence of inns, theatres, museums, picture-galleries, libraries, promenades, evening parties, and the ever-handy and comfortable café, is a privation which an European must always feel. A firman from the Grand Signior is on its way to us from Constantinople, Mr Barker having written for it on our arrival here. It will be useful in Asia Minor.

December 24.—The caravan from Sukne arrived this day, and we shall soon be off. We are to send the outlines of our tour to Lord Belmore for his guidance; but this we defer till we get to Palmyra. His lordship very kindly offered us a passage in his brig to any parts which might lie in his way, should we be able to embark with him from Syria; but there is no chance of this.

December 29.—We were to have set off this evening for Palmyra, by way of Sukne; when, accidentally meeting a merchant from Bagdad, a friend of Mr. Barker, he strongly dissuaded us from the measure, and urged us to go by the way of Hamah or Homs, as the Annasee Arabs are in the neighbourhood of Palmyra. We had understood that the cold had driven them all to the southward, towards the banks of the Euphrates; but as it appears there yet remain two tribes of them, Homs will be the best place to start from.

We accordingly prepared to depart in two or three days for Hamah, which place, as well as Homs, is distant only four days' journey from Palmyra, which we had sanguine expectations of being able to reach from either one or the other of these towns. However, we had two other strings to our bow; either to push on to Cariateen, which is only one day from Tadmor, and thence to steal to that city before the Arabs were aware of our intention; or to take

Turkish post-horses and an escort from Damascus, and go in spite of the Arabs. This last plan, however, would have been a very expensive one. Our constrained residence of six weeks at Aleppo made us fully acquainted with the city and its environs. It is pleasantly situated in a hollow surrounded by sloping hills, which are, however, uninteresting, having no trees, and the land not being inclosed. The houses are built of stone; the streets narrow and ill-paved, except the bazars, which are all roofed over with arches of the same construction as the houses, and are lighted from above. Thus you can walk all over the town on the terraces of the houses; the arches connecting the streets one with the other. We visited houses half a mile distant in this manner. The Franks and Christians have their separate quarters here, as in all Turkish towns. The city, the walls of which resemble those of Antioch, is surrounded with gardens, watered by small rivulets drawn from the main stream which supplies the town. We visited some Turkish houses, and were much struck with the beautiful ceilings of the apartments, which are decorated by Persian artists. They are curiously gilt, and painted. The decorations in carve-work, on the doors and window-frames, are also extremely curious. The society of Aleppo is good: the men and women make separate parties to the baths, where they have coffee and refreshments, and pass the evening. We greatly admired the neat and cleanly appearance of the butchers' shops, which are equal to those of London.

CHAPTER V.

Departure for Hamah—Letters of Introduction—Caravan from Mecca—Hamah—Khans—Georgian Slaves—Negotiations with the Arabs—Interview with them—Homs—Departure for Palmyra—Arab Camp—Interview with the Arab Chiefs—Arab Feast—Fine View of Palmyra—Disappointment on reaching the Ruins—Description of them—Return to the Arab Camp—Reach Homs—Expenses of our Journey—Traits of the Arabs—Their character for Dishonesty not deserved—Damascus—Sketch of intended Route.

January 3.—We started for Hamah; our kind and estimable host, and his brother, accompanied us on horseback for two hours outside the town. Such had been Mr. Barker's solicitude in our behalf, that he furnished us with letters to Selim, the governor's secretary at Hamah, and to Scander, the secretary to the motsellim of Homs; he likewise gave us a letter of recommendation to Hadgi Hassan, an elderly Turk at Homs, who has great dealings with the Arabs. All these people were requested to render us every assistance in their power to enable us to reach Palmyra. He gave us, besides, other letters to the Saraffs of the pasha of Damascus, urging them to assist us in getting horses, should we be obliged to travel post. Also, letters to Acre, Cyprus, and Smyrna; to Sir Robert and Lady Liston, and to several other persons at Constantinople. He lent us Maundrell's Travels in Syria, and a good map of Asia Minor and Greece; and, not contented with doing us all these good offices, furnished us, as I have before stated, with all the money we wanted.

At sun-set we stopped at the khan Touman, a spacious lodging, but filled to excess with the caravans for Damascus and Latachia. On the following morning we proceeded at daylight in their company; our road lay over naked plains partly cultivated. About three in the afternoon we stopped at Sermein. There are several villages in this quarter, and a few clumps of olives; otherwise the country is destitute of wood. Mount Cassius, whose summit was already covered with snow, was in sight on our right.

January 5.—We proceeded at sunrise, intending to go with the Latachia caravan as far as Shogher, and thence follow up the banks of the Orontes to Hamah; but being late, and seeing a caravan on our left, we branched out in that direction, joined them, and finding that they were in the straight road to Hamah, and bound to that place and Damascus, we continued with them. About ten, we passed the ruins of a square Turkish fortress, inclosing a village. Many of these places, on the skirts of the desert, are walled in, probably to afford them protection against the Arabs. Shortly afterwards, we met a very extensive caravan, being part of the hadj or pilgrimage to Mecca, on their return from Damascus—they had the green flag, the prophet's banner, flying. There were but few camels, the animals being mostly horses and mules, and having all bells attached to them, which made a merry ringing noise.* There were several tackterwans, the only species of vehicle in the East. We had seen one of them in the great Morocco hadj, which arrived at Cairo in September last; it resembled a sedan chair, supported before and behind by horses, instead of men: but of those which we saw to-day, one was a species of tent-bed, placed cross-way on the back of a mule; and another resembled two children's cradles, fitted like panniers on the back of a camel. These tackterwans are inclosed with curtains, and are generally used by women or sick people. Nearly the whole of this, and the next day, we continued to pass divisions of the hadj: all the animals were laden with some private venture of the pilgrims, who always join commerce with religion in these expeditions. They have among themselves an old adage "Beware of thy neighbour if he has made a hadj; but if he has made two, quickly prepare to leave thy house." The keenness with which all the peasants, near the khans, bargain for everything they sell, seems to agree with this. We saw to-day some few Roman ruins, and sarcophagi, formed of the stone of the country, apparently of the date of the lower empire. At 2 P.M. we stopped for the night at Marah, and slept in a very good khan. The next morning, Lebanon, now a mass of snow, lay before us; and Mount Cassius was shut in by the northern extremity of the Ansarian mountains. We passed several sites of ancient towns, tanks, sarcophagi, &c., everything much dilapidated, and little interesting, except as proving that the neighbourhood was more thickly peopled in former times than it is at present. The country was a succession of open plains, without a single tree, and inhabited by numerous gazelles, partridges, hares, bustards, &c. We passed the night at Khan Shekune, situated near an artificial hill, several of which we had seen during the day. They resembled those on Salisbury Plain, and other parts of England. We found the khan good, but very full of people, in consequence of the return of the hadj.

January 7.—Our road was still through open plains, partially cultivated, and running parallel with the range of the Ansarian mountains. Lebanon and Anti-Lebanon were before us. About 3 P.M. we arrived at Hamah. The road for the last hour was pretty, descending into a vale, through which the Orontes takes a winding course. One of its banks is cultivated, wooded, and here and there laid out in gardens; the other consists in most parts of perpendicular chalky cliffs. Here are immense wheels turned by the stream to raise the water for the irrigation of the soil. Hamah is the Epiphania of the Greeks and Romans, though it is, no doubt, the site of the ancient Hamath, mentioned in various parts of scripture; together with Damascus, Lebanon, and other contiguous places, it took its name from the sons of Canaan, fourth son of Ham, the son of Noah, which proves its very high antiquity. Hamah is delightfully situated in a hollow, between and on the sides of two hills, near the west bank of the Orontes; but in itself it presents nothing worthy of notice at this day. We took up our quarters in a khan. These buildings in the towns differ considerably from those on the road side. Like

* In that day there shall be upon the bells of the Horses, "Holiness unto the Lord." Zech. xiv. v. 20.

them, they surround an open square, but are differently constructed, being intended for travellers and merchants to lodge in during the time they remain in the towns to dispose of their merchandise, or settle any private affairs they may have to transact; whereas the khans on the roadside are only intended to afford a night's lodging and security to the traveller and his beasts. In these latter the squares are formed in open piazzas, in which men and animals are lodged indiscriminately, there being no division into apartments, cells, or any detached chamber whatever; and for their use no payment is required. The khans in the towns, instead of having open piazzas, are furnished all round with two stories of small apartments, each chamber, or rather cell, being about 12 ft. square, with a door (the key of which is given you), and an iron-barred window with wooden shutters, but no glass. I suspect they were originally intended as a gratuitous lodging for travellers, the same as those on the high-roads and in the villages; but as they have only one small entrance, and are thereby the most secure places in the towns, the lower rooms are generally filled with merchandise of the different resident proprietors. In front of these are arched piazzas for the horses, mules, &c.; and also a balcony, or terrace, with wooden railing, fronting the upper row of cells, which are totally unfurnished. You must provide for yourself a mat to lie on, cooking utensils, fuel, &c. There is a porter who generally rents the khan, and in the daytime attends the gate, which is locked at night; he makes his profit by the fees from travellers, and also by a rent for the merchandise. We paid two piastres (1*s*. 5*d*.) for admittance, or as it is termed, for the key of our room; four paras (one penny English) a day for the lodging, and one para a day for each horse. Our provisions we always got from the market, and we cooked them in our own room. Our principal meat was mutton. The Turks do not eat much beef, and therefore it is never good. While at Hamah we received by a messenger, express from Aleppo, a letter from Mr. Barker, inclosing the firman from the grand Signior, for which Mr. Barker had written to Sir Robert Liston. This firman empowers us to go with four servants through Syria, Cyprus, the islands of the Archipelago, Smyrna, Adana, Karaman, Karahissar, Kiutaya, to Broussa, and thence to Constantinople. We are to be treated in the most friendly manner; to be afforded every assistance, security, and protection, according to the imperial capitulations; and to be furnished with all necessary escorts whenever occasion may require.

While we were at this place, there arrived one evening four shabby-looking, ill-dressed Turks, attired somewhat like soldiers, and an elderly fellow better clad, though no better looking than the others. These people brought with them eleven Georgian girls, the remnant of between forty and fifty, as we were informed, whom they had stolen or kidnapped from their parents on the confines of Georgia. They were brought to be sold as slaves or mistresses to such wealthy Turks as could afford to pay high sums for them. The poor girls were lodged in the cells contiguous to ours. They were mostly between fifteen and twenty years of age; two were younger, being about twelve. All were exceedingly pretty, with black sparkling eyes, rosy cheeks, long black hair, and very fair complexions, contradicting the account which Volney gives of the Georgian and Circassian women, where he says, "that their fame for beauty arises more from the fancy of travellers, heightened by the difficulty they have always found to get a sight of them, than from any real charms they possess." The prices which were demanded and obtained for these girls is the best proof of the estimation in which they are held by the Turks. We were present at the purchase of one girl by a rich Turk; fourteen purses, each purse being 500 piastres, or about 18*l*., were demanded. He offered ten; but they would not abate one para. The poor girl, who was about fifteen, was standing up all the while, hearing the disputes about her purchase. They were all taken out four different times, and conducted through the town to the rich Turkish houses, to be viewed and bid for, the same as any other merchandise; and on two occasions considerable parties of the principal inhabitants came to our khan, and examined the unhappy creatures at the door of their cells; they being obliged to stand up in a row, while their several merits were discussed by the rival bidders. Several of the purchasers were upwards of fifty years of age; while the friendless objects of their choice were only fifteen. The food given to these unfortunates was of a character with the rest of their treatment, consisting only of a loaf of bread and a small piece of cheese twice a day; and although oranges were only two paras (a halfpenny) each, we never saw one given to them. Whenever the owners went abroad they locked their charge up in the cells and carried away the key. On their return from one of their tours through the town, we heard some bitter lamenting in the cell next to ours, and found that it proceeded from one of the young girls, who was about to be sold, and was bewailing her separation from her sister and companions. These poor girls are carried from town to town on horseback. In this manner they had been brought from Georgia, being exposed for sale at all the principal towns as they came along. They were now destined for Damascus, where it was thought a good mart would be found for them. They set out on their melancholy journey two days before we started. Bruce has given some account of the Georgian and Circassian women. I think he comes much nearer the truth than Volney does.

Nothing else worthy of mention occurred while we were at Hamah, excepting our negociations with the Arabs regarding our journey to Palmyra. Shortly after we arrived, our Maltese interpreter, when taking our letter of introduction to Selim, the governor's secretary, met at his house a man named Pierre, of Dar-el-Camar, in the employ of Lady Hester Stanhope, by whom he had been sent, as he said, to fetch two horses which had been presented to Lady Hester by the governors of Homs and Hamah. He was also charged with a present of one hundred piastres to Narsah, the chief of the Annasee Arabs. This man, who returned with our interpreter, told us that he had accompanied Lady Hester to Palmyra and was acquainted with the Arab chiefs, and that it was he who made the bargain for Mr. Bankes, who was obliged to pay 1200 piastres, besides being sent back once by Narsah, and kept in confinement by Sheikh Hamed, his younger brother, at Palmyra, who extorted another 200 piastres from him. Selim, as well as Scander, being both absent at Damascus, we were at some difficulty how to proceed, but resolved to await the return of the former, as Pierre expected he would be back in a few days. We had much conversation with this man regarding the Arabs, and about the prices which travellers had at different times paid for visiting Palmyra; for, although we had made up our minds to go *coûte qui coûte*, we determined to fight as hard a battle as we could, and pretended to be very indifferent about it. We soon saw that if this man assisted us, he would at least make us pay as much money as he could, for he talked of two, three, four, and even six hundred piastres as nothing. We, however, told him that four hundred was the utmost we would pay; and that we knew Sir William Chatterton and Mr. Leslie had visited Palmyra, by Cariateen, at an expense of only one hundred piastres, while the Arabs were making extravagant demands of Mr. Bankes. Pierre, on hearing this, observed, "that if Sir William Chatterton and Mr. Leslie had gone for that sum, they had *stolen* to Tadmor." Perceiving that he was not inclined to make a moderate bargain for us, we were undetermined what course to pursue, as we made no doubt that he would at all events give information to the Arabs of our arrival and intention. In the meantime, a Christian, who lives at Homs, came to us, asserting, that there was no difficulty in getting to Palmyra, and that he was acquainted with two others of his own creed at Homs, who with himself would engage to conduct us upon asses, at a moderate price, and without any danger from the Arabs. We did not place very implicit confidence in his account, particularly as we knew that our deceased friend, Sheikh Ibrahim, had been robbed and stripped in his first attempt, and we had Mr. Bankes' fate also before us; but as time was passing away, and we were doing nothing, we decided on going with him to Homs, leaving Pierre and everybody else, to whom we spoke on the subject, to suppose that we had given up all idea of going to Palmyra, in consequence of the expense attending it, and had decided on pursuing our journey to Damascus and Jerusalem.

We had intended to have set out on the morning of the 16th. It however turned out very wet that day, and we did not accompany the man, as we had no idea of getting wet through on such an uncertain excursion; but we promised him to follow as soon as it cleared up. During the afternoon Pierre visited us, and appeared to be much surprised that we had not set out for Damascus. We told him that we were prevented from quitting Hamah by the rain. He made no further observation, but shortly after retired, and in about half an hour returned with five Arabs, whom he said he had brought to us that we might make a bargain with them for going to Palmyra. The chief of these was Sheikh Salee, the nephew of Mahannah. He was a lad about fourteen or fifteen years of age, very dirty and ill-dressed, with a sheep-skin cloak. He sat down in our room with great composure, as did his four companions, three of whom were blacks. While smoking their pipes, they examined everything in our apartment with great attention; but we had purposely hid whatever was likely to attract notice, or give an idea of wealth. Their first demand was 3000 piastres, at which we burst out into an immoderate fit of laughter. They then came down to 2000, but we remained fixed at 400. At last they lowered their demand to 800. The lad now made signs that we should be robbed. We shewed all we meant to take with us; and said it was not worth fifty piastres, which indeed was true enough. He then made signs that we should have our throats cut. We told him that neither he, Mahannah, nor any of his tribe, would dare touch a Frank, furnished as we were with the imperial firman, which he knew we had. They do not care, however, much for the Grand Signior. It was not a little remarkable to hear such threats from a boy only fourteen years of age. At last they quitted us, saying they must have 800. After some deliberation, we sent to say that we would give them 600, including the hire of the camels; *but no part of the money to be paid until our safe return to Hamah.* After much prevarication, during which they endeavoured to make us give them a further sum for the camels, they at length consented to our terms, "for the love," as they said, "of the Malaka" or queen, for such they were pleased to call Lady Hester Stanhope, who had herself given 500*l.* for this trip. Had we paid them as much, no doubt they would have called us two kings; for, like the Nubians, money is their idol. The next morning we sent to the Aga to have the treaty ratified in writing. They now demanded 300 piastres in advance. We positively refused to pay a para until our safe return; and, finally, the Aga declined being responsible unless Mahannah or Narsah sent a written document to say we might pass safely. Thus the affair remained till the morning of the 19th, the Arabs still endeavouring to prevail on us to give them three, two, or even 100 piastres in advance; but as the smallest sum paid beforehand would have placed us in some measure in their power, and rendered our journey uncertain, we persisted in refusing.

January 19.—No message from Mahannah having arrived, we left Hamah at dawn of day, and arrived at Homs in about eight hours, the road still leading through rich plains destitute of wood. About half-way we crossed the Orontes, now diminished in breadth to a paltry stream. The river here winds through a chasm. There is a bridge of thirteen arches; and the water is kept up for the purpose of turning a mill. A cascade which it forms, the khan, the neighbouring village of Rastan, and a few trees on the bank of the rivulet, altogether make rather a pretty scene. Rastan stands on an eminence near the bridge, and the ancient Arethusia adjoins it, presenting an object of more interest than we had lately been accustomed to, though none of the buildings remain perfect. Part of the walls, the line of the streets, and the pedestals of some columns, being alone remarkable. We put up at a khan in Homs; and Pierre, who had followed us from Hamah, arrived soon after us.

January 20.—We had some conversation with the Christian we had seen at Hamah; but it appeared evident he was undertaking a task that he was unable to execute. In the evening one of the Arabs who had visited us with Sheikh Salee, came with a letter from Sheikh Narsah, who, he said, was encamped one day's journey from Palmyra. The letter stated, "that Narsah had heard of our arrival in Hamah, and of our wish to visit Tadmor; that he expected by the 24th that the Fidon and Isbaah Arabs under Sheikh Haleel, who were at war with the Annasees, would have removed from the neighbourhood of Palmyra; and that, at the expiration of that time, he would come to Homs with three camels to conduct us." This story we afterwards had reason to believe was a fiction, to persuade us of the absolute necessity of his protection. In the mean time he desired we would give the bearer twenty piastres. Upon this we made great difficulties; for, as our departure was not yet completely settled, it might very likely be money thrown away; and we thought that if we showed an easy compliance in giving small sums, we might soon receive a demand for large ones. In short, finding how tardily affairs were going on, we resolved to set out the next morning on foot, calling on Narsah on our way. To this plan the Arab consented, and everything was agreed on; he swearing by the most sacred oaths that all should go on well, and that we should have an ass to carry our bread, water, and sheep-skin coats.

January 21.—This morning the man came again, saying, he could not take us, as he feared Narsah would cut off his head for having undertaken the business without express orders. Therefore, after much discussion, this last arrangement also terminated unfavourably, and the Arab set off a second time for the camp of Mahannah, to bring the camels as soon as possible, and apprise his chief that we had removed to Homs. In the afternoon it came on to blow hard, with continued squalls of snow, sleet, and rain; and we were not sorry that our walking trip was put off. The bad weather continued without intermission night and day till the 24th, on the evening of which day the man returned from Mahannah with the three camels; we could not, however, arrange for starting till the 26th, as the motsellim (governor) could not ratify the bargain, being busily engaged in taking an inventory of the effects of the pasha, who had shortly before been beheaded. This pasha had been appointed to the command of the hadj, and had set off from Constantinople. While he was on his return from Mecca, a khat-sherriffe was despatched from the capital, ordering his head to be cut off and sent immediately to Constantinople; and the sentence was carried into execution before he reached Damascus. We hear that he was accused of intriguing with the Russians against the state. We paid 300 piastres into the hands of Hadji Hassan, as part payment to the Arab sheikhs, but it was agreed that they should not themselves receive any portion of it till our safe return to Homs. Sheikh Narsah's order was, that we should pay all before starting; but we persisted in refusing, and moreover, we made the Arabs consent, before witnesses, that no further demands beyond the 600 piastres were to be made upon us on any pretence whatever. The motsellim, who, like all the Turks, had a great and unnecessary dread of these people, observed, "Why will you trust yourselves amongst the Arabs? suppose they should destroy you!"

January 26.—At one P.M., after nineteen days' negotiation at Hamah and Homs, we started with our three camels and as many conductors, with two skin bottles, in which they had poured the melted butter bought with Lady Hester's present. We proved to them before departing that we had not a para in our pockets, thus preventing any temptation to pilfer. All our baggage consisted of a sheep-skin coat, the woolly side inwards, and the other side coloured red with ochre, and greased to keep out the rain. We rode for five hours, our guides nearly the whole time singing a favourite Arab song. On arriving at a Bedouin camp, we had some scruples about entering a tent, expecting they would have had many objections against receiving us. Instead of which, to our surprise, we were welcomed by both men and women; the latter smiling, said, we were Frangi (Franks), and retired to their part of the tent to prepare supper.

January 27.—Having been regaled with a substantial breakfast, we proceeded at eight A.M. and rode till four in the afternoon, when we stopped at another Arab camp, where we were again well received.

January 28.—We started at dawn of day, and saw many dwarf trees, of which the country had hitherto been destitute. It now resembled a heath covered by a plentiful stock of aromatic shrubs, with occasional hill and dale. We followed no particular road or track; but our general direction appeared to be easterly. This morning we had a striking instance of the value the Arab sets on his time, and of his impatience to accomplish a journey when once he has undertaken it. Suddenly one of our party quitting us, hastened on in advance, and was soon out of sight. On coming up with him we found he had collected brushwood and made a blazing fire; presently some butter was melted and sweetened with honey. In this we dipped our bread, and what with the Arab's voracious mode of eating, and these time-saving measures, our breakfast did not detain us above ten minutes. The same hurry was subsequently shewn on our wanting to drink some water from a small crevice in the rock close to us. We were prohibited and told there was plenty before us; but, as we knew that the camps were hours in advance, we were not to be controlled, and dismounting, quenched our thirst. The soil was excessively rich; but all appearance of cultivation had ceased when we had ridden a few hours from Homs. The scarcity of water is doubtless the cause of this. We could not help laughing at our principal guide, who with a rusty old match-lock and *no powder*, pretended to be very vigilant in reconnoitring from all the heights for harami (robbers), while we knew that he and his companions were of the most timid nature, and that they were well aware that we were going with the sanction, and under the protection of their own chiefs, who commanded the whole country. At noon we saw a wild boar, so large that at first we thought it was an ass. About four in the afternoon we opened the valley in which Mahannah's camp was pitched. The Arabs were obliged to inquire before they could find out the direction of the camp; and as they had been absent from it only a few days, some idea may be formed of the difficulty of tracking the tribes in the desert.

As we approached, we beheld a very animated and busy scene. The girls were singing, and the children busied in running down the young partridges with dogs; the birds being as yet only able to fly a short distance at a time. Presently we heard a hue and cry from all quarters, and soon perceived a large wild boar, with his bristles erect, beset by all the dogs; everybody running eagerly to the pursuit. He was found behind one of the tents. They chased him all through the camp; and two Arabs on horseback, with spears, joined in the pursuit. The animal, however, kept both men and dogs at bay, and finally got off with only one wound.

We now approached the sheikh's tent and found Mahannah and his two sons, Sheikhs Narsah and Hamed, together with about thirty Arab chiefs of various camps, seated round an immense fire. Sheikh Narsah was leaning on a camel's saddle, their usual cushion. He did not rise to receive us, although we afterwards observed that he and the whole circle rose whenever a strange sheikh arrived. We attributed this cool reception to the low estimation he held us in, in consequence of the unusually small sum we were to pay for visiting Palmyra, and from the plainness of our dress and appearance. Mahannah was a short, crooked-backed, mean-looking old man, between seventy and eighty years of age, dressed in a coarse robe. His son, Narsah, to whom he had, in consequence of his age, resigned the reins of government, was good-looking, about thirty years of age, with very dignified and engaging manners. He had the Koran open in his hand when we arrived, to give us, we supposed, an idea of his learning. He was well dressed, with a red pelisse and an enormous white turban. We observed much whispering going forward between Narsah and every stranger that arrived; and our guides were separately questioned in the same manner, to learn, as we conjectured, whether we had much money or not. Narsah alone addressed us. He inquired why the English wished so much to see Palmyra, and whether we were not going to search for gold? We told him he should have half of any we might find there.

As the evening advanced, the Arab guests increased to the number of fifty. Their mode of saluting their chiefs is by kissing either cheek alternately, not the hand as in Nubia. Narsah questioned us about Buonaparte and the occupation of France by the allied troops. I suspect his knowledge of these matters proceeded from his correspondence with Lady Hester Stanhope. On our inquiring after Sheikh Hamedy, a handsome young man, apparently between twenty and twenty-five years of age, with evident confusion in his countenance, acknowledged himself as that person; at the same time remarking that we had probably heard a bad account of him, but that the reports to his prejudice were not correct. It was this man who confined Mr. Bankes for a day, and obliged him to pay 200 piastres exclusive of the 1200 which he gave to Narsah for visiting Palmyra.

Some of the partridges which the children had caught, were now brought in. They roasted them on the fire, and part was given to us; Sheikh Hamedy *throwing* a leg and a wing to each of us. They afterwards gave us some honey and butter, together with bread to dip into it *. Narsah desired one of his men to mix the two ingredients for us, as we were awkward at it. The Arab having stirred the mixture up well with his fingers, showed his dexterity in consuming as well as in mixing, and recompensed himself for his trouble by eating half of it. At sunset, and again at eight o'clock, the whole assembly were summoned to prayers; a man standing outside the tent, and calling them to their devotions, in the same manner as is done from the minarets of the mosques of Turkish towns. Each man rubbed his face over with sand, a heap of which was placed in front of the tent for that purpose, to serve as a substitute for water in their religious ablutions. We could not but admire the decorous solemnity with which they all joined in worship, standing in a row, and bowing down and kissing the ground together. An immense platter of roast mutton was then brought in for supper, with pillaw of rice. The Arabs fed apart, while a separate portion was brought for Narsah and us. We observed the elderly men gave their half-gnawed bones to those around

* "Butter and honey shall he eat." Isa. vii. 5.

them, and we were told that they have an adage commending the custom. A black slave was perpetually pounding coffee from the moment we entered the tent till we went to sleep, and as he began in the morning at day-light, and was constantly employed, it would seem that the consumption of this article must be considerable. Late at night Narsah began to address the whole circle of sheikhs, who, we found, had been convened in order that they might hear his request that some portions of grazing land, called "The Cottons," might be delivered up to him. Being tired with the length of his discourse, we removed to a corner of the tent and fell asleep. We heard afterwards that his harangue lasted till three in the morning.

On the following day we wished to proceed, according to the promise to let us depart before sun-rise, which Narsah had given us the preceding evening, swearing by his head, and lifting up his hand at the same time. But as the chief had sat up so late he did not make his appearance till about ten o'clock, when, instead of letting us depart, he desired we would accompany him to a small vale contiguous to his tent. We found the Arabs assembling from all quarters, and following us in great numbers. We were quite at a loss to know the meaning of this; at first we thought it was intended to show off the numbers of his people. Presently, however, we came to a tent, and found an immense feast of rice and camel's flesh prepared for the whole assembly. We were conducted to a smaller tent apart, and had our share sent to us. We were in doubt what object the sheikh had in thus separating us; whether it was meant as an accommodation to us, that we might eat more comfortably and freely by ourselves than in the midst of a concourse of people; or whether he thought we were not fit society for him. Our dress was certainly of a much meaner description than that of any of the sheikhs: and as throughout the East a stranger is generally estimated according to the dress he wears, it is probable that our homely appearance had some weight with Narsah on this occasion. We found the meat both savoury and tender, being a portion of the hump, which is considered the best part. There was little fat, and the grain was remarkably coarse; however, we made a hearty breakfast. The feast was conducted with much order and decorum. The sheikhs fed apart in a double row, with several immense platters placed at equal distances between them, and a rope line was drawn round to keep the people from pressing in. Narsah was at the head of the row, with a small select circle, amongst whom he placed us after we had breakfasted, having perceived us amongst the spectators. When the sheikhs had finished, the people were regaled with the remains; independent of which, portions were distributed to the different tents of the camp. This latter arrangement was for the women and children. Several camels must have been cooked, judging from the immense quantities of meat we saw. This feast was no doubt intended to give weight to the proceedings of the former evening. We were asked whether Christians did not eat pigs' flesh; and, answering in the affirmative, were questioned if we did not also drink sow's milk, as they do that of camels: this, however, we stoutly denied. Mahannah made many signs for money, both for himself and Sheikh Alli, a very handsome little boy about five years of age, the son of Narsah. The Arab sign for money is rubbing the fore finger and thumb together. About eleven we set out. Our camels were changed for dromedaries of a heavy sort, which set off with us at full trot up hill and down dale, each of us having his Arab conductor mounted behind him. We had now an addition to our party; as one of Narsah's men, who was called a guard, accompanied us, mounted on a white dromedary, decorated with tassels, and armed with another old matchlock gun. We rode till four o'clock in the afternoon. We found the pace of the animals on level ground and up hill good enough, but in descending we were dreadfully jolted.

January 30.—At dawn we resumed our journey. Our new guard had endeavoured to make us start at midnight, but we would not submit to this, as the nights were very cold and frosty. We trotted this day at the same rate as on the preceding, and were jolted and bruised almost beyond endurance. At two in the afternoon we arrived at the object of our journey; our *useful* guard having previously lighted the match of his gun, and gone through the ceremony of loading, *but without ammunition.*

On opening the ruins of Palmyra, from the Valley of the Tombs, we were much struck with the picturesque effect of the whole mass, presenting altogether the most imposing sight of the kind we had ever seen, and rendered doubly interesting by our having travelled through a wilderness destitute of a single building. The ruins stand on a sandy plain, on the skirts of the desert; their snow-white appearance, contrasted with the yellow sand, produced a very striking effect. Great, however, was our disappointment when, on a minute examination, we found that there was not a single column, pediment, architrave, portal, or frieze worthy of admiration. None of the columns exceeded, in diameter, 4 ft., or in height 40. Those of the boasted avenue were little more than 30 ft. high; the epistylium is in no instance ornamented with carved-work, excepting now and then an ill-executed cornice. The plates of Wood and Dawkins are certainly well executed, but they have done more than justice to the originals. Taken as a *tout-ensemble,* these ruins are certainly remarkable, by reason of their extent (being nearly a mile and a half in length); and they are, moreover, less encumbered by modern fabrics; for except the Arab village of Tadmor, which occupies the peristyle court of the Temple of the Sun, and the Turkish burying-place, there is nothing to obstruct the antiquary. But when examined in detail they excite little interest; and we judged Palmyra to be hardly worthy of the time, expense, anxiety, and fatiguing journey which we had undergone to visit it. The projecting pedestals in the centre of the columns of the great avenue have a very unsightly appearance; there is also a great sameness in the architecture, all the capitals being Corinthian, excepting those which surround the Temple of the Sun. These last are fluted, and when decorated with their brazen Ionic capitals, were doubtless very handsome. The sculpture, as well of the capitals of the columns, as of the other ornamental parts of the door-ways and buildings, is very coarse and bad. Although the designs, as given in the work of Wood and Dawkins, are generally correct, we found that the execution of the sculpture is far inferior to what might have been expected, judging from their engravings. The three arches of the avenue at the end nearest the Temple of the Sun, so beautiful on paper, are excessively insignificant in reality; and the decorated frieze is very badly wrought: even the devices are not striking. These arches are not to be compared to the common portals of Thebes, although the Egyptians were unacquainted with the arch. Everything here is built of a very perishable stone; it does not deserve the name of marble; it is greatly inferior even to that of Baalbec; and we are inclined to think the ruins of the latter place are much more worthy the traveller's notice than those of Palmyra. We suspect that it is the difficulty of getting to Tadmor, and the fact that few travellers have been there, that has given rise to the great renown of these ruins. We give the preference to Baalbec, not only for the general superiority of the sculpture, but also for the extraordinary massive structure of the buildings; and while the columns of Baalbec, nearly 60 ft. in height, and 7 in diameter, supporting a most rich and beautifully wrought epistylium 20 ft. high, are formed of only *three* pieces of stone, the smallest columns of Palmyra, 3½ ft. in diameter and 30 ft. high, are formed of six, seven, and even eight pieces; those, however, surrounding the peristyle court of the Temple of the Sun, are about 40 ft. high, and 4 ft. in diameter, and are formed of only three or four stones; and in the centre of the avenue are four granite columns, about 30 ft. high, each formed of a single stone; only one of these is still standing. We found the tombs very interesting; their construction is different from that of any we had elsewhere seen. They consist of a number of square towers, three, four, and five stories high, and are situated without the walls of the ancient city. The most perfect are on the sides of the valley which leads to Homs and Hamah. These tombs are not ornamented on the exterior, with the exception of a few figures in basso-relievo over the door, and a tablet bearing a Greek inscription. There are generally five sepulchral chambers one over the other; and on each side are eight recesses, each divided into four or five parts, for the reception of corpses; the lower chamber, in some instances, fronts an excavation in the side of the hill contiguous to it. Some of these lower apartments are very handsome, the sides being ornamented with sculpture and fluted Corinthian pilasters, though the walls were of plain white stucco, without any figures or emblematical representation. The ceiling, on which the paint is still very perfect, is ornamented, like that of the peristyle court of the Temple of the Sun at Baalbec, with the heads of different heathen deities, disposed in diamond-shaped divisions. We were much interested by the remains of some mummies and mummy cloths, which appear to have been preserved very much after the manner of the Egyptians, only that the gum had lost all that odour resembling frankincense, which we noticed in Egypt. We found a hand in tolerable preservation; but these sepulchres are not in any way so interesting as the Egyptian burying-places. You here look in vain for those beautiful paintings, &c., which so well portray the manners and customs of the ancients. Over the inside of the door-way, we saw a tablet in basso-relievo, of seven or eight standing figures dressed in long robes, with their hands on their breasts; we supposed them to represent priests. We also noticed a sarcophagus, with the sides ornamented much in the same manner. The marble folding doors of some of the grander tombs, which are situated in the town, are still erect, but much dilapidated. They are carved in panels, but are ill-executed and unpolished. The lines of the streets and the foundations of the houses are distinguishable in some places. We agree with Mr. Bankes, that many of the small square rows of columns which Wood and Dawkins suppose to have inclosed temples, were no other than the open courts of private edifices, inclosing fountains. Mr. Bankes was led to this conclusion from there being one of only four columns, which never could have inclosed a temple or solid building within it: moreover, similar remains at Pompeii unquestionably belonged to private edifices. On the right hand, as you pass down the great avenue of columns, there is a door-way standing: within are the remains of the building it belonged to, having a Hebrew inscription on the architrave, which is interesting on three accounts; first, as the foundation of Tadmor was by Solomon; secondly, as Zenobia is said by some to have been of the Jewish religion; and thirdly, as Bishop Riddle states that in his time 2000 Jews dwelt at Tadmor. This inscription was discovered by Mr. Bankes. There is at Palmyra a tepid spring of mineral water, having a strong sulphureous taste and smell; a subterraneous aqueduct supplied the town. There is a great quantity of salt in the desert adjoining Tadmor, which forms a lucrative branch of commerce to the natives.

January 31.—Having finished our examination of the ruins, we started on our return at 2 P. M., and continued till ten at night. After dark the Arabs implored us not to sing, for fear the robbers should hear us, and appeared to be as fearful in their own desert, as it was possible for a stranger to have been.

February 1.—We moved at sun-rise, and did not reach Mahannah's camp until dark; we were conducted back by a different road, and met with two parties of his people on horseback, one of seven, and the other of twelve, most of them armed with spears; we also met a small party on dromedaries richly caparisoned, sent, as we thought, on purpose to show his importance. They asked us in passing, how much we had paid for visiting Palmyra, taking it as a thing of course that we were obliged to give money. Our change of road naturally gave some mystery to our proceeding. On our arrival at the camp, old Mahannah came out of his tent and began feeling the saddles; and took from the poor Arabs all the salt which they had purchased at Palmyra. We were pretty well received by the chiefs; Narsah had on the *old* robe this time, and his father the new one. We soon found out the meaning of this, as Narsah urged our interpreter to request us to give him a new dress; but the latter said it was a thing impossible, as we had made our bargain for six hundred piastres, and would give nothing besides. We obtained a promise that everything should be in readiness for us to depart early in the morning, and Narsah told us he should write a letter *to the King of England*, which we were to take with us. He sent one to his *dear friend* Lady Hester, with whom they all seem to be enchanted. They call her "El Malaka," (the queen;) some say she is "Bint-el Sultan" (daughter of the king,) and others favour her with the appellation of the Virgin Mary.

February 2 —We were detained until 9 A.M., and had much difficulty in procuring a draught of water before starting; but we absolutely refused to move without it. In consequence of this detention we were benighted before we had completed our day's journey, and had a bitterly cold bivouack in the open air, the Arabs being afraid even to light a fire. We, however, managed to lay down between two of our camels, which, from their kneeling posture, kept some of the cold air off; sleeping was out of the question, as it was freezing hard, with a strong, cutting wind.

On the 3rd, at dawn, we were on route; we saw twenty-three white gazelles, and witnessed the removal of an Arab camp; the movables were all placed on the camels' backs; the women, with the children slung over their shoulders, and the flocks followed, presenting altogether an interesting sight. At a small encampment we breakfasted off a thick mess of lentiles and bread,* highly seasoned with pepper, and very good. Towards noon we passed a valley, furrowed up in all directions, by the wild boars;† the soil had the appearance of having been literally ploughed up. In the evening we reached Homs; we were highly satisfied with our conductors, and therefore gave them each twenty piastres, as voluntary backsheeish. One of these men had already received twenty for carrying the message to Narsah, as before mentioned. We also sent a turban of the value of twenty piastres to the sheikh of Tadmor, for his civility to us, and gave 100 piastres to Pierre; so that our whole expenses in visiting Palmyra amounted to 800 piastres, 200 of which consisted of voluntary gifts.

The behaviour of these Arabs to each other, whatever may be their conduct to strangers, presents an agreeable picture of domestic harmony and comfort, and is in unison with all the ideas the poets have given of the peaceful contentment of the pastoral life; in fact, they are a nation of shepherds, and I question much if, in our most polished circles, more real dignity of deportment and urbanity of manners are to be met with than in the humble tent of the Arab. It appeared to us that all that was good amongst them was centred in the lower orders; the chiefs monopolising to themselves all that cunning and roguery which render them contemptible in the eyes of a stranger. An Arab, on arriving in a strange camp, goes to the first tent that comes in his way; he does not wait to be asked in, but without any ceremony makes his camel lie down, unloads it at the entrance, and, entering the tent with the simple salutation

* "Then Jacob gave Esau bread, and pottage of lentiles." Genesis xxv. 34.

† "The boar out of the wood doth waste it." Psalm lxxx. 13.

of salaam alikam (peace be between us), seats himself by the fire, no matter whether the host be at home or not. Should he be present, he immediately puts fresh wood on the fire, and begins to burn and pound coffee, generally offering his pipe to his guests in the mean time. His wife, or wives, after spreading mats, if they have any, for the strangers to sit on, retire to their part of the tent, which is divided in the middle by their sack of corn, and whatever other effects they have, and prepare the dinner or supper, according to the time of the day, without any order being given by the master, but as a matter of course; in the mean time the host chats with his guests, generally about their sheep, which are their principal concern. The coffee being ready, he pours out a cupful for each of his guests, and helps himself last. The meal generally consists of camels', goats', or sheeps' milk, boiled wheat and milk, lentil soup, or melted butter, and bread to dip into it; as soon as the meal is ready, the landlord pours out water for all his guests in turn, who there-with wash the right hand.* The ablution finished, every one commences; the host retires, not eating with his guests, but welcoming them with frequent exclamations of coula, coula, (eat it all, eat it all). The repast ended, the attentive master again brings the water for washing the hands, and then eats of what remains. On two occasions, when we arrived at a camp late at night, and halting before a tent, found the owner, with his wife and children, just retired to rest, having arranged their carpets, &c. for the night, it was astonishing to see the good humour with which they all arose again and kindled a fire, the wife at once beginning to knead the dough and prepare our supper, our Arab guides making no apologies, but taking it all as a matter of course. Surely this was a striking instance of Arab hospitality. It was a pleasing sight to see them bring in their flocks at night: the sheep always slept close to the tents of their owners; several Arabs, together with numerous dogs, remaining outside as guards. The lambs (for it was the lambing season) were placed inside the tents, in a small spot fenced round, to screen them from the inclemency of the night air. The first care in the morning was to let them out to their dams, when it was interesting to observe the numerous ewes recognise their offspring by the smell alone; the lambs not being gifted with the sagacity of their mothers, were willing to suck from the first ewe they met with.

The Arab having few wants is unacquainted with many cares, and is thus ignorant of the greater part of the troubles and difficulties which are experienced in more civilised society. Each man has a tent of his own, and is thus possessed of a freehold, and has nothing to do with rents or taxes; and the shrubs of the wilderness provide him with food for his flocks, and fuel for his fires. The labour of tilling and reaping is unknown to him, but much judgment and foresight is necessary in his periodical migrations with his flocks, which must be regulated and timed with due regard to the seasons, so that they may consume the herbage while they are advancing, and at the same time leave the land to itself sufficiently long to recover its verdure before they return. They contrive to be near their southern boundary in the winter, and at their northern limits in the summer. They are frequently obliged to pitch their tents at six or eight hours' distance from the wells, and then it is that their camels are of incalculable utility to them. Their behaviour to us was the same as towards each other; and I suspect that their character for robbing and pilfering arises from the conduct of some few of the worst part of the community, who infest the high-roads, rather than from any dishonesty in the generality of these people. The dread which the Turks have of the Arabs appeared to us quite unaccountable, as during the whole of our stay among them we did not see more than half a dozen old matchlock guns, and about eighteen spears. Narsah was

* "Except they wash, they eat not." Mark vii. 4.

imprisoned in Damascus a short time for some tricks he had been playing there. The pasha wished to cut off his head, but a strong remonstrance from the merchants of Aleppo and Bagdad, setting forth the disastrous consequences which would attend the execution of this man, by rousing the vengeance of the Arabs, procured his release; and, instead of losing his head, he was dismissed with a present of a robe and some backsheeish.

Requiring a little rest on our return from Tadmor, we remained at Homs till the 7th February, on which day we set out and travelled for about seven hours, passing over rich plains, and rounding the point of a mountain which we took to be the end of Anti-Lebanon. The next day we proceeded for nine hours through a mountainous country. On the 9th, after journeying for seven hours, we stopped at a khan in a plain, around which the mountains were barren, uninteresting, and partly covered with snow.

February 10.—Leaving this place we again entered a hilly country, when, on arriving at the brow of a descent, the extensive and beautiful plain of Damascus opened on our view, with the town surrounded by woods, amidst which were several villages. The land was highly cultivated; to the eastward the plain extends as far as the eye can reach; in other directions it is bounded by hills, Lebanon rising conspicuous above them all. In about two hours we reached the plain, and in five more arrived at the convent of the Terra Sancta in Damascus. For the last three hours of our journey, the road was extremely beautiful, passing through rich olive groves, and gardens inclosed by walls of sun-burnt brick, and surrounded and irrigated by streams of water, partly natural and partly conducted by art.

February 17.—Not having slept on a bed, or with our clothes off, since we left Aleppo, thirty-eight days ago, we now fully appreciated the luxury of good beds. Our time since the 10th has been occupied in writing letters, and in visiting different parts of the town, such as the place of the Vision of St. Paul outside the eastern gate; the place where he was let down the wall in a basket; the house of Ananias; the street called Straight, &c., alluded to in the Acts of the Apostles. The Turkish name for Damascus is Shum, or Shem, and the friars of the convent think it was originally founded by Shem, the son of Noah; the earliest information we have of this place is in the time of Abraham.*

We purpose proceeding to the Holy Land in a few days by Panias, near to which place is the source of the Jordan; thence crossing the bridge of Jacob, we shall go to Nazareth, Tiberias, Nablous, Jericho, and Jerusalem. In consequence of a letter from Mr. Barker, we have received great assistance from Monsieur Chaboceau, physician to the pasha of this place, and through his good offices have got another firman for the pashalic, and a letter to the governor of Jerusalem, from whom we hope to get guides to conduct us to Mount Sinai. Whether we succeed or not in getting to Mount Sinai, we shall return by Jerusalem to Acre, and then embark for Cyprus, whence we shall proceed to the coast of Asia Minor, beginning by Tarsus, which will conduct us to Smyrna, the site of Troy, and finally to Constantinople.

* Genesis xiv. 15.

CHAPTER VI.

Departure from Damascus—Source of the Jordan—Singular Lake—Panias—Abundance of Game—Safot—Its elevated situation—Vermin—Tiberias—Ancient Baths—Lake of Tiberias—Om Keis—Ruins around Tiberias—Bysan—Its Theatre and other Ruins—Ford of the Jordan—The Valley of Adjeloun—The Callah-el-Rubbat—Souf—Remarkable Ruins at Djerash—Agreement with the Benesuckher Arabs to escort us to Kerek—Uproar at Katty—Description of Djerash—Troubles with our Escort—Szalt—Disturbance at quitting Szalt—Escape from the Arabs—Difficulty in fording the Jordan—Nablous—Jerusalem—Visit of the Pilgrims to the Jordan—Future Route—Adventure at the "Tombs of the Kings."

On the 23d Feb. we quitted Damascus, and passing over a slight eminence entered a plain, through which runs a fine stream, but being destitute of wood, it has less beauty than the country around Damascus, though the soil is rich. About four in the afternoon, we stopped at the khan of the village of Sasa. Hitherto we had followed the road from Damascus to Jacob's Bridge, at that part of the Jordan which lies between the lakes Houle and Tiberias.

February 24.—We passed to the westward for Panias. The first part of the road led through a fine plain, watered by a pretty, winding rivulet, with numerous tributary streams, and many old ruined mills; we then began to ascend over very rugged and rocky ground, quite void of vegetation; in some places there were traces of an ancient paved way, probably the Roman road leading from Damascus to Cæsarea Philippi; as we ascended we had the highest part of Djebail Sheikh (Anti-Lebanon), on our right; we found the snow, occasionally, of considerable depth, and it was with difficulty we got our horses through it. The road now became gradually less stony, and we saw flocks of goats browsing on a rich herbage, in places from which the stones had been cleared away and piled up in great heaps. The shrubs gradually increased in number, size, and beauty, and we presently descended into a very rich little plain immediately at the foot of Djebail Sheikh. There is a conspicuous tomb in this valley, and a rivulet, which appears to take its source at the foot of the mountains, passes along the western side of the plain in a southerly direction, its course then turns more to the westward, and rushing in a very picturesque manner, through a deep chasm, overhung by shrubs of various descriptions, joins the Jordan at Panias; it is marked in Arrowsmith's chart as the real source of the Jordan, but the fountains at Panias, which are by far the most copious, though not the most distant from the Dead Sea, where the river terminates, are generally considered to be the source; an opinion in which both of us agree. From this plain we ascended up the southern side of Djebail Sheikh, and after passing a very small village about one o'clock, we saw on our left, close to us, a very picturesque lake, of little more than a mile in circumference, apparently perfectly circular, and surrounded by sloping hills richly wooded. The singularity of this lake is, that it has no apparent supply or discharge; its waters appeared perfectly still, though clear and limpid; a great many wild-fowl were swimming in it. This lake has been remarked only by Burckhardt and Seetzen, other travellers who have gone from Damascus to Panias having taken the route by Raschia and Hasbeya; Arrowsmith's map notices it by the name of the Birket-el Ram, on the authority of Seetzen. Josephus mentions it under the name of "Phiala" (a cup), in allusion to its shape. It was supposed by the ancients to be the real source of the Jordan; Josephus states, that they threw straw into the lake, which came out at the *apparent source* at Panias. A short distance from Phiala, we crossed a stream which discharges itself into the larger one which we first met with; the latter we followed for a considerable distance, and then mounting up the hill to the S. W. saw the town of Panias, the great Saracenic castle near it, the plain of the Jordan as far as the lake Houle, and the mountains on the other side of the plain, forming altogether a fine *coup d'œil.* As we descended towards Panias the country became extremely beautiful; great quantities of wild flowers, and a variety of shrubs just budding, combined with the rich verdure of the grass, corn, and beans, showed us all at once the beauties of spring, and conducted us into a climate quite different from that of Damascus, or of the country which we had passed through since we left that city. About 5 P.M. we entered Panias, crossing a causeway constructed over the rivulet, which as before stated flows from the foot of Djebail Sheikh. The river here rushes over the rocks in a very picturesque manner, its banks are covered with shrubs, and there are the ruins of ancient walls, but whether Saracenic or not I cannot say. The present town of Panias is small, the ground it stands on is of a triangular form, inclosed by the Jordan on one side, the rivulet on the other, and the mountain at the back. The situation being thus compressed, it is evident that the ancient Panias, afterwards Cæsarea Philippi, could not have been of great extent. Josephus, in his "Jewish Antiquities," mentions a temple built by Herod, but we could discover no trace of it. The *apparent* source of the Jordan is in a cave at the foot of a precipice, in the sides of which are several niches with Greek inscriptions.

The neighbourhood of Panias is very beautiful, richly wooded, and abounds in game; we devoted a part of the morning of the 25th to shooting, but had poor sport, though we saw plenty of partridges, wild ducks, snipe, &c. Having been directed to follow the Jordan to the lake Houle, we left Panias at 11 o'clock, and took that route. The beautifully wooded country did not continue for more than two miles, and we then entered into open rich plains. We found the ground very marshy: after wandering about to find fords over the numerous streams which water the plain, we crossed the Jordan itself; but the country on the other side was as full of marshes and swamps as that we had left, and in several places we nearly lost the horses; at last we succeeded in reaching the road to Safot, which runs at the foot of the hills on the other side of the plain, and to have reached which, we ought, in the first instance, to have passed round the north end of the valley. In consequence of the loss of time in these bogs, we got no further on our journey this evening than a village by the side of a hill, near the N.W. end of lake Houle; the banks of which are low, the hills not approaching it in any part.

February 26.—We ascended from this point to Safot. The plain which we had quitted was literally covered with wild geese, ducks, widgeon, snipe, and water-fowl of every description. There is a village at the foot of the steep ascent to Safot, in which are a few Roman ruins. As we ascended, the lakes of Houle and Tiberias opened to us with much grandeur, and part of the plain of the Jordan being also visible, added to the beauty of the scene. The country in the mountains is, for the most part, cultivated. Safot is beautifully situated; the castle stands by itself on a small hill, at the foot of which is the town, which looks like four distinct villages. The approach is very fine, and the country abounds in olives, vines, and almond trees, which are now in blossom. The lake of Tiberias is visible from some parts of Safot, which, from its elevated situation, Maundrell thinks is the city alluded to by our Saviour.* Its ancient name appears in Arrowsmith's map as Japhet. We were detained here by rainy weather, until the afternoon of the 28th, when we started for Tiberias, but only reached an old ruined khan, about two miles to the north of the village of Madjdala by the lake's side. Here we were dreadfully bitten by a

* "A city that is set on a hill cannot be hid." Matt. v. 14.

species of vermin, which attacks both men and camels in this country; it was red, and soft like a maggot. In the morning we found ourselves studded all over with deep crimson spots, from which it would appear that there is much venom in the bite of this disgusting animal. A traveller in these countries, however much the thought may shock him at first, must make up his mind to be constantly covered with lice and fleas; we kill every day from ten to twenty of these gentry, which are always to be found on every mat or cushion used in the country. These nauseous visitors seldom get into the head, but crawl about your shirt and clothes. Every native you see is covered with them, and if you ask why they have such a plentiful store, while we are comparatively so little attacked, they tell you "it is the curse of God on them." The other day I cut my foot, and our Arab Seys (who has accompanied us all the way from Yaffa), and is a very cleanly person, washing himself constantly, tore off a small piece of the sleeve of his shirt to apply to the wound; the piece was about three inches long, by two wide, and before using it, I killed on it three lice and two fleas! This will speak more strongly than all I can say on the subject. Bugs are also very plentiful; in Egypt our rooms were full of them.

March 1.—The greater part of our road this day was a descent, passing through a beautiful and wild country covered with shrubs of various descriptions, and occasionally crossing valleys and rivulets. About four miles from Safot there is a picturesque cliff, the sides of which are perforated with a great number of caves, at present inhabited by goatherds; we supposed them to be ancient sepulchres, as indeed did other travellers who, from their ruined appearance, have not thought them worthy of examination; but Mr. Bankes, who leaves nothing unexplored, inspected them, and pronounces them to be only natural cavities. About eight o'clock we reached Tiberias, having travelled for two hours along the side of the lake. More pains appear to have been taken to construct the road where it was very rocky, than in most parts of Syria which we had visited. The modern town of Tiberias is very small; it stands close to the lake of Gennesaret, and is walled round with towers equidistant from each other. At the northern extremity are the remains of the ancient town, which are distinguishable by walls and other ruined buildings, as well as by fragments of columns, some of which are of beautiful red granite. South of the town are the famous hot baths of Tiberius; they consist of three mineral springs. We had no thermometer, but we found the water too hot to admit of the hand being kept in it for more than fifty seconds; we endeavoured to boil an egg in it, but without success, even though we removed the shell. Over the spring is a Turkish bath close to the lake's side, which is much resorted to, particularly by the Jews, who have also a great veneration for a Roman sepulchre, excavated in the cliff near the spot, which they say is the "Tomb of Jacob." Beyond the baths a wall runs from the lake to the mountain's side, which rather perplexed us when we were taking the measurement of the ancient walls of Tiberias; but we are now convinced that the walls of the town did not extend so far to the south, and that this wall was part of the fortifications of Vespasian's camp; indeed, Josephus places the camp in this position. The lake of Tiberias is a fine sheet of water, but the land about it has no striking features, and the scenery is altogether devoid of beauty; but it is interesting from the frequent allusions to it in the Gospels. We were lodged, as Frank travellers usually are, in the small catholic church, which is under the charge of an Arab priest; this they tell you was the house of St. Peter; but after we had been there a few days, we observed that one of the stones of the building had part of an Arabic inscription upon it, inverted, which proves it to be of much more modern origin; Dr. Clarke, however, seems to believe the assertion of the natives. We found the church so full of fleas, that we preferred a small open court in front of it for our lodging. The natives have a saying, that "the king of the fleas has his court in Tabaria." We here lived on fish, which is most excellent; there is not much variety, but the best sort, and it is the most common, is a species of bream, equal to the finest perch. It is remarkable that there is not, at present, a single boat of any description on the lake; the fish are caught by the casting-net from the beach, a method which must yield a very small quantity compared to what would be obtained with boats. I imagine this to be the reason why fish is so dear, being sold at the same price per pound as meat. It was on this lake that the miraculous draught of fishes took place.* There is a current throughout the whole breadth of the lake; the passage of the Jordan through it is observable by the smoothness of the surface.

March 2.—To-day, Mr. Bankes arrived after having made a complete tour of the Haouran, and passed round the lake of Tiberias. He proposed that we should join him in a journey, which he contemplates making beyond the Jordan, and round the Dead Sea to Jerusalem; he had expressed a wish to this effect at Aleppo, and had left a letter for us at Damascus to the same purport. We have accordingly resolved to accompany him; we had totally abandoned all idea of making the tour of the Dead Sea, as a hopeless undertaking, notwithstanding we had our poor friend Burckhardt's notes to aid and assist us; Mr. Bankes was, however, resolved to make the attempt alone if we could not have joined him. While he made a short visit to Safot, which he had not yet seen, we determined to inspect Om Keis (the ancient Gadara), in the country of the Gadarenes.

March 4.—We quitted Tiberias at eleven, and following the shore of the lake till we came to the site of the ancient Tarichea; forded the Jordan close to the ruins of a Roman bridge, a few hundred yards from the end of the lake; thence we passed by the village of Semmack (the Arabic for fish) at the south end of the lake, and turning to the southward, in about half an hour crossed the river Yarmack or Hieromax, a very pretty stream, tributary to the Jordan. There is here a small ancient town, but it contains nothing of interest; the map marks it "Amatha." From this point we ascended the mountains by a very steep road, and before sunset arrived at Om Keis. The natives inhabit the ancient sepulchres. We were very kindly received by the sheikh. The tomb in which we lodged was capable of containing between twenty and thirty people; it was of an oblong form, and the cattle, &c., occupied one end, while the proprietor and his family lived in the other. The walls of the ancient Gadara are easily discernible; within them the pavement of the city is still very perfect; and the traces of the chariot wheels are visible on the stones. We found the remains of a row of columns which lined the main street on either side; two theatres, in tolerable preservation, are within the walls; and without, to the northward, is the Necropolis; the sepulchres, which are all under ground, are hewn out of the rock; the doors are very massive, being cut out of immense blocks of stone; some of these are now standing, and actually turn on their hinges. The hinge is nothing but a part of the stone left projecting at each end, and let into a socket cut in the rock; the face of the doors are cut in the shape of panels. From this place we had a fine view of the lake of Tiberias.

March 5.—In the morning we descended to the N. E. into the plain of the Yarmack, to visit the thermal springs there; they are not so hot as those of Tiberias. One of them is inclosed by palm-trees, in a very picturesque manner; it is of great depth, and its surface is covered with a species of red moss, somewhat resembling sponge before it has been purified: this the natives told us they apply to their camels when suffering under certain cutaneous disorders. Here are

* Luke, v. 4—9.

the ruins of a Roman bath. We found several sick persons at these springs who had come to use the waters. From this point we followed the Yarmack until we came near the place where we had crossed it the preceding evening, and returned by dusk to Tiberias. Mr. Bankes having rejoined us, we employed ourselves from the 6th to the 10th in measuring the circuit of the ancient city, and in making researches in the neighbourhood. Mr. Bankes had discovered a curious ancient fortification, situated to the west of Magdala. On the north side of the entrance of a ravine there is a high perpendicular cliff which, from its projecting situation and steep sides, forms a natural barrier on two sides of a triangle, the other side being defended by a wall of rough masonry, with numerous projecting turrets. Mr. Bankes made a plan of it; we were two days in taking the measurements. The natives call it Callah-el-Hammam, (Castle of the Pigeons,) but we are not aware that any ancient authors mention it, or give a clue to its origin. It may possibly be the ancient "Jotapata" where Josephus was taken, and which he states to have been demolished by Vespasian. It is certainly of very ancient date—prior, Mr. Bankes thinks, to the time of the Romans. The village of Erbed, in which there are a few Roman ruins, stands in a plain at the foot of the Mount Beatitude, on the opposite side of the ravine. There are some curious old convents in the side of the cliff, on the left in going from the village of Majdil (the ancient Magdala) to the Callah-el-Hammam. These convents are very singularly constructed, being excavated several stories high in the perpendicular cliff, with galleries, &c. About two miles south of Majdil are the ruins of six Roman baths; the springs are mineral, but only of a luke-warm temperature. The baths are circular, from 15 ft. to 20 ft. in diameter, inclosed with a wall about 12 ft. high within, and 6 ft. without; at present there is no apparent means of ingress or egress. Their position is very picturesque, being close to the lake, and overgrown with shrubs, weeds, and wild flowers; the water is perfectly clear, and about 6 ft. or 7 ft. deep, with pebbles at the bottom; there are also fish sporting about in them; the spring discharges itself into the lake, subterraneously, through the wall. We swam to the Scorpion rock mentioned by Josephus, but saw no scorpions on it.

March 10.—In the forenoon we left Tiberias, and observed, in following the borders of the lake, one of the circular towers, with part of the wall of the ancient town on that side. We left the hot baths about noon. Drawing towards the southern extremity of the lake, we saw, on our right, at the foot of the hills, an extensive aqueduct; at the entrance are traces of the walls of Tarichea, which appears to have been situated on two eminences, one on the right of our road, and the other bordering on the lower end of the lake, by the Jordan; this latter appears to have been artificially surrounded by water on the other sides. The Jordan winds extremely here, but has little current. The ruins of the Roman bridge which we saw in going to Om Keis, had ten arches: from this point the road continues through rather a naked country, with occasional views of the river. About 3 o'clock we came to a khan near a bridge; and, an hour's ride beyond this, we observed, by the road-side, a Roman mile-stone but there were only two or three letters distinctly visible on it. Farther on, the pavement of the ancient road is perceivable, and about two miles from Bysan we saw a sarcophagus, on the brow of a slight eminence on the right of the road; here we crossed a small stream, and ascended to Bysan about dusk. During the latter part of this day's journey we remarked a great number of Arab camps. Bysan is supposed to be the Bethshan of Scripture, afterwards called Scythopolis, the largest city of the Decapolis, and the only one that side of the Jordan. It was to the wall of Bethshan that the body of Saul was fastened after he was slain.*

March 11.—This day we employed

* 1 Sam. xxxi. 10.

ourselves in inspecting the ruins. The most interesting is the theatre, the walls of which can be distinctly traced, although every part of it is completely filled with weeds. It measures across the front about 180 ft., and is remarkable as having those oval recesses half way up the theatre, mentioned by Vitruvius as being constructed to contain the brass sounding tubes. We had never seen these in any other ancient theatre, and we were, at the time, quite at a loss to conjecture to what use they were applied. There are seven of these cells, and Vitruvius mentions, that even in his day very few theatres had them. We were very careful to take a correct plan of this theatre, attending to every minute particular.

We found twenty-four sculls and numerous bones in one of the most concealed vomitories; in one of the sculls a viper was basking, with his body twisted through the sockets of the eyes, presenting a good subject for a moralist. At this place the tombs lie to the N. E. of the Acropolis, without the walls; the sarcophagi remain in some of them; we here found niches of a triangular shape, for the lamps; some of the doors were still hanging on the ancient hinges of stone, and in remarkable preservation. Two streams run through the ruins of the city, almost insulating the Acropolis; there is a fine Roman bridge over the one to the S. W.; beyond it may be seen the paved way which led to the ancient Ptolemais, now Acre. The plains extend in this direction to the sea-coast, without any intervening mountains. On the other side, a little below where the streams unite, the walls of the town cross the rivulet in a singular manner; a high arch in the centre, with a smaller one on each end, appear to have formed a bridge, and the wall of the city was continued along its edge. It would seem as if there had been a grating across the centre arch; the outer part of the two smaller arches was walled up. On the hill near this bridge the ruins of one of the gates of the city are very distinguishable, and amongst the remains are prostrate columns of Corinthian architecture. The Acropolis is a high circular hill, on the top of which are the traces of the walls which encompassed it. The people are a fanatical set.

March 12.—At eight o'clock in the morning we left Bysan. Near the town are the ruins of many subterranean granaries. Taking guides from an Arab camp to show us the proper place for fording the Jordan, we reached its banks in one hour and twenty minutes. They are very prettily wooded, although the more distant parts of the plains are quite destitute of trees. Near the ford, about half a mile to the south, is a tomb called "Sheikh Daoud," standing on a round hill resembling a barrow. The stream of the Jordan is here much swifter than in the part near the lake of Tiberias. The water at the ford reached above the bellies of the horses. The breadth of the river we found to be 140 feet. We bathed here. From the Jordan we turned to the right of the path to see Tabathat Fahkil, which we reached in about half an hour. Here the ruins of a modern village stand on a hill, bearing E.S.E. from the Acropolis of Bysan; and in a plain to the west of it are the ruins of a square building, with a semicircular end, which appears to have been surrounded by columns. On the east and south sides of the hill are considerable ruins of some ancient city which must have been of great extent. The situation is beautiful, being on the side of a ravine, with a picturesque stream running at the bottom. As this place appears to be as ancient as Scythopolis, and full two-thirds of its size, it seems unaccountable that history should not mention a town so near "the principal city of the Decapolis" as this is. We searched for inscriptions, but in vain. The ruins of a fine temple are situated near the water-side, and amongst the columns are found the three orders of architecture, Doric, Ionic, and Corinthian. The river passing to the south falls into the Jordan. Crossing the rivulet, and following a path to the southward, we entered a small plain very thickly covered with herbage, particularly the mustard plant, which reached as high as our horses' heads. To the eastward we observed several excavations in the side of the hills. These are probably the Necropolis, for there are several tombs in this direction, resembling those at Bysan and Om Keis. Finding no path, we re-crossed the rivulet, and proceeding to the north rejoined the track from the Jordan, which we had originally quitted to visit Tabathat Fahkil; from this point we began to ascend, passing occasionally over hill and vale, well wooded, the country gradually increasing in beauty. On our left we saw the spot where Elijah was fed by the ravens.* There are many villages in this direction.

March 13.—We slept at Hallawye. In the morning we continued our route, and passed through some most beautiful woodland scenery, with the gall oak, wild olive, arbutus, &c. &c., in great luxuriance, and a variety of wild flowers, such as the cyclamen, crimson anemone, &c., on a rich soil. We arrived, in three hours, at a village called Cafringee, situated at the southern extremity of the valley of Adjeloun.† There are sufficient fragments amongst the rubbish and buildings of Cafringee to show that there was once a Roman town or some large edifice on the spot. We remained here about an hour, and then sending our baggage forward to the village of Adjeloun, proceeded, in company with the principal sheikh of the neighbourhood, to the Callah-el-Rubbat, which is situated, to the N.N.W., on an eminence, at an hour's distance. About half way up the hill we were shown a great cave, the most extensive one we had seen in Syria; this is, probably, the "cave of Makkedah," in which the five kings were discovered, and afterwards buried.‡ The Callah-el-Rubbat commands, by its elevated situation, a most extensive view of the plain of the Jordan, the lakes Asphaltes and Tiberias, and a vast tract of country in every direction. Indeed, for several days we had this castle constantly in view from every quarter. Unfortunately, the weather was too hazy to admit of our profiting much by our lofty situation. We fully examined every part of the castle; it is entirely of Turkish architecture, and has an Arabic inscription in one of the centre stones. The building is constructed out of the rock, which has been excavated to form the moat round it: there are some tanks near the castle.

On descending to the village of Adjeloun, we found, in the court of an old mosque, a Roman mile-stone, and in the building itself, several fragments of Roman sculpture. The next day, half an hour after quitting Adjeloun, we passed through the village of Eugen; here are some Roman tombs, and two sarcophagi cut in the rock. From Eugen the road led through a narrow and picturesque valley with a fine view of the Callah-el-Rubbat behind us. This vale opened into a plain, whence the road passes through a woody, uneven country, extremely beautiful. We here observed several arbutus of great beauty and unusual dimensions; the trunk of one was about 6 ft. in circumference. In some instances the Valonia oak and arbutus andrachne were growing grafted together, probably from the acorn or berry of the one having dropped into some crack, in the stem of the other, and there taken root. The Roman road is discernible as you advance into a plain near Souf. We saw, likewise, three Roman mile-stones near to each other. Souf is a small village, situated on the side of a hill, about two hours and a half from Adjeloun; in the vale below it is the source of a stream which runs through the valley. At the fountain is an imperfect Greek inscription, and in the ruins of a church in the village are a mile-stone, and an altar having a Greek inscription. At 3 P.M. we went with three armed natives of Souf to Djerash. We took the shortest

* "And the ravens brought him bread and flesh in the morning, and bread and flesh in the evening; and he drank of the brook." 1 Kings, xvii. 6.

† "Sun, stand thou still upon Gibeon; and thou moon in the valley of Ajalon." Joshua, x. 12.

‡ Joshua, x. 17—27.

road over the hills; and after taking a general view of the ruins, returned to Souf by a valley lying to the N.E. This latter road is very beautifully wooded, and runs by the side of a picturesque stream, the banks of which are covered with the oleander. We found the natives of Souf a rude set, constantly annoying us with stories about dytchmaan, or enemies, alluding to the Salhaan Arabs, who are encamped near Djerash; this was evidently done with a view to induce us to have a strong escort every time we went to Djerash; for which service they asked two piastres per man each trip. In consequence of all this, when we went again, on the 15th, to Djerash, we took with us the sheikh and ten of his people. We took measures of one of the temples; our escort annoying us all the time with absurd remarks on the importance of their protecting us against the Arabs. During the day two of these said Arabs arrived on horseback, armed with pikes; but they were very quiet. We returned to Souf rather early in the afternoon.

March 16.—It rained hard, and the natives of Souf refused to attend us any more to Djerash, going over again the old story of their terror of the dytchmaan. In the afternoon Mr. Bankes' interpreter, and the soldier who attended him as a guard, arrived with a young prince of the Benesuckher Arabs, named Ebyn Fayes, and ten of his tribe. The prince was attended by his mace-bearer; the mace was of iron, hollow, and about two feet long. All the party were well mounted and armed, and as they galloped down the hill, firing their pistols and manœuvring with their spears, they formed a curious and interesting sight. Mr. Bankes had dispatched the interpreter and soldier from Adjeloun to the Benesuckher camp, to obtain a guard to conduct us to the several places which we wished to visit, lying east of the Jordan and Dead Sea; he had a list of the places which Burckhardt had visited, and a note of his route by Kerek and Wady Mousa, and intended to pass from the latter to the south end of the Dead Sea, and by Hebron to Jerusalem. The interpreter, however, could only make a bargain with these people to escort us as far as Kerek, as they said they were at war with the tribes beyond that place, and could go no further. As the places beyond Kerek were the most beset with difficulties, there seemed to be little hope of performing the whole of the journey under their protection; we, however, kept them for the present, hoping if we reached Kerek with them, to pursue our journey by other means; especially as the natives of Kerek are mostly Christians, and are in the habit of making their pilgrimage to Jerusalem by the route we were anxious to take. Volney was told by the Arabs, "that there are to the S. E. of the lake Asphaltes, within three days' journey, upwards of 300 ruined towns absolutely deserted; several having large edifices with columns." This was the country of the Nabatheans, the most potent, says Josephus, of the Arabs and of the Idumæans, who, at the time of the destruction of Jerusalem, were almost as numerous as the Jews. Our lamented friend, Sheikh Ibrahim, states in his notes, that three days south from Kerek, in the Wady Mousa, are the ruins of Petra, the capital of the ancient Arabia Petræa. Here, to use his own expression, are wonderfully fine temples cut out of the rock, and more than 200 sepulchres. Since the death of poor Burckhardt, no European has seen this place, or indeed the others to the S. E. of the Dead Sea. Hebron is the ancient Kiriath Arba, and is said to be of higher antiquity than Memphis; to see the site of such a place, excites no ordinary degree of interest. Abraun or Hebron, is the place where Abraham died. The terms agreed on with the Arabs were, that they should conduct us safe to Kerek for 1000 piastres; most unfortunately, Mr. Bankes paid the whole of the money beforehand, and to this ill-advised step we owe all the tricks they afterwards played us.

March 17.—We quitted Souf with our Arab guard, and passed the day in taking further measurements at Djerash. It was here that the Arabs induced Mr. Bankes to pay *all* the money in advance, and immediately commenced a regular train of impositions and falsehoods, which in the end compelled us to leave them and to abandon the journey. In dealings with these people not a single para should ever be paid them in advance; it should be stipulated *that they are to receive nothing till they have completed their contract.* They are a cunning set, and behave well when they are kept in check in this manner; but if paid anything before hand, they continually teaze you for more, and when once they have received the whole of the money they consider that you are completely in their power, and that they may do as they like with you; since Lady Hester Stanhope *spoiled the market*, by overpaying them when she went to Palmyra, few people, going to that place, have succeeded so well with them as we did; and this was certainly owing to our persisting in not paying a single para till their part of the agreement was fulfilled. In the evening we reached Katty, a village lying in a beautiful situation, to the W. N. W. of Djerash, at about an hour's distance. The Arabs here demanded money to buy provisions for themselves; we were obliged to give them 30 piastres a day.

March 18.—This morning we again went to Djerash, and measured the walls of the town, and the principal temple. Some of the Salhaan Arabs appearing in the distance, our Benesuckher friends galloped off to parley with them, and, as usual, we were again teazed about the dytchmaan. We went this night, by the desire of our conductors, to a small camp of the Salhaans, although they had been continually calling them their enemies; it lay one hour and a half to the S. E. of Djerash. On the way they tried to persuade Mr. Bankes to give a horse to the Salhaans; this request was made in a valley about half an hour distant from the camp, and was propounded in a very *mysterious* manner; on his refusing they at first stopped, and said they would not go on, but finally conducted us to the camp, saying that they would give up one of their own horses, and even went through the ceremony of parading their present before the tent we were in. We never ascertained the fact, but fully believe that it was a mere attempt to rob us of one of our horses.

March 19.—We went in the morning to examine a place called Reashy, but found nothing there of interest. The Benesuckher Arabs refused to go to Djerash, excusing themselves by saying they feared the Salhaans; we were very anxious to finish the plan of Djerash, nothing having ever been published regarding these antiquities; indeed, they were unknown to Europeans until Mr. Seetzen discovered them in 1806. I believe Mr. Bankes, Sir W. Chatterton, Mr. Leslie, Sheikh Ibrahim, and Mr. Buckingham, are the only Europeans who have seen them. The Arabs were now told that Mr. Bankes would give up the researches he had intended to make on the banks of the Zerka, and go to Djerash instead. We accordingly set out in that direction with three of the Arabs, the remainder proceeding with our baggage from the Salhaan camp to Katty. In our way we ascended to Nebi Hood, a village situated on the summit of a hill, S. S. E. of Djerash; the village is at present deserted; we found a Greek inscription on an altar in the court-yard of one of the houses. We were about to proceed to Djerash, when one of our three Arabs who had advanced a little in front, returned to inform us that six Salhaans were waiting near Djerash to intercept us. We accordingly returned to join some more of the Benesuckher party, after having first reconnoitred for ourselves. We soon met the remainder of our escort on their way to Katty, and therefore proceeded with them all, and had a parley with the six Salhaans, who, after some conversation, in which they said that "they wanted heads, not money," told the Benesuckhers that we had *their* permission to remain at Djerash till the afternoon of this day. Their being able to bring only six armed men to intercept us, was no great proof of their force; and our Benesuckher friends now joined us in laughing at them. We endeavoured to finish our task at Djerash this day, but though we were at work till dark (Irby and myself measuring, and Mr. Bankes drawing, copying inscriptions, &c.), we could not complete our work. In the course of the day Mr. Bankes was robbed of his cap by an armed Arab, who, having concealed himself amongst the ruins of the great theatre, stole on him unperceived, while he was drawing. We passed the night at Katty; just as we arrived a grand quarrel arose between the Benesuckhers and the villagers; the scene of action was on the house tops. It is a custom of the country, that for one night travellers are provided with provisions gratis; and there is in every Turkish village a room to lodge them in. Europeans on departing generally make a present to the servants, at least equivalent to what has been consumed. I mentioned before, that we had given the Arabs thirty piastres a day for their food; these cunning fellows, however, wanted to force the villagers to feed them, although they had been there before on the night of the 17th, and as the poor people had to feed the horses gratis, as well as the men, it came very hard on them. We paid for everything *we* got; and we assured the villagers that the Benesuckhers were provided with money to pay for all *they* had. This was the subject-matter of the quarrel,—battle there was none; for although there was much appearance of anger and rage, and the greatest noise and confusion imaginable, men, women, and children, being all mixed together pell-mell, nevertheless, every one was cautious to avoid coming to blows, and the affray ended to the advantage of the poor natives, the Benesuckhers retreating from the village.

March 20.—We went in the morning to Djerash to finish our operations; a very singular circumstance here took place. Mr. Bankes' soldier from Damascus, whom he had always found very useful and attached, had within the last two or three days very much altered his manner and conduct, and exhibited strong proofs of fear, both in words and actions; on our way to Djerash he told us frequently that the Arabs would strip us of everything, and while Mr. Bankes was taking a copy of an inscription near the north gate of the city, the soldier very slowly, without making any further observations, walked off, and was never seen by us again. On the preceding evening he said he had received information of some Damascus troops having arrived at a town a few hours' distant, and asked permission to depart in the night to procure their protection for us; however, he did not then go, as the villagers persuaded him to the contrary; we, of course, imagined that this was his object in setting off, and, that finding the report false, he had returned to Damascus. Two spy-glasses were found missing, which Mr. Bankes had brought with him, for presents; we did not, however, suspect the soldier of any roguery in this respect, although he certainly took the interpreter's gun, leaving his own, which was worse. The theft, however, we afterwards heard was proved against him; the Arabs denied having taken the telescopes. It was two o'clock in the afternoon before we had completed our operations at Djerash. It has been a splendid city, built on two sides of a valley, with a fine stream running through it; the situation is beautiful. The town was principally composed of two main streets, crossing each other in the centre at right angles, as at Antinoe. The streets were lined with a double row of columns, some of which are Ionic and some Corinthian. The pavement is exceedingly good, and there is an elevated space on each side for foot passengers; the marks of the chariot wheels are visible in many parts of the streets. Djerash, supposed to be either Pella or Gerasa, but in some respects answering to neither, can boast of more public edifices than any other city we have seen. There are two theatres, two grand temples,—one, as appears by a Greek inscription, dedicated to the sun, like that at Palmyra, and not unlike that edifice, being constructed in the centre of an immense double peristyle court. The columns of the temple are five feet in diameter, and of a proportionate height; the capitals are Corinthian, and well executed. One singularity in this edifice is a chamber under ground, below the principal hall of the temple, with a bath in the centre. Five or six smaller temples are scattered about the town; and a magnificent Ionic oval space, of 309 feet long, adds greatly to the beauty of the ruins. The scene of the larger theatre is singularly perfect; there are two grand baths, and two bridges crossing the valley and river. The temples, and both the theatres, are built of marble, but not of a very fine sort. Three hundred yards from the south-west gate is the circus, or stadium, and near it the triumphal arch. The cemetery surrounds the city, but the sarcophagi are not very highly finished; upwards of two hundred and thirty columns are now standing in the city. To the north-east, about 200 yards from the walls, are a very large reservoir for water, and a picturesque tomb fronted by four Corinthian columns; near which is an aqueduct. There are numerous inscriptions in all directions, chiefly of the time of Antoninus Pius; most of them are much mutilated. The Greek inscription, before alluded to, was on the propyleum of the Temple of the Sun, which must have been a grand piece of architecture. The city has three entrances, with richly ornamented gateways; and the remains of the wall, with its occasional towers, are in wonderful preservation. On the whole, we considered Djerash to be a much finer mass of ruins than Palmyra.

At two o'clock in the afternoon, having completed our operations, we set out in a south-west direction for Szalt. In an hour and twenty minutes we crossed the Zerka, a small stream winding prettily in a narrow valley; there are the ruins of a small building on the front of the hills near the ford. Ascending from the rivulet, we passed the sites of some small towns, possessing nothing of interest; and at five in the evening we arrived at a camp of the Salhaans, where we passed the night.

March 21.—This morning we proceeded, but coming to a cross-road, the Benesucklhers said they could not reach Szalt that day, but would conduct us to a camp of their own; although we knew that Szalt could be only a few hours distant. We positively insisted upon their escorting us to Szalt, which, after much altercation, they said they would do, if we would give two hundred piastres to each of the sheikhs of Szalt, Heshbon, and Kerek, and also to themselves five days' advance of the thirty piastres a day. All this we positively refused, excepting the thirty for to-day; and, after further discussion, the Benesuckhers endeavouring by their threats to frighten us into a compliance with their demands, the dispute ended by our going to Szalt, accompanied by the prime minister (as we termed him) of the young prince, the chief of the party. The minister is a very great rogue; he is not an Arab born: we thought he had much the appearance of a Levantine, of European extraction.

It was he who put every bad idea into the minds of the prince, and the rest of the Arabs, who were mostly very young men, and not so well versed as himself in the art of cheating. We did not succeed in getting to Szalt, until the interpreter, and the Arab Seys who took care of our horses, frightened by the threats and gesticulations of our escort, had given the Arabs sixty piastres, of which we told them they must themselves be the losers. The prince and his party now quitted us for their own camp, as they said they could not enter Szalt, being at war with the inhabitants. We crossed over some small hills into a spacious valley called Bayga, in which are the ruins of a large square cyclopean building, perhaps a fortress; on quitting which, we ascended to the westward over some rugged rocks, and thence descended into some picturesque valleys most beautifully wooded. From these valleys we traversed some more barren soil, and again descending, passed on the left some vineyards, inclosed with stone walls; whence turning to the right, we had the first view of Szalt, not ten minutes distant from us. The castle is situated on the top of a hill, on the sides of which is the village, nearly surrounded by a valley and by high hills, forming a very picturesque object. The neighbourhood abounds in vineyards and olives. We found the finest raisins here that we had seen in Syria. The inhabitants of Szalt are numerous, and more than one-third of them are Christians. We arrived wet through. The people showed us great attention, drying our clothes before the fire. We first went to the travellers' room, but were soon after conducted to the house of a Christian. The weather continued bad the whole of the next day, but on the 23rd became fairer. In consequence of the treachery of the Arabs, we wished to be quit of them, and, if possible, to get the natives of Szalt to conduct us to Kerek. The *prime minister* made some extravagant demands; however, he was paid up to the day, and told that his services and those of his comrades were no longer wanted. He now tried all he could to induce us to consent to go to their camp, but this would have been a very imprudent course to have taken. Finding that he could not, either by good or bad words, prevail on us to go, he went off in a huff, saying, that his companions would take care that we did not stir from Szalt until we consented to his scheme. To show how little we feared these threats, we took a walk of two hours, and returned in the evening. Some of the Mahommedan natives of Szalt insulted us on our return. We wished next day to go to Amaun, but the son of the sheikh of the town told us his father was gone to the Arabs, and that nothing could be done till his return.

March 24. — This morning the sheikh's son and five other guards accompanied us to visit some places in the neighbourhood. The first was a village called Athan, situated two hours distant to the N.N.W. There is a ruined village here. We saw no remains of antiquity; but in ascending from it, we observed some sarcophagi cut out of the rock. We afterwards went to a place called Gilhad Gilhood, said by the natives to be the birthplace of the prophet Elijah. There are here two old tombs; one of them has been used as a Christian chapel; also some sarcophagi cut out of the rock, and other antique remains. We visited, in all, five ruined villages, which serve at least to show that the country lying five or six miles to the north of Szalt, was once more populous than it is at present. Szalt has been thought to be the ancient Amathus, but we are more inclined to believe it to be Machærus, where John the Baptist was beheaded. The country in general is extremely beautiful and woody. On our return to the town we found a black messenger from the Benesuckher prince, inviting us to go to his camp and adjust our differences; but we had determined, if the natives of Szalt refused to conduct us to Kerek, to recross the Jordan on the following day, and proceed to Jerusalem, where we could adopt other measures for carrying our plans into execution.

March 29.—In the morning, at nine o'clock, we quitted Szalt, in the middle of a great dispute amongst the natives, whether they should or should not deliver us up to the Arabs. The tops of all the houses were covered with women and children to see the result of the fray. On quitting the house, our interpreter was missing, and after some delay, we found him concealed behind the door, crying bitterly. The first person we met was the prime minister, whom we had not seen since the 23rd. He was in company with the black, and another Benesuckher Arab; and mounting their horses they immediately joined us, and endeavoured all in their power to persuade us to go the wrong road; in which they were joined by all the Turkish natives of the place, who kept bawling to us that we were going wrong. Fortunately, when walking out one day, we had made inquiries, and had discovered the right road to Jerusalem; which, in spite of all their remonstrances, we accordingly took. The plan of the prime minister was, doubtless, to lead us to the Arabs' camp, and there detain us until they had got what they wanted. As we ascended the hill, followed by the Arabs, we soon got a view of the Dead Sea, the neighbourhood of Jericho, and the plain of the Jordan. We had given out that our intention was to pass through Jericho on our way to Jerusalem; but having deviated from the right path shortly after we began to descend, we thought of passing on to Bysan. One of the Arabs quitted us on the brow of the hill; and when they saw that we had ceased to keep the road to Jericho, the black man went also. Both departed, no doubt, to give information to the prince and his party of the track we had taken. A little after mid-day, when we had nearly descended to the plain, to the minister's surprise and vexation, we turned short off to the ford of the Jordan, which we saw in the distance, and quitted him, notwithstanding his numerous remonstrances. Indeed had we continued long in the track we were going, we should soon have been amongst some of the Bene-suckher camps, as we had shortly before passed five or six small camps, but of what tribe we did not know. We now pushed straight for the Jordan, and reached its banks about two o'clock. At the foot of the mountains we observed some singular, and certainly very ancient tombs, composed of great rough stones, resembling what is called "Kitt's Cotty House," in Kent. They were built of two long stones, for sides, with one at each end, and a small door in front, mostly facing to the north. This door was cut in the stone. All were of rough stones apparently not hewn, but found in huge flakes, such as are still seen about the spot: over the whole was laid an immense flat piece projecting both at the sides and ends. What rendered these tombs more remarkable was, that the interior was not long enough for a corpse, being only 5 ft.: both the front and back stones being considerably within the ends of the side ones. There were about twenty-seven of these tombs, very irregularly situated. The plain, about half way from the foot of the mountains, is tolerably level, but barren; it then becomes very rugged, consisting of hills, vales, and deep chasms, in a dry saltish soil, of a very white appearance. This continues to within a quarter of a mile of the river's bank; whence the rest is a rich, flat plain to the margin of the river, which is at the bottom of a deep ravine, beautifully wooded, and so overgrown, that the stream is not seen till you are close to it. The Callah-el-Rubbat bore N.E. half N. from the ford. Hereabouts it would be interesting to search for the twelve stones erected by the Israelites to commemorate their passing the river.* The water was too high for us to make the search; and, indeed, we were not sufficiently at our ease, with the idea of the Arabs being in chase of us. We were detained till nearly three o'clock before we could cross the river, which we were surprised to find very much swollen. An Arab, on horseback, arrived shortly after us, and as he had no baggage, was well mounted, and likely to be acquainted with the ford, we requested him to cross first, that we might profit by his example: but, like the peasants on Mount Lebanon, he refused to lead the way. We therefore crossed one at a time, the others, from an eminence on the banks, directing his progress. The stream was exceedingly rapid, and so deep, that we were obliged to swim our horses, which, as they had our fire-arms and our baggage, as well as ourselves on their backs, was no easy task. We all got completely wet through, and our papers, pocket-books, &c., were totally spoiled. From the river we pursued a direction W.N.W. for two hours, into a rich valley: there was no road or track. On the right we passed a great cave with an artificial door. A labourer misinformed us, and directed us up the dry course of a torrent in search of a village. After vainly wandering about till dark, we came to the termination of the valley, and saw no signs of any path or habitation. Heavy rain came on, with thunder and lightning,

* "And Joshua set up twelve stones in the midst of Jordan, in the place where the feet of the priests which bare the ark of the covenant stood; and they are there unto this day." Joshua, iv. 9.

and we were glad to take shelter for the night in a cave used occasionally by the shepherds.

March 26.—At day-light we were forced to retrace our steps, and return to the valley we had left, which we found was called Wady Zeit (Oil Valley); in it is a village called Agrarba, which we did not see. On entering Wady Zeit, the peasants all came out, armed with six muskets and their instruments of agriculture. Seeing a mounted party, issuing out of an uninhabited valley, so early in the morning. they had mistaken us for Bedouins. We obtained a guide for Nablous. From these people we learnt that the Arabs had crossed the Jordan the preceding evening in chase of us, and not being able to get any information, had returned to the other side of the river. We, therefore, owe our escape to the circumstance of having lost our way. We observed that this rich valley ends abruptly at the foot of the hills to the westward. We followed the principal road, which led us out by a ravine, to the S. W., and continuing in this track till about 11 o'clock, we crossed over the hills to the westward. About half an hour after mid-day we reached the village of Bait Forage, situated by the side of a rich extensive plain, having six other villages on its borders, many olive-yards, and much corn. We were glad to get some breakfast here, after a twenty-eight hours' fast, with the exception of a few dirty raisins, which we found in the bottom of one of our hourges. We remained till 2 o'clock, and then proceeded for Nablous, about two hours distant. In twenty minutes we arrived at a ruined village, called Kaffer Baiter, around which are several old Roman tombs and tanks. In one of the tombs, the mouth of which was closed with rubbish, we found some dead bodies concealed. Thence we went to Nablous, the road leading us by Jacob's Well, a short distance from which, a valley, in a southern direction, unites with that in which stand Bait Forage and the six other villages. Maundrell says, these rich valleys are supposed to be "the portion of land given by Jacob to his son Joseph." Nablous is the ancient Sychem. We went to the summit of Mount Gerizim, and found the ruins of a large town, with a tank, near a conspicuous tomb.

On the 28*th* of *March* we quitted Nablous, and reached Jerusalem the next day. For an excellent description of Nablous, and also of all the objects of interest at Jerusalem, I must refer the reader to Maundrell. We took his book in our pockets, and visited every place which he mentions, most of them three different times. Once by ourselves, once as ciceroni to Lord Belmore and his family, and once with Mr. Legh, the gentleman who has published his Journey in Nubia. . . We have been to Bethlehem and St. John's, visited the Holy Sepulchre at the Greek Easter, and saw the celebrated trick of the holy fire, &c.

May 1.—After staying for more than a month at Jerusalem, we started for the Jordan with all the pilgrims, escorted by the governor and a body of troops. The sight was most impressive. The immense number of Christians, from all quarters, the various costumes of the Greeks, the Copts from Egypt, the Abyssinians from Æthiopia: some of the pilgrims on camels, with double cradles on their backs; some on mules, also with cradles; some on horses; some on asses; in all amounting to about 5000, presented a most curious and interesting scene, winding amongst the hills, in a line as far as the eye could reach, and sometimes through different openings in the mountains, appearing in two or three divisions. In the evening we arrived at the camp near Jericho. We could trace no remains of the Hippodrome which Josephus places here.

May 2.—At two this morning we started by torch-light for the Jordan, which we reached at 7 A.M. Here we found the pilgrims bathing in the river, men, women, and children, all mixed together. They immersed their clothes in the river, gathered boughs off the trees, and filled bottles with the water to take home, in commemoration of their pilgrimage. We went, attended by two Arabs, to the Dead Sea, and bathed in it; the water was bitter and buoyant. Those of our party who could not swim, floated on the surface like corks; on dipping the head in, the eyes smarted dreadfully, and we were much surprised to observe, on coming out of the lake, that the water did not evaporate from the body, as is the case on emerging from fresh water, but adhered to the skin, and was greasy to the touch. At night we returned to Jerusalem.

We propose starting to-morrow with two Arabs to make the tour of the Dead Sea, and search for the sites of the cities that are known to have stood in that direction. Our party will consist of Messrs. Legh and Bankes, with their attendants, and Captain Irby and myself. We have plenty of arms, and shall muster altogether eleven persons, including two Arabs. The trip will probably take us about three weeks. We have all dressed ourselves as Arabs of the desert, to excite less observation.

Lord and Lady Belmore and their party have been here about three weeks. They came from Cairo by land, having taken the same route as we did. Their party is very strong, and they had the brother of a famous Arab chief to protect them. They are all now attiring themselves as Arabs, and are going to visit Baalbec, Damascus, &c., after which they embark in his lordship's yacht for Europe. The friars of the convent had a serious dispute in the Holy Sepulchre the day before yesterday. They were performing one of their ceremonies, when the Greeks attacked them, wounding several of them. There has been much disputing before the governor in consequence, and a Tartar has been sent with their complaints to Constantinople. In Maundrell's time there was a similar fray between the Greeks and Latins, and the jealousy has existed ever since. A rather singular adventure befel us while at Jerusalem. There is amongst the sepulchres, which travellers have designated as "the Tombs of the Kings," an excavated vault with an oblong portico. The only visible entrance to this vault is at one end of the portico, while from its construction there is every reason to suppose that a corresponding entrance would be found at the other end, which is now filled with rubbish. Mr. Bankes was so thoroughly convinced of this, that when at Constantinople he used every exertion, but in vain, to procure a firman authorising him to excavate and ascertain the fact. We now endeavoured to obtain permission from the governor of Jerusalem to dig there, but without success. As we could not procure legal authority, we determined on prosecuting the undertaking secretly in the night, and accordingly purchased privately some pickaxes and other implements. Late in the evening we quitted the town, singly, and from different gates, to avoid suspicion; and assembling at the rendezvous after dark, found that we mustered a party of ten persons, viz., Messrs. Bankes and Legh, Captain Corry, and ourselves, together with five servants, including two of Lord Belmore's sailors, whom his lordship had allowed to join us. We divided our party into two watches, and worked hard four hours at a time during the whole night, digging and clearing away the rubbish. We were obliged to station one of the servants as a sentinel near the road side, to apprise us of the approach of any one In the morning we had removed the rubbish to a depth of about 10 ft., when we came to an immense block of stone, apparently in the very spot where we expected to find the entrance to the tomb. As we were unable to move this mass, we returned to the city, pretty well fatigued, having been obliged, for want of spades, to clear away the rubbish with our hands. The next day Captain Corry, Mr. Bankes, and Mahomet his janissary, acting on the suggestion of Lord Belmore, succeeded in breaking the stone by heating it, and then pouring cold vinegar on it; but, unfortunately, shortly after this was done, our proceedings were discovered by some Turks, and reported to the governor, who put a very effectual stop to our researches, by ordering the whole of the portico to be walled in.

CHAPTER VII.

A TOUR TO PETRA AND THE DEAD SEA.

Difficulties attending our proposed Visit to Petra—Our Party—Our assumed Names and Costumes—Departure from Jerusalem—The Mountain of the Franks—The Labyrinth—Tekoa—Hebron—Its Governor—Difficulty in obtaining a Guide—Jellaheen Arabs—Plain of the Dead Sea—Salt Hills Singular Trees and Plants—Favourable Reception by the Ghorneys—Beautiful Geological Specimens—Stopped by Arabs—The Castle of Kerek—Description of Kerek—Christian Church—Reception at Kerek—Skeikh Yousouf—His openness of Character—Departure from Kerek—The Wahabees Mahannah—Mote—Ruins at Dettrass The Wady-el Ahsa—Ruined Temple—Gharundel Volcanic Mountains—Shobek—Abon Raschid—His Dispute with the Sheikh of Wady Mousa, who refuses to permit our Advance—Noble conduct of Abon Raschid—View of Wady Mousa—Conferences of the Rival Chiefs—Preparations for Hostilities—Reinforcement from Kerek—Hindi—Failure of Negotiations—The Enemy suddenly withdraw their opposition.

Great were the obstacles which presented themselves, and innumerable the difficulties which we had to surmount before we could commence our journey to Petra. It had for some time been the wish of Mr. Bankes to undertake this tour, as the only two Europeans who had ever been either at Kerek or Wady Mousa (Valley of Moses or Petra) were both dead, viz., Sheikh Ibrahim and Mr. Seetzen. Both these indefatigable travellers performed this journey alone and in disguise, and were consequently obliged to conceal their papers, and make all their observations by stealth, which must necessarily have rendered their remarks very brief and cursory, compared to what they would have been had the writers been unrestrained. Seetzen travelled as an Arab, calling himself Moosa, but never got so far as Petra.

Although we are of opinion that Mr. Bankes could not have succeeded in accomplishing this journey without his junction with Mr. Legh and ourselves, still he has the merit of being the first person travelling as a European, who ever thought of extending his researches in that direction; and from his profound knowledge of ancient history, as well as his skill in drawing, he was by far the best calculated to go on such an expedition. When Mr. Bankes applied at Constantinople to have Kerek and Wady Mousa inserted in his firman, the Turkish Government returned for answer, "that they knew of no such places within the Grand Seignior's dominions;" but as he and Mr. Frere, the British minister, pressed the point very much, they at length referred him to the Pasha of Damascus, who, equally averse to have anything to do with the business, passed him on to the governor of Jerusalem. This latter tried all he could to dissuade us from the undertaking, though Mr. Legh gave him a handsome spy-glass to induce him to assist us. He advised us to apply to Mahommed Aga, the governor of Yaffa. The communication between Egypt and Mousa being usually through Gaza, which is under Mahommed Aga's government, it was supposed that he would have the greatest influence over the Arabs about Wady Mousa, inasmuch as he possessed the means of punishing them for any violence they might commit, either by stopping their supplies from Egypt, or by making prisoners of such of their people as came within his reach. The governor of Yaffa, however, not only evaded the affair altogether, but in order to put a stop to our journey, ordered us to return the horses which he had lent us. A second visit to the governor of Jerusalem seemed to promise as little as the preceding. We all four called on him. On this occasion, a former motsellim, who had been twenty years in office, and was sitting with the governor, pledged his word to us that the Arabs are a most savage and treacherous race; and to prove it, added, that they think Franks' blood a good medicine for their women when sick, and that they would make use of ours for this purpose. All that we could procure from the governor was a promise to write to the Sheikh of Kerek to apprise him of our coming. When we went with the Greek pilgrims to Jericho and the Jordan, the governor sent a man to us, whom he thought fit to call the Sheikh of Kerek, congratulating us on the obstacles to our going to that place having been overcome. This man, however, was no sheikh, and we suspect the motive of the motsellim for sending the *counterfeit*, was to obtain another present. Finding that there was no getting any of the public authorities to render us any assistance, we determined to proceed, trusting to our numbers and force, and to try our fortune with the Sheikh of Hebron. Each of the party procured a Bedouin Arab dress of the most ordinary description, and we all bought horses for the journey, except Mr. Bankes, who was already provided. Our party consisted of Mr. Legh, attended by an interpreter, a Tartar from Constantinople, and a seyes (hostler); Mr. Bankes, who had with him a soldier of the Pasha of Egypt, and ourselves with a Christian Arab servant. We had for our guides an Arab named Mahommed, who lived near Jericho, and a native of Hebron. We took the precaution of having as little baggage as possible with us, and sent the greater part to Acre with one of Mr. Legh's servants. We assumed Eastern names for the journey: Mr. Legh was called Osman; Mr. Bankes, Halleel; Captain Irby, Abdallah; and I, in remembrance of Collins' beautiful Eclogue of the Camel Driver, chose the name of Hassan. Our dress consisted of a frock and drawers of very coarse linen; the frock being fastened round the waist by a red leathern girdle, about 4 in. broad. The head-dress was a handkerchief of mixed silk and cotton, coloured with broad stripes of alternate red, green, and yellow. This was doubled into a triangular form and thrown over the head, to which it was attached by a double girdle of brown worsted rope. One corner of the handkerchief hangs down over the back of the neck the other two cover the ears, and come down over the shoulders. When the weather is cold, the Arabs tuck up these corners under the chin, and cover the whole face with the exception of the eyes. Over all we had the woollen abba, which we had long worn, and which we procured at Yaffa. As regards arms, we had amongst us six muskets, one blunderbuss, five braces of pistols, and two sabres. Our money, consisting of small gold coins, was concealed in leathern belts round our waists next the skin.

In the evening of the 6th of May, we left Jerusalem two hours before dark, our party consisting of eleven persons, all mounted. We slept at Bethlehem.

May 7.—At 8 A.M. we proceeded to "Solomon's Pools," and thence down the valley towards the Mountain of the Franks, which we ascended. We found it hollow on the top, with walls round it, and four towers, all much in ruins. This post is said to have been maintained by the Franks forty years after the fall of Jerusalem. Though the place is too small ever to have contained one halt the number of men which would have been requisite to make any stand in such a country; and the ruins, though they may be those of a place once defended by Franks, appear to have had an earlier origin, as the architecture seems to be Roman. From the Mount of the Franks we could see part of the Dead Sea, and Kerek on the other side of it. We took the following bearings by compass: Abou Jane, a village on the right, between Bethlehem and the Frank Mountain, West.—Bethlehem, N.W.—St. Elias, N.N.W.

We now proceeded to see the labyrinth. On approaching it, we left our horses at the ruins of a village called Hariatoon, and proceeded on foot, by the side of the cliffs on the southern side of a deep and picturesque ravine, to the mouth of the cave, which is entered by a long, winding, narrow passage, with small natural chambers or cavities on either side. We soon came to a large chamber, with natural arches of a great height; from this chamber there were numerous passages leading in all directions, occasionally joined by others at right angles, and forming a perfect labyrinth, which our guides assured us had never been thoroughly explored, the people being afraid of losing themselves. The passages were generally four feet high, by three feet wide, and were all on the same level. We saw but few petrifactions; nevertheless, the grotto was perfectly clear, and the air pure and good. In the large chamber we found some broken pottery, by which it would seem that this place had once been inhabited, probably it had served for a place of concealment. We observed a few English names written with charcoal. We now returned to the horses, and proceeded to the southward, to visit the ruins of Tekoa. They stand on a slight eminence, commanding several bursts of the Dead Sea, and cover a considerable extent. This place was built by King Rehoboam.* We could not find the remains of any distinct temple or public edifice, though there are a few fragments of columns. From Tekoa we passed through a plain of cultivated land, and thence all the way to Hebron, through a much prettier country than that near Jerusalem, the sides of the hills being richly studded with shrubs and dwarf trees in full verdure. The prickly oak, arbutus, and Scotch fir, were most abundant. About five o'clock we passed a village called Sipheer, by the side of a well-cultivated valley. There are about nine Roman sepulchral caves near this village. From this point we crossed a rugged road into another plain, where are the ruins of a small convent, called by the Jews "the House of Abraham." We now ascended considerably, and passing between numerous vineyards, with a watch-tower in each, (some of which appeared to be very ancient,) we reached Hebron at dusk. It appears by sacred history, that "Hebron was built seven years before Zoan in Egypt."† Josephus makes it not only older than Zoan, or Tanais, but also than Memphis. Here Abraham, Sarah, and Isaac died.* We had this day passed many camps of Arabs; towards evening some of them invited us to pass the night in their tents. The Sheikh of Hebron received us very kindly. We were lodged in a small prayer-room attached to the khan; it was furnished with mats and carpets for us, and we were presently served with a beverage we never before saw in the East,—"warm rice milk with sugar." It was handed round before coffee, and in the usual small cups. The Turks of Hebron having little intercourse with Europeans, are extremely jealous of Franks, not one of whom is allowed to live in the town, and I believe very few travellers have ever visited it; in consequence we found it impossible to gain admission into the mosque, in which is said to be the "tomb of Abraham." The lower part of this building is very curious, evidently antique, being formed of great stones, some of which are upwards of twenty-five feet in length; it has sixteen pilasters on each side, and eight at either end, without capitals, excepting a sort of ornamental summit which extends along the whole building, and is a species of cornice. Above this is a continuation of modern masonry. The approach to the entrance of the edifice is by a long flight of steps between it and other ruined buildings which stand on its S.E. side. I imagine that the outside walls only inclose the court which surrounds the mosque, and are not part of the mosque itself. The town of Hebron is not of large dimensions, though its population is great. The country all round it is cultivated to a considerable extent. The streets are winding, and the houses unusually high. We visited a manufactory of glass lamps, which are exported to Egypt. We were told by the governor of Hebron, that there is a regular party of pilgrims who set out from hence every year, without any escort, depending entirely on their own strength. They arrange so as to fall in with the great Damascus hadj, near to, or at Mecca, which is at the distance of thirty days.

* "He built even Bethlehem, and Etam, and Tekoa." 2 Chron. xi. 6.

† Numbers, xiii. 22.

* Genesis, xxiii. 2; xlix. 31.

From a merchant of Cairo we ascertained the existence of vast ruins at Abdi, in the Desert to the south, about three days' distance.

The first evening the governor of Hebron made no difficulty about our going to Wady Mousa, and Kerek, saying, "it was an easy matter, and he would undertake it." On the seventh, however, difficulties began. We visited, after dinner, the house of the Jewish priest. There are one hundred Jewish houses in Hebron; we found their quarters excessively clean, and neatly whitewashed; that of the priest was particularly so; it had a very nice divan, and commanded a fine view of the country. The Jews were very civil, and offered us letters to the places we were going to. On our return to the khan, from visiting the synagogue, Mr. Bankes presented a watch to the governor, who took it without making any remark at the time, but soon retired; shortly after a messenger arrived to say, that the motsellim was not content with his present, and had given it to the Jewish priest. Soon, however, another person made his appearance, saying, they wished to arrange the bargain for paying the guides, &c. Three hundred and fifty piastres were offered, but immediately rejected, as three thousand would have been at the first offer. After a second visit to the Jew's house, where we again found the governor, four hundred piastres were paid down, and we were to proceed the following morning. After supper, the governor called at the khan; he appeared to be shuffling a good deal, altering the order in which the different places were to be visited; but as he did not make any material change, *still placing Wady Mousa before Kerek*, we did not much care about it. He looked at all the firmans, boyourdees, &c., but did not appear to pay as much respect as is usual to the firman of the Grand Seignior. On observing Mr. Legh's Constantinople Tartar, he said, but in a good-humoured way, that a few years ago, if a Tartar had come to Hebron, he would have had his head cut off, but that it was not so now. We requested to proceed on our journey early in the morning, but he said that arrangements could not be made for our departure till an hour after sunrise; and soon afterwards left us.

May 8. — The governor did not make his appearance till after eight o'clock, bringing with him the three men who were to be our conductors, and the Jewish priest. He was shortly after followed by his brother, who had previously inquired in an indirect manner, why he had not received a present as well as his kinsman. Lastly came all the law officers, and heads of authorities. These, together with the motsellim, advised us to go to Kerek direct, and not to Wady Mousa. The governor, however, told the guides that there were 400 piastres for them if they chose to take us; but these people, who had, in all probability, previously received instructions to the purpose, declined conducting us. Finally, seeing there was no dealing with such people, we mounted our horses and left the town. In justice to the governor, it should be mentioned that he not only returned the 400 piastres but the watch also. When we had got outside the town we held a consultation together, and finding it impossible to proceed alone, without a guide to shew us the road, we sent into the town to say we would consent to visit Kerek, first, in the mean time we retired to a neighbouring olive-yard. Our messenger returned with word from the governor, "that he would have nothing at all to do with our concerns." A man on horseback offered to show us the road, and we accordingly proceeded with him, but had scarcely advanced half an hour, when two men came galloping and hallooing after us; upon which we stopped in a corn field, whilst we sent Mr. Bankes' soldier, Mahommed, with them into the town, as the governor wished to communicate with us; this was about mid-day. Towards two o'clock, Mahommed the Arab, who had accompanied us from Jerusalem, quitted us. About three o'clock Mahommed the soldier returned with one of the Jews, the sheikh having consented to send us to Kerek, with a letter to Sheikh Yousouf. He likewise sent as a guide one of the Jellaheen Arabs. In return for this the motsellim demanded 300 piastres, or the watch and 200. The watch and 150 were given, as the former was of more value than they imagined. Two roubees (five piastres and a half) were given to the Jew, and he begged one for the governor's brother. A roubee is less than two shillings value.

We now proceeded. The country was *ugly* enough, but tolerably well cultivated with corn. We passed several ruined sites. One of them, which they called Hagee, stands on a hill, and has a large square building, which appeared partly perfect. We saw another on our right, and a column which was too far off to be visited. We afterwards passed two Roman excavated tombs, with porticoes in front, not very interesting. There are two ruined sites near them, to one of which they probably belonged. About five o'clock we reached a well, where we gave our horses water, as the camp where we were to sleep was ill-provided. They called this well "Al-baid;" there are two pools. One is small with green water, the other a fountain in the rock. There is an ancient site N.W. of it, with a wall of large construction, and some good masonry. There are slanting passages cut in the rock, leading to caves which have probably served for tombs.

We reached a Jellaheen camp of thirty tents about dusk. It was situated on the summit of a hill, an unusual position, as they generally pitch their camps in valleys. The harems, or parts of each tent allotted to the women, were covered in front, and they all appeared carefully veiled. We found these people extremely poor in appearance, though they had plenty of sheep, goats, and camels. The camp was placed in a desert country, the cultivated land having ceased about the well Al-baid. We had mutton for supper, but were obliged to find our own coffee. An Arab journeyman tailor arrived, and was employed making coats of sheep-skins, which he dyed red with ochre, or some such substance. These people said that in years of scarcity they retired to Egypt. Our course from Hebron to this camp was in a south-easterly direction.

May 9.—We wished to make a bargain with the Jellaheens to conduct us to Wady Mousa. But nothing would induce them to consent. After much bargaining, they agreed to take us to Kerek, if we would give seventy-five piastres to the chief, and fifty to the five guides, who were to accompany us with muskets. Though these people had for a long time refused to accept this sum, they all, when it was agreed to, began fighting who should go. After we had descended from the camp, we offered 500 piastres if they would conduct us to Wady Mousa; but nothing could induce them to consent. They said they would not go if we would give them 5000 piastres! observing, that money was of no use to a man if he lost his life, and that the people of Wady Mousa were a treacherous and cruel race, and always attacked strangers by firing at them from rocky eminences, which concealing the hostile party gave the others no chance. Seeing that all our endeavours were fruitless, we ceased to press the subject. We left the camp about eight, and at nine we arrived at a well where we watered our horses. We remained here about half an hour and then proceeded, when our conductors began their tricks, by saying they would go no further unless we gave them 500 piastres, the sum which we had offered if they would conduct us to Wady Mousa. After much altercation, seeing that nothing would bring them to reason, we said we would go alone, which they defied us to do. We, however, left them, taking a course in the desert about S.E. by the compass, and trusting to our good fortune to meet with some Arabs or tents in our way. We had proceeded in this manner till eleven o'clock, when one of the guides appeared in the rear, waving his turban, and making all possible signs for us to stop. In about half an hour two of them joined us. We were greatly rejoiced to see these people return, but affected to be quite indifferent about it, to prevent further roguery. We now proceeded a little more to the south, and about mid-day had, from a slight eminence to the left of the road, a fine view of the southern extremity of the Dead Sea, together with the back-water and plain at the end of it. The lake Asphaltes appeared not to be nearly so long as is usually supposed, or as all the ancient authors have made it out to be. We now began a continued descent into a deep, barren valley, and did not get to the bottom till near five o'clock, passing with considerable difficulty over a path so rugged, barren, and full of great stones, that we were obliged to lead our horses. At last we reached the ruins of an old Turkish fort, standing on a single rock to the left of the road; to the right there is a pool of green water, fit only for horses, but of which we were glad to drink, although an old man was stripped and washing himself in the middle of it at the time. Beyond the fort, on the same side of the road, the cliff is excavated at a considerable height with loop-holes, possibly meant for a post whence a sentinel might see all passengers, and apprise those in the castle of their approach. It would appear that this was a sort of "barrier," where duties were levied on the passers-by; they call the place El Zowar. From hence we passed through a pretty, gravelly ravine, with bushes of the acacia, and a tree bearing a small stone fruit, resembling in taste a dried apple; the Arabs call it "doom," though it is a very different tree from the doom palm. About six we entered the great plain at the end of the Dead Sea; for about a quarter of an hour we passed a few bushes, but afterwards found the soil sandy and perfectly barren. On our right we had a continued hill of a sandy soil, running in a S.E. and N.W. direction towards the middle of the plain. At dark we stopped for the night in a ravine at the side of this hill, much against the wishes of our guides, who strongly urged the want of water, and the dread of the dytchmaan, as inducements to make us proceed. We collected a quantity of wood which the Dead Sea had thrown up at high-water mark, and endeavoured to make a fire in order to bake bread, as we had flour. The wood was, however, so impregnated with salt, that all our efforts to light it were unavailing, and we contented ourselves with drinking the flour and water mixed, which, though not very palatable, served to appease our hunger. All night our guides, not being able through fear to sleep themselves, endeavoured to prevent us from sleeping by alarms of the dytchmaan. On the 10th, at the very dawn of day, we proceeded across the plain; for the first half hour we had still the sand hill on our right. We found, beside the saline appearance left by the retiring of the waters, several large fragments of clear rock-salt lying on the ground, and, on examining the hill, we found it composed partly of salt and partly of hardened sand. In many instances the salt was hanging from cliffs in clear perpendicular points, like icicles; and we observed numerous strata of that material of considerable thickness, having very little sand mixed with it. Strabo mentions, "that to the southward of the Dead Sea there are towns and cities built entirely of salt;" and although such an account seems strange, yet when we contemplated the scene before us, it did not appear very improbable. The torrents, during the rainy season, had brought down immense masses of salt, and we observed that the strata were generally in perpendicular lines. Leaving this hill, the plain opens considerably to the south, and is bounded at the distance of about eight miles by a sandy cliff, from 60 to 80 feet in height, which runs directly across and closes the valley of El-Ghor, thus forming a margin for the uttermost limits of the Dead Sea to the southward. We were told that the plain on the top of this range of cliffs continues the whole way to Mecca. It appeared to us that the mountains to the westward of the Dead Sea gradually decreased their height to the southward, while those to the eastward continued to preserve the same altitude as far as the eye could reach, and appeared to be of a reddish colour, resembling granite. Leaving the salt hill, our track led for an hour and a half across the barren flats of the back-water, now left dry by the effects of evaporation. We passed six drains into that part more contiguous to the sea, where the water still remains; some were wet and still draining, others were dry. These had a strong marshy smell, similar to that usually arising from the muddy flats in salt water harbours, but by no means more unpleasant. I imagine this to have given rise to the reports of the ancients, as to the disagreeable smell of the waters of the Dead Sea. The water on the main body of the lake is perfectly free from any smell whatever. We now entered into a very prettily wooded country, with high rushes and marshes; leaving these, the variety of bushes and wild plants became very great, some of the latter were rare and of remarkable appearance. Occasionally we met with specimens such as none of our party had ever seen before; a botanist would have had a fine treat in this delightful spot. Amongst the trees which we knew, were various species of the acacia, and in some instances we met with the dwarf mimosa; we saw also the doom mentioned before, the tamarisk, and the plant which we saw in Nubia, and which Norden calls "the oschar." There was one curious tree which we observed in great numbers, and which bore a fruit in bunches, resembling in appearance the currant, with the colour of the plum; it has a pleasant though strong aromatic taste, resembling mustard, and, if taken in any quantity, produces a similar irritability in the nose and eyes. The leaves of this tree have the same pungent flavour as the fruit, though not so strong. We think it probable that this is the tree our Saviour alluded to in the parable of the mustard seed, and not the mustard plant, which is to be found in the north; for although in our journey from Bysan to Adjeloun we met with the mustard plant growing wild, as high as our horses' heads, still, being an annual, it did not deserve the appellation of a tree; whereas the other is really such, and birds might easily, and actually do, take shelter under its shadow. We passed the wild cotton plant amongst an infinity of others that we neither knew how to name or describe. In about half an hour we arrived at the little river, which is marked in the map, and improperly placed as the Futlet; the people told us it was the "Nahr-el-Hussan," or horse river; there was plenty of corn cultivated in the open grounds, between the bushes. Our guides told us not to talk, lest we should be discovered by the natives: but this was what we wanted, in order to get something to eat, the flour and water of the preceding night not having been very satisfying. We soon met some of the natives taking in the harvest; they were a wild-looking people, and wore leathern aprons reaching to the shoulders, a dress we had never before seen; they addressed us with great civility, and on our telling them we were soldiers of the Aga of Jaffa, going to Kerek, they said they wished that more would come amongst them, as they were much oppressed by the Bedouin Arabs, whom they described as a bad set of people, caring neither for God nor the saints. They took us to their bivouac in the thicket, saying that their village was some way off, and that they were only remaining here to take in the harvest. They gave us some doom, dried and pounded into a sort of coarse meal and mixed with butter; we found it exceedingly good; about half an hour afterwards they brought us bread, butter, and milk. We were annoyed here with large horse-flies, which were in great numbers, and some of our animals were streaming with blood from their bite. We were told at Kerek, that these flies were "a plague sent by the Almighty at the destruction of Sodom and Gomorrah." These people are called Ghorneys, and differ materially, both in manner and appearance, from the Arabs, as well as from the natives of the towns; they adhere to one place of abode, and cultivate the land in its vicinity. They do not live in tents like the Arabs, but build huts of reeds, rushes, and canes; they construct their buildings contiguous to each other, and form their villages in the shape of a square, with only one entrance for the cattle, which are thereby prevented from straggling, and are kept more collected for protection during the night. These people treated us very hospitably, which they would naturally do, taking us to be soldiers of so powerful a ruler as Mahommed Aga; but we never heard any other than a bad character of them ever after. Before we left them, they threshed out, with great sticks, some corn for our horses. The women commenced the labour, but as they could not work *and hide their faces* at the same time, the men dismissed them and did the work themselves. When about to take our leave, we offered them a handsome reward for what we had had, but they absolutely refused, and held out for a good quarter of an hour, notwithstanding all our entreaties; at last we threw the money amongst them, when a most furious battle took place about the mode of sharing it. We could not refrain from laughing most heartily at so odd a scene, and at eleven left them fighting and beating each other most furiously. We now crossed the Houssan; our horses, smarting from the bites of the unmerciful flies, quietly laid down in the middle of the stream, leaving us no alternative but to dismount and walk out. We proceeded along the foot of the mountains which bound the east side of the plains, and continued doing so till near five in the afternoon, our track being rugged and barren in the extreme, with innumerable fragments of red and grey granite; grey, red, and black porphyry; serpentine stone; beautiful black bazalt, breccia, and many other kinds of stone scattered in every direction, all fragments from the neighbouring mountains. It may be presumed that from this neighbourhood the ancients procured materials for the numerous handsome columns which one finds in Syria, and which now adorn the Turkish baths, mosques, &c. Our two companions made a collection of all the specimens they met with; some of these were beautiful, and well adapted for vases or other ornaments. We found that the chain of mountains under which we were passing was chiefly composed of sand-stone and bad marble. At five, we had reached the tongue of land which lies between the south end of the Dead Sea and its back-water, and from hence we began to ascend the hills on our right. At six we stopped in a beautiful shady ravine, watered by the river "El-Dara," whose banks are covered in profusion with the palm, acacia, aspine, and oleander, in full flower and beauty, perfuming the whole place, and rendering it a most delightful spot, particularly when contrasted with the desert appearance of the neighbourhood. I will here insert the relative distances of the principal objects we passed this day. Two hours and a half from the western cliff of the Ghor to Rahk, the first salt-water drain; half an hour to Szafye, or Ahsa, the Nahr-el-Hussan; three hours from Saphy to the Honey river, Nahr-el-Assel; from thence two hours to Mare; and two more to El-Dara, where we passed the night.

May 7.—This morning, shortly after the rising of the sun, we began to ascend the mountain; the road was very rugged and stony, with hardly a vestige of vegetation. The rocks were of a dark-coloured sand-stone. On our left there was a deep ravine. Three men shouted from a height, and asked where we were going to?—they had only one musket. About eight o'clock we reached a commanding point, where the road turns in its ascent; here we had an excellent bird's-eye view of the south end of the Dead Sea and the back-water. The time which we expended in taking a sketch of it, enabled the men who had hailed us to come up; two were blacks; they accosted us very roughly, and examined us attentively. They were armed; but still we were as strong as they were. Mr. Bankes, Captain Irby, and I, had only our Christian Arab servant with us,—Mr. Legh and his party having gone on before: the strangers remained with us. As soon as the sketch was finished we began to ascend to join the rest of our party, and in our way were surprised by seeing five other men armed with muskets, peeping from behind a rock at some distance from the road; after hesitating a moment, they came forward, and questioned us as to where we were from, the place of our destination, &c. By this time we had joined Mr. Legh and the rest of the party; and having satisfied the curiosity of these people, we proceeded on our journey.

Our road now was on a sort of terrace scarped out on the side of a romantic ravine. Vast fragments, each as large as an ordinarily sized house, which had been detached from the sides of the precipices, were lying below in confused heaps; some were only just cracked off, and not yet fallen. About a quarter of an hour after meeting the strangers, we came to a small pool of water, under an olive tree; here some of the same men we had left behind came up with us again, and called out loudly to us to come and eat bread with them; but as we did not like their appearance or conduct, the rest being visible in the distance, running to join their comrades, we continued our route. As we advanced, we found ourselves among corn fields with cattle grazing in the valley on our left, through which the river Souf Saffa runs towards the Dead Sea. We observed the ancient mill-courses, but the river itself was hid by the richness of the vegetation on its banks; the purple oleander was in full blossom. The castle of Kerek now opened on our view, but not any part of the town, as it lay behind the castle. The ruins of the castle on this side, that is the N.W., present two principal features; a great mass at the south angle of the town, and, more towards the north, a great building called the Seraglio of Meleh-e-daher. Between these two is the only gate of entrance on this western side. It is merely a plain, narrow arch, with an Arabic inscription over it, erected at the mouth of a natural cavern, or passage in the rock, which leads with a winding course *through* a high ridge of the natural rock, and has thus been made to serve as the principal avenue to the fortress. The entrance thus formed has a very singular effect. High as the town is placed, it is commanded on every side. In our approach we descended a little into the narrow valley at the foot of the castle hill, where runs a stream with a narrow line of gardens on its banks, in which we observed olives, pomegranates, figs, and vegetables. The ascent from hence is steep and toilsome: we all dismounted. Entering at the cavern gate already described, we found ourselves within the walls, with the seraglio on our left hand; the houses do not come very close upon that part of the fortification, though there are ruins and foundations everywhere, seeming to announce a greater population formerly. There are also the remains of a mosque with pointed arches, and an octagonal minaret, with a band of black stone carried round it: the whole is much in ruins. Over the door-way is a pointed horseshoe arch, like that at the khan at Bysan; and amongst the ornaments is the cup repeated several times. The houses are of one story, terrace roofed, and so constructed that the roof at the back is, in many of them, not above the level of the ground; in many instances you may pass over the houses, even on horseback, without being aware of it; some have a little court before them. The principal chamber in the best buildings has two arches thrown across it, on which rest the rafters, not squared, and very smoky. A small hole in the centre serves as a vent for the smoke; and immediately under it, in the centre of the room, is a circular hearth with a rim raised round it. In the recesses between the opening of the arches are raised platforms which serve as shelves; there are also receptacles for corn, with bung-holes, in the manner of casks, for taking it out. The walls are daubed with rude paintings in red and black: we observed particularly an attempt to represent a horseman, and, in another instance, a kneeling camel, with a man mounting it. There is not a vestige of antique work in the castle; but, considered as Mahommedan architecture, it is good, especially at the south end, where the rock has been cut down in order to detach the ridge from the hill to which it was by nature joined. Two sides are left standing across this artificial ravine in the manner of walls. The most remarkable thing that we observed was a Christian church within the circuit of this part of the castle; it is very ill constructed with small stones; and some pillars are laid horizontally into the masonry, forming quite a contrast to the Mahommedan work, which is of large, well cut stones, laid in regular courses. This church has small narrow windows, and a circular end and arched front, resembling that at Tiberias, which is called the house of St. Peter, but which is evidently posterior to the first Mahommedan conquest, as there is an Arabic inscription built upside down into the present walls. It is probable, therefore, that both are the works of crusaders; and as Godfrey de Boulogne took Kerek, and called it Mons Regalis, it is probable he or some of his successors may have built this church. There are remains of paintings of large groups of figures on the stuccoed walls; one seems to have represented a king in armour; another the martyrdom of some saint; and there is an imperfect inscription with letters of the Gothic form. The castle seems to be more ancient than the church. We found a few remnants of antiquity; a small column of deep-coloured red granite, well polished but ill shaped; another of grey granite; and not far from it, close to a well, a great wing sculptured in basso-relievo, bearing much resemblance to those which we had seen attached to the globe in Egyptian buildings. We could form no conjecture what it originally had been; there was no trace of a globe; possibly it was the wing of a Roman eagle; its length was 7 ft., and its breadth 4. Near the mosque are three capitals, resembling no regular order of architecture, but similar to some which we saw at Hamah. We found two Greek inscriptions, but neither of them interesting. The place is well supplied with water by numerous cisterns. Sheikh Yousouf was absent at a camp about half a day distant, passing the honey-moon with a young Arab wife he had just married; but we were very well received by Abdel Khader, his son. Few questions were asked, and we excited less attention than might have been expected. There was a merchant from Damascus present, and another from Hebron. The women here do not keep out of sight, nor cover their faces at all; the utmost they ever conceal is the point of the chin. We sat and conversed familiarly with several of them. We and our horses were well fed for nothing. Amongst our company was a man who represented himself as a great traveller; he had been to Tripoli, Aleppo, Mardyn, and Cyprus; he had never been to Constantinople, and said he had no desire to go there, because he had heard that a man could not beat out his pipe without burning the house down; and that justice was so strictly administered, that persons ran the risk of having their heads cut off while they were talking in the streets. It was also an instance of the liberty of speech in these remote corners, in our traveller saying, "that people respected the sultan because it was their interest to do so, on account of commerce, &c.; but as to the pashas, they were no better than themselves, and that it was a degradation to stand in a humiliating posture with the head stooped, and the hands hidden, before one of them; when here, a man might loll at his ease in his own house, and stand or lie in whatever posture he pleased." Indeed, few of the people in the place appeared to know even the name of the present sultan. We were invited to dine one day at a Turk's house, and were treated to a boiled sheep, without bread, or anything but the meat itself; this custom we first observed at Szalt, and to our great annoyance found that it was the same on the east side of the Dead Sea, &c.; not only amongst the Arabs, but in the towns and villages.

It appears that the Wahabees made an attempt on Kerek, and were encamped for several days on the heights south of the town; one of them was sent in to parley; and the inhabitants boast of having killed about forty of them, from the loop-holes of the castle, with their muskets.

May 13.—Towards the evening, Sheikh Yousouf arrived without his bride; he was a fine looking old man, apparently nearly sixty years of age; he had lost his front teeth, and his beard was white. Upon being told the motive of our travelling in these mountains, he asked rather roughly "whether this was the country of our fathers;" but we soon found him to be a plain, blunt honest old man, of very few words. Only one man in the town could read, and he was the Greek priest. He read to Yousouf the letter from Sheikh Eysah of Hebron, without which we have reason to think we should have had a much colder reception. It appears that the governor of Jerusalem deceived us, and never wrote to Kerek at all. We got the Greek priest to assist us in arranging the business with Yousouf, and as we had for once to deal with an honest man, we had not much trouble; for, in fact, the negotiations the next morning were hardly closed, before the horses were ordered to be in readiness. Four hundred piastres were paid down as the price of a safe conduct through several places, specified in a list, as far as Wady Mousa, to the south, and Szalt, to the north; but the old man could not undertake to free us from some incidental tributes on the road. Yousouf pledged himself to accompany us through the whole journey.

During our stay at Kerek, we saw the dowry of a young woman going to be married paid at the sheikh's house; it amounted to about one hundred piastres, in white Constantinople money. This I believe was only what she was to wear as her head ornament, as the ladies here decorate their foreheads with dollars and different kinds of money; sometimes the coins hang down to both ears, and must be a great weight. The amount of a dowry is, in some instances, as high as four purses!

There are about as many Christian inhabitants in Kerek as Turks; the former boast of being the strongest and bravest, and are able to produce four hundred men bearing arms; they are on very good terms with the Turks, and appear to enjoy equal freedom with them. It was said, that at the time of the French invasion in 1799, there was a project for disarming the Christians and driving them out, which the present sheikh prevented. We saw, and were recognised by several of the suspicious people we had met on our road the day of our arrival; they asked us why we did not stop to eat with them? but their suspicious conduct, and the manner in which they first came upon us, looked as if they meant no good.

May 14.—In the afternoon we set out from Kerek to the southward; we descended into the ravine which surrounds the place, having the main body of the castle close on our right hand, the base of which is here a slanting casing of the rocks as at Homs, Aleppo, &c. Hence we passed up the side of a narrow ravine to its very end. On each side there are caverns and wrought tombs. In one of these, which had externally all the appearance of a natural grotto, we observed places for sarcophagi; it is probable that the whole is the burying-place of the ancient town. In this ravine is a spring of water, with a small Turkish building.

Here we were joined by an Arab from Djebal, who had been forced away by the Wahabees, and had lived and served with them. Almost all his fellow-townsmen had been put to death. He had been upwards of a month at Dareyah, their capital, which he described as being larger than Kerek. The houses, he said, are all built with mud, and the fortifications are formed of mud and palm trees; there are cannon on the walls, and an immense treasure buried and concealed. He said that the Wahabees greatly prefer silver to gold, for which no reason was given. He confirmed the story of their horses being fed, at times, entirely on camel's milk. He was mounted on one of these horses, a light leggy animal, very different in appearance from those of the Arabs; he seemed to think the Wahabee sect very general, and said, jokingly, that Sheikh Yousouf was one, which the other denied with apparent horror.

We ascended into a country of downs, with verdure so close as to appear almost turf, and with corn fields at intervals; there were not many rocks, though the surface was sprinkled over with stones. In an hour and a half we reached a camp belonging to the people of Kerek, under Sheikh Ismayel, Yousouf's youngest son. After taking some leban (sour milk) and bread, we proceeded to the N.W., about a mile across some corn land, to a ruined village called Mahanna. The ruins are mostly those of ordinary buildings, but it is evident that one of them had been a Christian church. Another ruined site to the westward was called Dgellgood. The following ruined sites are visible from this point—Machad. Arti-Musshut, (which is the single building supposed to be the tomb of Abou-Taleb,) Harnahta or Mote, Toor, Howeeh, and Marrowhich. We now went due east for an hour to Medin, from whence we could see the following ruined sites, most of them on slight eminences—Imriega, E. by N., Hadad, Shirsee, Behlanah, Suhl, and Nehkill; in short, the whole of the fine plains in this quarter are covered with sites of towns, on every eminence or spot convenient for the construction of one; and, as all the land is capable of rich cultivation, there can be little doubt that this country, now so deserted, once presented a continued picture of plenty and fertility. Having finished our survey of the neighbouring ruins, we returned to Ismayel's camp, where we slept.

May 15.—This morning we were off before sun-rise; the same downs continued, with numerous Arab camps in various directions, the ruined sites being still visible in all directions. In about a quarter of an hour we came to the site of Hamahta or Mote, which last name, signifying death, it acquired from the circumstance of all its inhabitants having been exterminated by Abou Taleb, whose supposed tomb, "Musshut," is a building upon arches, standing in a small inclosure, less than half a mile distant to the W.S.W. Near this spot is a Roman mile-stone, inscribed in Latin, the number of miles is thirteen, but the rest of the inscription is indistinct. In about a quarter of an hour from Mote we reached the tomb of Sheikh Jaffa; here the Mahommedans of our party alighted, and entered the tomb to pray. Mahommed, the soldier, reported, that within there are two dark granite columns, well polished.

A quarter of an hour farther we reached the camp of Sheikh Sahlem, who commands, or has influence, at Djebal, and over all the country as far as Shobek. This man asked us two hundred piastres instead of thirty, which old Yousouf said was all he would require. We refused it, and Sahlem persisting, we mounted and retired to a distance. Upon our leaving the tent he expressed a wish "that we might be struck with lightning before we reached Kerek," and added, "that had not Sheikh Yousouf been present with us, he would have had our money by force." Finding, however, that he did not follow us, we sent back to offer one hundred and fifty piastres; the bargain was struck, and the money counted into his hands. He mounted his horse, and accompanied us, together with his son, a fine young man. In about half an hour he brought us to another large camp of his tribe, of thirty-three tents. Having remained here a short time, we proceeded, unattended, about two miles off, to visit the ruins of Dettrass. At the foot of the hill are many cisterns; the ruins are indistinct and of no interest, except three piles of buildings, which appear to be of Roman architecture; one was evidently a temple; the others, though large, are so much ruined that it is impossible to ascertain what they had originally been. While we were examining these ruins, the people from the neighbouring camps flocked round us in considerable numbers, but were very civil. We returned to our camp in the evening, and observing that all the old women, and many of the young ones, had their cheeks covered with blood and scratches, we inquired the reason, when they told us they had mourned the day before for a death in one of the harems.

May 16.—We recovered the track which we had quitted, where it falls into a deep ravine, which has steep, rocky sides. At the extremity, where we turned out of this track to follow a more rapid descent into the Wady-el-Ahsa, we saw upon our left hand, on the height, the remains of an ancient fortress, which seems to have commanded the pass. It is of dry masonry and large stones, and is no doubt antique. They give it the name of Acoujah. As we proceeded downwards, there was on our right hand a great quantity of lava and black volcanic matter, which seem to have issued from the side of the neighbouring ridge of mountains. We presently reached the little rivulet called El-Ahsa at the bottom of the ravine. It has in some parts cut out for itself a very deep channel in the rock, and there are occasionally some small picturesque water-falls, from 10 to 15 feet in height. The oleander, as usual upon the banks of most streams in this country, was in great beauty and profusion. From hence we began to ascend a steeper acclivity than that we had come down. It is observable that the sides of this valley El-Asha are more destitute of verdure than the plains above. We continued our course up a slanting hollow, in which we noticed the stones gathered into heaps, and converted into fences, in a manner which seemed to denote an abandoned cultivation, and we observed a field or two of corn near a little spring. A little further, upon the point of a sort of promontory of high land that stands between the fork of two valleys, are the ruins of a small but rich building. Little or nothing is left entire, and the fragments are lying around in confusion. There are rich arabesque borders of vines and foliage, much in the taste of Diocletian's buildings at Palmyra, or the triumphal arch. The capitals are not of any regular order, but fanciful, and loaded with ornaments. The execution is sharp and neat. The temple appears to have fronted S.S.W., and there were apparently four semi-columns attached to the front wall, 3 feet 5 inches in diameter. Amongst the fragments are pieces of columns of a smaller size. Near this there are other vestiges of buildings, but nothing that gives reason to suppose there ever was a town. The great dark mass of volcanic matter which we passed, bears from these ruins N.N.E., it is called Elabahn, which is also the name of a clear spring issuing from the rock a little south of it. There are old mill-courses in the low ground. The ascent still continued for a short distance, when we reached the level of the high plain in a S.S.W. direction. There were reapers at work, who informed us that the chief persons of the town of Djebal were encamped at no great distance. This induced our two sheikhs to turn to the southward, out of the great track, towards the encampment. At one in the afternoon we reached a camp of thirty-three tents. A feeble attempt was made here to extort money from us under pretext that the sheikh was independent. Upon our mentioning our intention of visiting their village, Djebal, which was two hours distant, objections were raised against our doing so. We therefore left it till our return. There were some specimens of volcanic stone in the valley near the camp, but not in any great quantity. Near this place we visited some uninteresting ruins called El-Hagre. Some person in the camp secreted a spy-glass which had dropped from Mr. Bankes' pocket. After confessing that it had been found, and was in the camp, they attempted to force him to give an extravagant reward. This was obstinately refused, and by the intervention of Sheikh Yousouf it was at length restored on the payment of two rubees.

May 17.—After we had set out, Daoud, a relation of the Sheikh of Kerek, missed his sword, and rode back for it, but the rogues refused to restore it to him. Passing to the southward, in about half an hour we saw the village of Bsaida about a mile distant. About and beyond this village there are hanging woods of some extent, but the trees are small and stunted. From hence, in three hours, the descent becoming more considerable as we advanced, we reached the ruins which are called Gharundel. They are situated on the slope of a hill, and their extent is very considerable. Towards the centre of the ruins are the remains of two parallel rows of columns, of which three are standing in one row, and two in the other. Their diameter is 2 feet. None have capitals. There are also, near to this spot, fragments of columns of 3 feet diameter. The capitals appear to have been of bad Doric. A spring of water runs close below these ruins from Gharundel. We passed up a valley to an Arab camp. They were Bedouins of the tribe of Hadjeyah. While we were eating with these people, there was an alarm of an enemy having made an attempt to carry off some of their flocks. The women cried out and waved their scarfs from the top of the hill. We rode up but saw nothing of the robbers. Our road was now S.W., and a white line in the desert, at a distance to the left, as far as the eye could reach, was pointed out as the hadj road to Mecca. We noticed three dark volcanic summits, very distinguishable from the sand. The lava that had streamed from them forms a sort of island in the plain. Close on the right of the road was another volcanic mount, covered with scoriæ of a reddish colour and extremely light. There was much black porous stone below it. Soon after we found an ancient Roman highway paved with black stone. The edges, and a line down the middle, were paved pretty regularly. On the right, at intervals of about a mile and a half, are ruins of square stone buildings. In one of them there was a cistern. They were probably intended for the use of travellers. Proceeding in a direction parallel to this road, we saw towards the S.W. a large mass of ruins, called El-Gaig, they offered no objects of interest. We found three mile-stones; the last only was erect. All the inscriptions were effaced by time and the climate. From one of these stones we turned off, about a mile from the road, to examine some buildings, but found them Turkish. One had an Arabic inscription over the door, which appeared ancient. Some crosses were scrawled about the door, and these signs are three times repeated +λιι. Seeing some Arabs in the distance to the south, we rejoined our companions, who had advanced just a Roman mile on the road, and were waiting at another mile-stone. We followed the road till we came to the edge of a deep vale. Here we deviated to the right and descended, the original road continuing straight on the height. At the S.W. end of the vale rises a hill, upon which stands "Showbec," like a gigantic mound. At its foot the ground is terraced out into gardens, and thickly planted with figs, now in full leaf. There are numerous caves in the side of the hill. Nearly at the bottom of the descent we passed a sheikh's tomb, called "Abou Soliman." Then passing a ravine, we approached the town on its N.E. side by a zig-zag path, which seems to be the only one leading to it. It appeared that almost all that side of the castle-hill by which we ascended has once been covered with buildings. Our coming seemed to excite considerable alarm amongst the natives, who stood on the walls shouting and throwing down stones. We entered at an iron gate, when the inhabitants seeing Sheikhs Yousouf and Sahlem with us, received us very civilly, some crying out, "Go and get bread and fire-wood for these poor fellows, who are come to lodge a night amongst us." We were carried up to a sort of divan, in the open air, constructed upon what seemed to be the ruins of a church of crusade architecture, standing due east and west. The tower of the castle has Arabic inscriptions upon it. The three doors of what we supposed to have been a church are square-topped, and the centre is under a pointed arch, and has more the air of Mahommedan than Christian architecture. We had a most extensive view from hence, comprising the whole skirts of the desert, with the volcanic hills which I have mentioned. The inhabitants brought us figs split and dried, of a green colour and delicious flavour, tasting nearly like the fresh fruit. They told us they were on the trees when the pilgrims arrived at Damascus. This was in December. We observed much kissing in the salutations. Each party generally kissed the right cheek first, once, and then the left four or five times. They evinced their good breeding in suppressing their curiosity as to the motive of our journey, whence we came, &c., though evidently labouring under the greatest anxiety to know every particular. Shortly after our arrival we had an alarm of Arabs. Thirty men with muskets immediately ran out. Others drove in the flocks in great haste. They returned in about an hour, saying, the Arabs had killed forty of their goats, but that they would find an opportunity of returning the compliment. We, however, doubted the truth of this story. The name of Showbec, or Shobek*, occurs among those who sealed the covenant. After a diligent search for inscriptions, we found one in the architrave of the principal door. It is in Latin, and though imperfect, Mr. Bankes made so much of it out as to leave no doubt that it relates to one of the Frank kings of Jerusalem. One of their principal strongholds, somewhere in this direction, was called "Mons Regalis." This might either be Kerek or the place in question; though Miletus, extending their conquests still further, says, that this name was applied by them to Petra, and, relying upon some passages in Diodorus Siculus, adds, that it seems to have borne that name in the historian's time. The most remarkable circumstance is, that while the interior parts of this church are in the pure Gothic style, resembling that of the same age in Europe, the ornaments of the inscribed doorway are of the genuine eastern taste, exhibiting that border of convex fluting which is common in Turkish buildings. The pointed arch itself inclines slightly inwards at the bottom, in the manner of a horse-shoe. The construction also has more of the Oriental than the Norman style. The transome, instead of consisting of a single stone, being composed of many, irregularly locked together by dove-tails and angular inequalities. In the walls, at the gates of Antioch, there are similar examples, and certainly of the time of the crusades.

May 18.—Quitting Shobek, we wound by a spiral road into the valley which surrounds it, and observed that the road had been artificially deepened, and in some parts cased with masonry. Thence we ascended to the S.W., and soon came to a brook which contributes to the watering of the gardens below Shobek, but is not the only supply. Upon the two parallel ridges, between which our road led, we noticed stones arranged in fences and gathered into heaps, denoting the boundaries of former fields and gardens; and near the spring there appeared the remains of a village. Our course continued much in the same direction, between west and S.W. for about a mile, gently ascending till we arrived at a large Arab camp, situated upon high ground, with still higher about it. Here we expected to have found the Sheikh "Mahommed Abou Raschid," that is to say, Mahommed the father of Raschid, which latter is the title he goes by. Most of the sheikhs have some denomination of this kind to distinguish them. "Mahommed Aga," for instance, is called "Abou Nabout," (the master of the mace or stick); and in Sir Sydney Smith's transactions at Acre, his principal coadjutor, the

* Now those that sealed were . . . . Hallohesh, Pileha, Shobek. Nehemiah, x. 24.

pasha, was surnamed "Dgezar," which in Turkish signifies the "Cutter." Shobek, and the district about it, is commanded by Abou Raschid. He was absent, but messengers were dispatched to acquaint him with our arrival. From this camp we saw another to the southward, and beyond it a hill thinly scattered with trees. We were hospitably received. A merchant whom we had known at Hebron came in, complaining that he had been robbed of twenty-eight pieces of merchandise, which he had brought to sell amongst the Arabs, who had laid hands on the goods in their tents, and refused to give them up. At particular seasons of the year the inhabitants of these tents are in the habit of passing to Cairo, whence they carry on the charcoal trade between that city and Suez. They said it was a five days' journey from hence to Suez. In passing into Egypt they usually take the road to Gaza, though they seem to be fully aware of the shorter way; it is, therefore, only for the sake of security. At Shobek there was a small caravan which was to set out on the day of our departure; the leader of it offered to carry us to Cairo in eight days.

May 19.—About noon Abou Raschid arrived. He was a middle-sized man, with very marked features, having a dark complexion, very dark beard, black piercing eyes, and aquiline nose; his age might be about thirty. He was full of life and spirits, but a man of few words, and plain, unaffected manners. Ever since our arrival we had heard him spoken of in great raptures in the camp. Having dined with us, the Hebron merchant pleaded his cause before him, when he presently gave orders "that his goods should be restored to him." With regard to ourselves, he very soon came to terms with us, assuring us that he would willingly conduct us to Wady Mousa for nothing, for the sake of Mahommed Ali, Pasha of Egypt. Soon after a great dispute and tumult arose in the tent, Abou Zatoun (the Father of the Olives), the Sheikh of Wady Mousa, declaring, with violent gestures, and swearing "by the beard of the prophet," and "by the honour of their women," that, we should not go forward; and seeing that, notwithstanding his violence, both Abou Raschid and ourselves were preparing our horses, he quitted the tent, uttering threats and execrations, and rode off for Wady Mousa, determined to prevent our going. All the Wady Mousa people also quitted the camp, joining in their chief's hostility, and repeatedly exclaiming, "Let the dogs go and perish if they please;" and swearing we should neither drink of their water nor pass into their territory. While this was passing, our good old friend Sheikh Yousouf's resolution was shaken, and both he and Sahlem of Djebal strongly urged us to return and give up the business, saying that all further perseverance would be fruitless. Abou Raschid twice dismounted to answer the arguments of his people, or to overcome their opposition, for they had surrounded him in numbers, imploring him to desist, and asking him "why he risked himself for the mere gratification of the curiosity of fellows who were only Christians." The sheikh seeing that all his arguments had no effect, seized his spear and sprang on his horse, exclaiming, "I have set them on their horses; let us see who will dare to stop Abou Raschid." We presently descended in a S.W. direction, through a ravine, whose sides, rocky as they are, have in former times been terraced and cultivated. The Wady Mousa people rode in a parallel line with us, keeping on the high ground on our left. In about half an hour (four o'clock) we reached a spring that issues from the rock, and is called Sammack. Here we were joined by a host of people, all armed, and subject to our sheikh; some were on horseback and some on foot. Sheikhs Yousouf and Sahlem still remained behind at the camp. Abou Raschid, on the coming up of his people, took an oath, "By the honour of their women," and "by the faith of a true Mussulman," that we *should* drink of the water of Wady Mousa, and go whithersoever it pleased him to carry us. Thus were the rival chiefs pledged to completely opposite courses in regard to us. To the honour of Abou Raschid it should be said, that as yet he had not received, or even stipulated for any pecuniary or other reward whatever. As we advanced down the ravine, a wild and romantic view opened to us, terminated by the peaks of the black and rugged ridge of Mount Hor, the same that is alluded to in Scripture, and by a boundless extent of desert, which we have hardly ever seen equalled for singularity and grandeur. We turned up out of this valley to the eastward, and remarked as we quitted it, that there were two small masses of ruins upon the two opposite points which command it: they were, probably, forts. Our road through a circular plain, covered with corn, and bushes of whitethorn just coming into blossom, conducted us to a valley with the sides prettily studded with turpentine trees, so clustered and grouped together as to give it a very park-like appearance. Here we perceived traces of a paved way, constructed similarly to that we had quitted when we were descending into Shobek. We supposed it to be a continuation of the same. At sun-set we alighted at a camp of sixty-eight tents, pitched in three adjoining circles, on the highest point of a pass. Our whole journey this day was S.W. The pass just mentioned was not between two mountains, but over the highest summit of one of them, great part of these heights being so steep as to be almost inaccessible, except by the beaten tracks. One of these precipices was close to our camp to the westward: it commands a most magnificent view, in which the foreground is a circular, but uneven hollow, in part cultivated, with several circular camps pitched in different parts of it; and the little village of Dibdeba, with a grove of fig-trees about it, bearing S.W. The dark ridge of Mount Hor, which appears to be altogether composed of a sort of sparry flint, broken into masses and seamed with wide crevices, with scarcely any verdure to vary its deep purple colour, forms the boundary of this hollow to the southward, and also, to the westward, that high peak, upon which is the reputed tomb of Aaron, (the Arabs call it Nebi Aaroon, Prophet Aaron) rearing itself above all the rest in the middle of the picture. This craggy ridge does not, however, terminate the landscape, the mountain from which we viewed it being considerably higher, and commanding an almost boundless view beyond it, over an expanse of country of a whitish hue, which is varied here and there with other coloured ridges rising like islands upon it, or jutting forward into it like promontories. The violent rains of the night of the 21st and 22d supplied the feature of water to this varied landscape, forming a glittering line in the distant plain. S.W. by S., as far as the eye could reach, is a range of mountains in which the natives pointed out Mount Sinai. We were told it was at the distance of four days. They also reported "Agaba," an inhabited place on the Red Sea, as distant a day and a half from us; and Mahn on the hadj road one day off. A place which the Arabs call Gereye was likewise mentioned as being four days to the eastward, or S.E., where are very extensive ruins. In front of our tent there was an ancient road. No remains can be traced of pavement, but merely two parallel lines of low, dry wall, set at the distance of about 25 ft. apart.

May 20.—We followed the road in its passage downwards to the S.W. for half an hour, when we reached another camp, subject, in some measure, to our chief. We had passed over the sites of two others abandoned by the adverse party during the night. These sites are always distinguishable by the fires and bed-places of the Arabs; the former are marked by little holes filled up with ashes, the latter by stones laid in oblong circles, with dried heath and dead boughs laid on them.

An eminence, nearly S.W. of this last camp, commanded a view over Wady Mousa, bearing south; it seemed an inconsiderable village, in a low situation, with a few fig-trees about it. Nebi Aaroon, and Dibdebar, were also visible from this point, but we were admonished to go to the brow of the precipice, only one at a time, and were afterwards prohibited to do so at all. There were some very strange looking people in this camp, some of the men having long hair of a tawny colour, plaited in small plaits, very much in the Nubian manner, but without grease, and a handkerchief of a brown colour, instead of the usual gaudy stripes, confined, in lieu of the plain cord, by a brown, flat band, worked in with patches of coloured woollen, and standing up above the head. Their sandals, which, however, are not peculiar to them, as we had observed them in many other instances, are simple, having a thong coming up on each side of the foot from the sole, and another between the toes ; a single tie fastens them on. The women had a singular way of plaiting their braided hair across the forehead, which had the air of a formal wig. The female children had the same leathern aprons, ornamented with shells, &c., which are common in Nubia.

From the break of day we had been apprised that the adverse party were fully prepared to stand to their word in opposing us ; that they had removed several of their camps, and that a large party of them had abandoned their village of Wady Mousa to occupy a height which commanded it. We could see the tents which they had pitched there, as the distance from our advanced camp was very moderate: they had also moved their cattle with them. Messages, sometimes of persuasion, but oftener of defiance, were continually passing. A small detachment of the hostile party passed our tents, but refused to eat in them. They were suffered to go on unmolested. In the afternoon a large deputation arrived, sufficient to fill the whole tent. A conference immediately commenced. The deputies never personally appealed to us ; but carried on the conversation with Abou Raschid only. It was in vain that the authority of the sultan, or of the pashas, was dwelt upon in our favour. They got rid of the firmans, by insisting that they did not understand Turkish ; and when a boyourdi of Sali, pasha of Damascus, was placed in their hands, they said it was a fabrication of the Jews, who are the pasha's ministers. Not argument only, but even artifice and falsehood were employed in our favour; our friend Abou Raschid asserting that we had with us a person on the part of Soliman, pasha of Acre, (our servant was the person whom he pointed out as such,) and a letter from the governor of Yaffa; which, although we might easily have procured it, we were not provided with. The adverse party, in some of their conferences, insisted much on seeing something under the hand of the last-mentioned governor, whose recommendation, we have reason to think, would have gone farther in this country than that of any other person. It was, however, in this instance only captiously asked for, on the presumption that we had it not to produce.

Abou Raschid urged repeatedly, that in the event of their not complying, we could use our influence with the several pashas to cut off their communication entirely, with Mahn, Gaza, and Egypt; and he insisted upon our taking down the names of the refractory chiefs, which were, Abou Zatoun (Father of the Olives), Sheikh of Wady Mousa, and commanding the Howetatt Arabs; Kali Phee, of the same place ; Lehaddineh Hinde, and the adherents of Ebn Jarzee, although he, himself, was rather disposed to our side. Our champion advised us, in the presence of these people, to instigate Mahomed Ali to lay hands on some of them whenever they should come to trade at Cairo. These people said on their first coming, "that we were very lucky in the protection of the chief who accompanied us, for otherwise we should never have returned." They pretended to believe that we had a design of poisoning the water.

In the evening there was a very violent thunder-storm; and as all that could be said or threatened seemed to have no effect upon our opponents, and as there was neither food for us, nor forage for the horses in the tents, we returned, and slept at the same camp as on the preceding night. It was the full of the moon, a dismal cold rain came on, which, for the space of two or three hours, penetrated the covering of our tent, and until a trench was dug along the inside of the back curtain, it flowed in upon us from the high ground; the goats and sheep were continually encroaching, and at last even a cow walked in.

May 21.—A thick fog prevailed, so that the opposite side of our camp was not visible. We heard very noisy councils in the adjoining tents, and it was soon after announced to us, that "war was positively determined on," as the only alternative of our not being permitted to see what we had desired, and to drink of the water. Messengers were dispatched to the camps, under Abou Raschid's influence, and to Shobek, to apprise them of the circumstance, and to request immediate reinforcements. The presence of Sheikh Yousouf and Sahlem was also required. A poor woman, in the other half of our tent, was looking over the partition with her child in her arms, shedding tears occasionally, and throwing in arguments of dissuasion. It was in vain that we agreed to give up Wady Mousa altogether, and declared that we had no desire to taste of the water. The antiquities, which are distant from the village, being the only object of our curiosity; but our chief stood always to his point, and declared that we should not only see the place, but *even bathe* in the waters; and, that if fair means could not compass this, he had sworn to accomplish it by force.

The messages which arrived in the course of the morning from the opposite party, were only a renewal of protestations and oaths against our entering their territory; and they even threw out menaces of cutting off our return from the place where we then were. Thus situated, we could not but compare our case to that of the Israelites under Moses, when Edom refused to give them a passage through her country.* The circumstance must likewise have occurred nearly in the same place, as the tomb of Aaron on Mount Hor† was now before us. About mid-day, when the weather was somewhat clearer, we perceived a number of armed men, some mounted, coming up the valley from the north-eastward. The horsemen were Sheikhs Yousouf and Sahlem, with their own attendants, and some few others with lances. The infantry followed, with their matchlocks and muskets, to the amount of upwards of sixty. They drew up into something like a line near the camp, and approached it shouting, the women answering with their usual screams of exultation from the tents, lee, lee, lee, lee, &c., for they were not suffered to stand exposed in the way, and such as had come out were rudely warned back into their tents by the men. The Sheikhs of Kerek and Djebal were conducted, each by separate openings, into the camp, to the tents allotted to them. We found them dispirited and discomposed at what had happened, and at the consequences which were likely to ensue. They reminded us of their having dissuaded us from pressing the matter any further at the camp where we had last parted; and in their conferences with Abou Raschid, gave him such advice as might be expected from persons of their years. Old Yousouf, particularly, like Nestor in the Iliad, dwelt much upon what had passed in his youth, and upon the wars in which he had engaged and had found reason, when too late, to repent of. He spoke with a great deal of grave action; but his counsels had more effect upon the rest of his audience, than on the spirited young Arab to whom they were addressed, who continued stanch in his determination of waging war, and could not be induced even to shift his ground so far as to confine his demands in our favour to the sight of the antiquities only; strenuously persisting that, as we had put ourselves under his protection, we should go wherever he was pleased to carry us.

A deputation arrived from the enemy, and the old sheikhs tried every argument that experience could suggest to induce them to permit us to go forward. They were denounced as rebels in the case of non-compliance,

* Numbers, xx. 14--22.
† Ibid. 28.

and the consequences were painted in the strongest colours. No effect was produced by these conferences. Our party was continually gaining strength by armed persons dropping in from various directions until night. The reinforcements were distributed amongst the different tents, and rations were refused to such as had not brought muskets or spears. The camp now began to assume a very warlike appearance. The spears stuck in the sand, the saddled horses before the tents, with the arms hanging up within, altogether had an imposing effect.* Perceiving that such a concourse of strangers must impoverish the camp, we begged to be permitted to pay for our food and that of our horses, but Abou Raschid would not hear of it. All was freely given to us, and our animals had abundance.

One circumstance seemed to turn in our favour. Hindi, an Arab chief of very poor and ordinary appearance, and almost blind, was represented to us as a man of great power and influence, who could command two thousand muskets: and though this was probably an exaggeration, yet from the effect which his interference appears to have had in the sequel, it seems probable that he was a chieftain of considerable power. He had been upon ill terms with Abou Raschid; yet from the time of our first conference with him at the advanced camp, he had seemed disposed to favour our views, and to dissuade the hostile party from their obstinate opposition. He professed great respect for the written orders of the Turkish government. On the other hand, it was said that there was a strong party among his adherents inclined to prevent his co-operation. However, towards the evening of this day, he made a solemn peace with our chief, and passed into the enemy's quarters, with the intention of bringing all his men to act in concert with Mahommed Abou Raschid, in open war against them, in case of their persisting to oppose us. Some communication was also made by letter, but in whose name we did not learn. The answer was expected, but did not arrive this night. Towards dark there went a rumour throughout the camp, that our opponents had given in, and that we should be at liberty on the morrow to go where we pleased. We laid down with this impression on our minds, and it was pretty general throughout the camp. Our chief seemed proud of matters having been brought to a favourable end so soon, and said exultingly, "that there were some who had the talent of carrying their point with saying very little, while others who made a great noise were obliged to give way, and behave like cattle."

The same dismal weather continued. About midnight there was a cry of thieves in the camp, and it was found that they were very quietly sitting at our fire; but as there were some of our people not yet asleep, we lost nothing. In the morning we heard that two spies had also been detected in the camp, but it did not appear that any further measures had been pursued against them than their dismissal.

May 22.—The fog was thicker than ever. We were surprised to find that this weather was not deemed unusual or out of season. It was now announced to us that the men of Wady Mousa did not adhere to their agreement, but in the plainest terms had declared, "that they would oppose us by main force, and that we should pay with our lives for any attempt that we should make to advance within their limits." It appeared that they had even thrown up some sort of fortification about the well. Upon our declaring that we did not wish matters to be pushed to extremities, and would willingly confine our desires to the sight of the antiquities only, Abou Raschid would hardly listen to the bearer of the message, and scarcely came to see us during the whole day. Armed reinforcements in small numbers were continually dropping in.

In this predicament we found ourselves on the morning of the 23rd. The

* "And behold Saul lay sleeping within the trench, and his spear stuck in the ground." 1 Samuel, xviii. 6.

result of Hindi's declaration was expected with impatience, and almost every one seemed to think that it must have great weight with the enemy. We, however, heard that their party had also had an accession of two neighbouring tribes of Arabs who had declared against us. To-day old Yousouf was unusually eloquent in our favour, giving out that we were believers in Mahommed, and that our only motive in wishing to advance was to pay our devotions at Aaron's tomb; thus giving a very plausible turn to the motive of our journey. When asked if we were of the true faith, he always replied "they are English." He recapitulated the list of the documents with which we were furnished; roundly asserting that we had recommendations from Yaffa and Egypt, though he knew that we had them not, and he attached much importance to the presence of our soldier and Tartar from Constantinople. He mentioned all the places we had visited in the country, particularly Palmyra and Szalt; adding that this was the first time we had been stopped. True to the character of an old chieftain, he dwelt again on the events of wars that had happened in his early days. His object was to carry matters by fair means, if possible, and to restrain the impetuosity of Abou Raschid, whom he warned of the usual effects of hasty measures, and, for the first time, alluded to an old grudge which the people of Wady Mousa bore towards him, on account of the fate of three or four of their fellow townsmen whom he had beheaded at Kerek. The tone, however, of old Yousouf was considerably changed, and he seemed not altogether so adverse to hostilities as he had hitherto been. He said, "I, too, could bring out the men of Kerek;" and he spoke of their numbers and courage, but he did not pledge himself to bring them out.

In the course of this morning it had been discovered that one of the ruins which we were in quest of was in sight from our mountain. It proved to be that which we called the palace; it was discernible through a narrow strait formed by two craggy cliffs, which gave it a very picturesque appearance. By following the brow of the mountain, we gained a sight also of the theatre cut out of the rock, and of several of the tombs. Though they were at a considerable distance, we could make them out pretty well with the help of a spy-glass. This sight was a great encouragement to us, as it appeared possible to reach the spot without passing at all near the enemy's quarters; and we began to concert among ourselves some means of getting there secretly in the night, should all other expedients fail.

While we were deliberating on this subject, we saw a great cavalcade entering our camp from the southward. There were many mounted Arabs with lances, and we observed that there were some amongst the horsemen who wore richer turbans, and of more gaudy colours, than is usual amongst Bedouins or peasants. As the procession advanced, several of Abou Raschid's Arabs went out, and led the horses of the chiefs by the bridles into the camp. The whole procession alighted at the tent of our chief, and kissed his turban; this was the signal of pacification. Peace was immediately proclaimed throughout the camp, and notice was given that the men bearing arms who had come from a distance, many of whom had joined us that very morning, were to return to their respective homes.

Our late opponents were now willing to consent to our setting out that afternoon, but by the general wish it was deferred until the next day. We heard music and singing in several of the tents. One of the chiefs of the party who had been adverse to us, came very shortly to pay us a visit; amongst other things, he said in his excuse that he had misconceived the object of our journey, having supposed us Frenchmen who came with a design of poisoning the water. They dissembled the real motive of their change of conduct, which there can be little doubt was fear, and imputed their concessions entirely to their respect for the sultan and the pashas. To make the matter more formal, there came with them a person who was in the employ of the Pasha of Damascus, with two attendants, to read and examine our papers. It proved, however, that he was wholly unacquainted with the Turkish language, and in consequence confined himself entirely to the boyourdees of the two pashas, which he declared to be satisfactory and sufficient, although, in point of fact, they were altogether foreign to the question, being addressed to persons and places in quite a different part of the country. This man, in recompense for this favourable decision, attempted in the course of the evening to lay claim to some remuneration, but Yousouf fought off his pretensions, by asserting, that for his own part he had not *seen* the colour of our gold, which was so far true, that the four hundred piastres were deposited in the hands of the Greek priest at Kerek.

In the evening we were visited by Abou Raschid, who was in high spirits; the weather had been considerably clearer, but it was still much colder than might have been expected at this season of the year. During the day we had explored the high land to the eastward of the camp, and found it covered, upon both its sides and on its summit, with lines of dry wall, and solid masses of masonry. These walls appeared to have inclosed cultivated grounds: the solid ruins seemed to be only the remains of towers for watching in harvest and vintage time. The whole neighbourhood of this spot bears similar traces of former industry, all which seem to indicate the vicinity of a great metropolis.

CHAPTER VIII.

Wady Mousa—Encampment of the Inhabitants—The Necropolis of Petra—Remarkable Tombs—Narrowness of the Valley—Description of the Architecture—Romantic Pass—Representation of an Altar—Scene of the Murder of thirty Pilgrims—Course of the Stream—Magnificent Temple—Singular appearance of the Rocks—Ancient Authors on Petra—Buildings in the Valley—Houses—Tombs—Visit to the Tomb of Aaron—View from the summit—Strange liberality of the Natives—Compelled to quit Petra—Parting with Abou Raschid—Locusts—Wady-el-Ahsa—Kerek—Mountains of the Franks—Start for the Dead Sea—The Ghorneys—The Oskar plant—The Dead Sea—Salt on its Shores—Lumps of Nitre and Sulphur—Absence of living Creatures—Scene in Ismayel's Tent—Optical illusion—Wady Modjeb—Country of the Amorites—Mayn—Visit to the Hot Springs—A Vapour Bath—Ebn Fayes—His violent threat—The Pools of Heshbon—Palace of Hircanus—Parting from Yousouf—His character—Djerash—The Valley of the Jordan—Tiberias—Acre—Observations on the Character and Customs of the Arabs—Arrival at Constantinople.

THE morning of the 24th May was less unfavourable than those which had preceded it. Soon after sun-rise we set out from the camp; we were in all about fifty persons, including the deputation from Wady Mousa and the men of Damascus, who had passed the night in the tents of our chief. The first part of our road was that by which we went to the advanced camp on the 20th; but before we reached that spot we turned off in an E.S.E. direction, constantly descending. We then passed into a rocky and steep defile, where the footing is extremely bad, and the passage so completely commanded from the sides, and so obstructed by huge masses of sandstone that had rolled down from above, that it was obvious a very small force would be capable of holding it against a great superiority of numbers. Towards the lower extremity of this pass the path branched off into two roads; it had previously been whispered to us by our chief, that, without seeming to take any notice, we should let the men of Wady Mousa go their way, while we should follow one of his men, who would go forward and guide us in a different direction. When we reached the point of separation, the others, not being apprised of this determination, said all they could to induce Abou

Raschid to ascend to their tents, and even came to high words with him, but they could not prevail, he having sworn an oath, that neither we nor himself should eat or drink at their expense, or within the limits of their territory. Some few followed us for a time, hoping to persuade us to turn back with them, but before we reached the valley of Wady Mousa they had all withdrawn.

The defile brought us directly down into this valley, the name of which had become so familiar to us; it is, at the point where we entered it, stony but cultivated, of moderate size, without much character or beauty, and runs from E. to W. A lesser hollow, sloping down to it from the southward, meets it at an angle; at the upper end of the latter valley is the village, seen over stages of hanging fruit-grounds and gardens, which are watered by a rivulet. At the point of junction of these valleys a spring issues from the rock and forms a brook, into which the rivulet flows: to this Abou Raschid pointed, with a look of exultation, observing, "there is the water about which there has been so much contention and dispute." It flows towards the westward, and is, in point of fact, the head of the stream which Pliny has dignified with the name of a river. We approached no nearer to the village than this point, but as the distance did not exceed a quarter of a mile, we could plainly perceive that there was nothing ancient there; that the houses were mean and ragged, and not more than forty or fifty in number. On the summit of a broad, green hill, rising above it, we could not only distinguish the large encampment to which the inhabitants had retired on the night of the 20th, but could plainly see them collected in great numbers on the brow looking down at and watching us.

Some hundred yards below this spring begin the out-skirts of the vast Necropolis of Petra. Many door-ways are visible, upon different levels, cut in the side of the mountain, which towards this part begins to assume a more rugged aspect; the most remarkable tombs stand near the road, which follows the course of the brook. The first of these is on the right hand, and is cut in a mass of whitish rock, which is in some measure insulated and detached from the general range. The centre represents the front of a square tower, with pilasters at the corner, and with several successive bands of frieze and entablature above; two low wings project from it at right angles, and present each of them a recess, in the manner of a portico, in which are two columns, whose capitals have an affinity with the Doric order, between corresponding antæ; there are, however, no triglyphs above. Three sides of a square area are thus inclosed; the fourth has been shut in by a low wall and two colossal lions on either side of the entrance, all much decayed. The interior has been a place of sepulture for several bodies. On the front are cut little niches and hollows, as if for the reception of votive offerings. Further on, upon the left, is a wide façade of rather a low proportion, loaded with ornaments in the Roman style, but in a bad taste, with an infinity of broken lines and unnecessary angles and projections, and multiplied pediments and half pediments, and pedestals set upon columns that support nothing. It has more the air of a fantastical scene in a theatre than an architectural work in stone; and for unmeaning richness, and littleness of conception, might, as Mr. Bankes observed, have been the work of Boromini himself, whose style it exactly resembles, and carries to the extreme. This remark is applicable, more or less, to every specimen of Roman design at Petra. The doorway has triglyphs over the entablature, and flowers in the metopes. The chamber within is not so large as the exterior led us to expect; it has a broad, raised platform round three sides, on which bodies were probably disposed. Immediately over this front is another of almost equal extent, but so wholly distinct from it, that even the centres do not correspond; the door-way has the same ornaments. The rest of the body of the design is no more than a plain front, without any other decoration than a single moulding. Upon this are set, in a recess, four tall and taper pyramids; the effect is singular and surprising, but they combine too little with the rest of the elevation for it to be good. Our attention was the more attracted by this monument, as it presents, perhaps, the only existing example of pyramids so applied, though we read of them as placed in a similar manner on the summit of the tomb of the Maccabees, and of the Queen of Adiabæne, both in the neighbouring province of Palestine. The interior of the mausoleum is of moderate size, with two sepulchral recesses upon each side, and one in form of an arched alcove at the upper end; a flight of steps leads up to the narrow terrace upon which it opens.

The sides of the valley were now becoming very precipitous and rugged, and approaching nearer and nearer to each other, so that it might rather deserve the name of a ravine, with high detached masses of rock standing up here and there in the open space. Of these the architects had availed themselves. In some instances large and lofty towers are represented in relievo on the lower part of the precipice, and the live rock is cut down on all sides, so as to make the resemblance complete. The greater number of them face the high road, but there are others which stand back in the wild nooks and recesses of the mountain. All seemed to have been sepulchral, and it was here that we first observed a species of architecture that is, perhaps, to be found nowhere else.

To erect quadrangular towers for sepulchres, seems to have been the fashion in several inland districts of the east; they abound at Palmyra, and are seen in the valley of Jehoshaphat near Jerusalem, &c.: but the details and ornaments of these universally betray an imitation of Roman architecture, whilst at Petra they bear all the marks of a peculiar and indigenous style; their sides have generally a slight degree of that inclination inwards, which is one of the characteristics of Egyptian edifices, and they are surmounted by the Egyptian torus and concave frieze. A very remarkable superstructure rises above as a parapet. Two corresponding flights of four or six steps are represented in relievo, ascending in opposite directions, from two points near the centre; they are connected together by a horizontal line drawn between the uppermost steps. At the angles are pilasters, which in many instances have a considerable diminution upwards; the capital is very peculiar, and appears like the rough *draft* of an unfinished Ionic capital as it comes from the quarry. It is, however, almost universal on these tombs, and may be called the *Arabian order* of architecture. An entablature and frieze, little differing from the Ionic or Corinthian, rests upon these pilasters; above that is a blank space, in the nature of a low attic, which is surmounted by the Egyptian torus and frieze, bearing the superstructure which I have described. There is one single example, near the theatre, of an upper door-way; it opens into this attic, to which there is no visible access; there may possibly, however, be some stairs in the interior; the lower door-way being unluckily choked up, we could not ascertain this. In some instances there are as many as four pilasters in the front, which are rounded instead of being angular. The part least peculiar in the details of these Arabian elevations, is the decorations of the door-ways, which have in many instances a pediment not distinguishable from those of Roman buildings, and in others a plain horizontal architrave with the same sort of mouldings. It is remarkable, that in very many instances the whole frame and ornament of the door has been of separate pieces, and *grafted* on upon the solid rock. Sometimes there are cavities for pegs or rivets, which would seem to have fastened decorations in metal or in wood; in others they seem to have been of marble or some fine sort of stone, let into grooves, which shew, in the hollow, their exact form. We were at a loss to account for the apparent conformity of this single portion of the building to the rules of the Greek and Roman architecture; it seems too strong to be accidental; and if we suppose the imitation to have taken place so far back as the first Macedonian expedition into this country, it will still make the tombs more recent, by many ages, than it is probable that many of them really are; since, from the days of Rekem, King of the Midianites, who passes for the founder of Petra, to those of Alexander the Great, there must have been a long line of kings, and these monarchs probably had excavated tombs. Yet if this form of the door-ways be considered sufficient to prove them decidedly posterior to that period, it is so general, that few, if any of the larger sort will remain for that early dynasty. If we bring them still later, and suppose them a Roman innovation, the difficulty is increased, because we must then believe a much greater lapse of ages to have passed in a flourishing kingdom, without any considerable monuments, although architecture was not unknown. It is possible such of the door frames as were not cut in the solid rock, may have been added afterwards, but this does not appear very probable, nor does it entirely remove the difficulty; especially, as in some instances in the higher parts of the design, broad bands seem to have been attached in a similar manner, which very probably bore inscriptions.

It is surprising, amongst such a multitude of tombs, to find so few with any inscription recording for whom they were constructed. We only met with two instances; one was on the tomb, near the theatre already described; it is much mutilated; the other, which we copied, is on the left hand side of the track leading towards Dibdebar, on a large front of pure Arabian design, with four attached columns. In this monument, the architect, from failure, or a defective vein in the sand-stone, has been obliged to carry up the lower part in masonry, so as to meet the upper, which is sculptured on the face of the mountain; in this part, also, there were flaws, and pieces have been let in to make up what was defective; these last remain, but the whole substructure has disappeared entirely, and the upper part is left hanging from the rock above, without any base whatever. This is not the only proof that is to be found, among the remains at Petra, that those who wrought on the rock, contrary to the necessary practice of builders, began their work at the top. To return to the inscription; it is upon an oblong tablet, without frame or relief, but is distinguished from the rest of the surface by being more delicately wrought; there project, from each of its ends, those wings in form of the blade of an axe, which are common both in the Roman and Greek tablets, and which would seem to have been intended originally to receive screws or fastenings, without encroaching on the part inscribed. Although the whole tablet is in the solid rock, there is upon each side a stain of metal caused by studs of bronze driven in, to give the whole tablet the appearance of a separate piece. The letters are well cut, and in a wonderful state of preservation, owing to the shelter which they receive from the projection of cornices, and an eastern aspect. None of our party had ever seen these characters before, excepting Mr. Bankes, who, upon comparing them, found them to be exactly similar to those which he had seen scratched on the rocks in the Wady Makootub, and about the foot of Mount Sinai. He subsequently found a passage in Diodorus Siculus, wherein he speaks of a letter written by the Nabathæi of Petra, to Antigonus, in the *Syriac character;* though this, perhaps, is no proof that the Syriac was in use with them, since they may have chosen that language only, as more familiar to the court they were addressing. The tablet has five long lines, and immediately underneath a single figure of a larger size, probably the date; the same occurs at the bottom of the Hebrew characters on the tomb of Aaron. The interior of the tomb on which this tablet is placed, has two chambers, with recesses for bodies, but no peculiarity worthy of notice; the front is crowned with a double flight of steps in the usual form. In many instances, in lieu of two flights diverging from each other, they are brought to meet in the form of pyramids, being reduced to a much smaller scale, and repeated in the manner of battlements, to the number of three, or five, with the half of one at each extremity.

We have preferred collecting into one view, the most remarkable features of these tombs, before we advance further, without confining ourselves strictly to those which are met with in the approach from Wady Mousa to the city, in order to generalise the description, and avoid interrupting the narrative by alluding to them as they present themselves, which they do, not only in every avenue to the city, and upon every precipice that surrounds it, but even intermixed almost promiscuously with its public and domestic edifices. As we advanced towards the eastern approach to Petra, the natural features of the defile grew more and more imposing at every step, and the excavations and sculpture more frequent on both sides, till it becomes at last a continued street of tombs, beyond which the rocks gradually approaching each other, seemed all at once to close without any outlet. There is, however, one frightful chasm for the passage of the stream, which furnishes, as it did anciently, the only access to Petra on this side. It is impossible to conceive anything more awful or sublime than such an approach; the width is not more than just sufficient for the passage of two horsemen abreast, the sides are in all parts perpendicular, varying from four hundred to seven hundred feet in height, and they often overhang to such a degree, that without their absolutely meeting, the sky is intercepted, and completely shut out for one hundred yards together, and there is little more light than in a cavern.

The screaming of the eagles, hawks, and owls, who were soaring above our heads in considerable numbers, seemingly annoyed at any one approaching their lonely habitation, added much to the singularity of this scene. The tamarisk, the wild fig, and the oleander, grow luxuriantly about the road, rendering the passage often difficult; in some places they hang down most beautifully from the cliffs and crevices where they have taken root; the caper plant was also in luxuriant growth.

Very near the entrance into this romantic pass, a bold arch is thrown across at a great height, connecting the opposite sides of the cliff. Whether this was part of an upper road upon the summit of the mountain, or whether it be a portion of an aqueduct, which seems less probable, we had no opportunity of examining; but as the traveller passes under it, its appearance is most surprising, hanging thus above his head betwixt two rugged masses, apparently inaccessible. Immediately under it are sculptured niches in the rock, destined probably for statues; and we suspect that on careful inspection inscriptions might be found there; but the position in which they are viewed is disadvantageous, and the height so great, that it would require a good glass to distinguish them. Farther down, upon a much lower level, there is an object frequently repeated in sculpture along the road side, which we were at a loss to understand. An altar is represented in a niche, upon which is set a mass of a lumpish form, sometimes square, and sometimes curved in its outline, and rising to a sharper or obtuser cone; in one instance, three of them are placed together in one niche. It may possibly be a representation of the god Terminus, or perhaps one of the stones which were objects of worship amongst the Arabs, down to the time of the coming of Mahomed. The number of these representations on the face of the rock is very considerable; in some instances there are many, almost contiguous, with Greek inscriptions on them, all of which are too much defaced to explain their object. The ravine, without changing its general direction, presents so many elbows and windings in its course, that the eye can seldom penetrate forward beyond a few paces, and is often puzzled to distinguish in what direction the passage will open, so completely does it appear obstructed. The exact spot was not pointed out to us, but it is somewhere amidst these natural horrors, that upwards of thirty pilgrims from Barbary were murdered last year, on their return from Mecca, by the men of Wady Mousa. The cloak of one of them was afterwards offered to us for sale, at Ipseyra, and one of their watches at Zaphoely. Salvator Rosa never conceived so savage and suitable a haunt for banditti. The brook has disappeared beneath the soil from the dryness of the season, but the manner it which its occasional overflowings have broken up the antique pavement, and the slippery passes which the running of the waters have made, by polishing the rock where it had been cut away to form the road, sufficiently prove the necessity of providing another course for its waters. A trough, carried along near the foot of the precipice upon the left hand side, was destined to confine the water, and to convey it upon a raised level to the city. At a considerable distance down the ravine, this water-course crosses over to the opposite side ; and towards its extremity may be traced, passing along at a great height in earthen pipes, bedded, and secured with mortar, in horizontal grooves cut in the face of the rock, and even across the architectural fronts of some of the tombs, which make it probable that it is of a later date.

We proceeded along this narrow passage for nearly two miles, the sides increasing in height as the path continually descended, while the tops of the precipices retained an uniform level. Where they are at the highest, a beam of stronger light breaks in at the close of the dark perspective, and opens to view, half seen at first through the tall, narrow opening, columns, statues, and cornices, of a light and finished style, and looking as if fresh from the chisel, without the tints or weather stains of age, and executed in a stone of a pale rose colour. At the moment we came in sight of them, they were illumined with the full light of the morning sun. The dark green of the shrubs that grow in this perpetual shade, and the sombre appearance of the passage from whence we were just issuing, formed a fine contrast with the glowing colour of the edifice. We know not what to compare this scene with ; perhaps there is nothing in the world that resembles it. Only a portion of a very extensive architectural elevation is seen at first; but it has been so contrived that a statue with expanded wings, perhaps of Victory, just fills the centre of the aperture in front, which being closed below by the sides of the rock folding over each other, gives to the figure the appearance of being suspended in the air at a considerable height ; the ruggedness of the cliffs below setting off the sculpture to the highest advantage. The rest of the design opened gradually at every pace as we advanced, till the narrow defile which had continued thus far, without any increase of breadth, spreads on both sides into an open area of a moderate size, whose sides are by nature inaccessible, and present the same awful and romantic features as the avenues which lead to it : this opening gives admission to a great body of light from the eastward. The position is one of the most beautiful that could be imagined for the front of a great temple; and the richness and exquisite finish of the decorations offer a most remarkable contrast to the savage scenery which surrounds it.

It is very lofty, the elevation comprising two stories. In some respects the taste is not to be commended; but many of the details and ornaments, and the size and proportion of the great door-way especially, to which there are five steps of ascent from the portico, are very noble. No part is built, the whole being purely a work of excavation ; and its minutest embellishments, wherever the hand of man has not purposely effaced and obliterated them, are so perfect, that it may be doubted whether any work of the ancients, excepting, perhaps, some on the banks of the Nile, have come down to our time so little injured by the lapse of ages. There is, in fact, scarcely a building of forty years' standing in England, so well preserved in the greater part of its architectural decorations. Of the larger portions of the architecture, nothing is deficient excepting a single column of the portico; the statues are numerous and colossal. Those on either side of the portico represent, in groups, a centaur and a young man. This part of the work only is imperfect, having been mutilated, probably by the fanaticism of early Christians, or Mussulmen, directed against idolatry, and particularly against images in the human form. In the upper tier the figures are females; two are winged, and two appear to be dancing, with some instruments lifted above their heads, of which that on the left hand seems to be the Amazonian bipennis. Unfortunately, the centre figure, which was doubtless the principal one, is much defaced; and there is nothing in the ornaments that could enable us to discover to what divinity the temple has been dedicated. The principal chamber of the interior is large and remarkably lofty, but quite plain, with the exception of the door-frames and architraves, of which there are three, one at the farther end, and one at each side, all opening into small plain cells. There is also a lateral chamber on each side, of a rude form, opening from the portico. The centre of the superstructure, which comprises the second story, is a circular elevation surrounded by columns, with a dome surmounted by an urn. This urn has not failed to excite the covetousness of the natives. We heard of it, at Jerusalem, as the deposit of a vast treasure, "Hasnah-el-Faraoun" (Treasure of Pharoah; and that it has been repeatedly fired at is proved by the marks of bullets in the stone. No one, however, seems to have succeeded in reaching it by climbing, which would, indeed, be a difficult task. The green stains on either side would lead to the supposition that the handles had been of bronze. One of the perforations, caused by a musket-ball, would seem to prove that the urn is hollow. Above the monument the face of the rock is left over-hanging, and it is to this that the excellent preservation of its details is to be ascribed. The half-pediments, which terminate the wings of the building, are finished at the top with eagles, which, combined with a style of architecture differing little from the Roman, can leave no doubt that this great effort of art is posterior to the time of Trajan's conquest.

Some of the heights, whose steep sides inclose the area in front of the temple, are rendered accessible, though with great difficulty, by flights of steps cut in them. We found the ascent, in some instances, so steep and slippery that we were obliged to take off our shoes, and to use our hands nearly as much as we did our feet. Some small pyramids hewn out of the rock are on the summit of these heights; and we discovered a much higher conical point of mountain, to whose summit there is a regular spiral staircase cut with great care and neatness; it is the same peak, possibly, as that on which we saw, from another point of view, a single pillar, or obelisk. We first observed, also, from the heights above the temple, the great vase which crowns another monument to the N.W.

The wide space which constitutes the area before the temple is about 50 yards in width, and about three times as long. It terminates to the south in a wild precipitous cliff, rendered accessible by the steps abovementioned to the N.N.W. The defile assumes, for about 300 yards, the same features which characterise the eastern approach, with an infinite variety of tombs, both Arabian and Roman, on either side. This pass conducts to the theatre, and here the ruins of the city burst on the view in their full grandeur, shut in on the opposite side by barren, craggy precipices, from which numerous ravines and valleys like those we had passed, branch out in all directions. The sides of the mountains, covered with an endless variety of excavated tombs and private dwellings,* presented altogether the most singular scene we ever beheld; and we despair of being

* "O thou that dwellest in the clefts of the rock!" Jer. xlix. 16.

able to give the reader an idea of the singular effect of rocks, tinted with most extraordinary hues, whose summits present us with Nature in her most savage and romantic form, whilst their bases are worked out in all the symmetry and regularity of art, with colonnades and pediments, and ranges of corridors sculptured on the perpendicular surface.

The short notice of Petra, by Pliny, is as follows: "The Nabatæi inhabit a city called Petra, in a hollow somewhat less than two miles in circumference, surrounded by inaccessible mountains, with a stream running through it. It is distant from the town of Gaza, on the coast, six hundred miles; and from the Persian Gulf one hundred and twenty-two." Book vi. c. 28, Strabo says, "The capital of the Nabatæi is called Petra; it lies in a spot which is in itself level and plain, but fortified all round with a barrier of rocks and precipices, within, furnished with springs of excellent quality for the supply of water and the irrigation of gardens; without the circuit, the country is in a great measure desert, and especially towards Judea. Jericho is at the distance of three or four days." He adds, that one of the royal lineage always resided at Petra, and had a sort of counsellor attached to him who was entitled his brother; he describes their laws and customs.

It will be seen that these two ancient geographers, in characterising the position of the city, not only agree with one another, but are sufficiently correct in their statements; though, strictly speaking, the situation can neither be called a valley with Pliny, nor a plain with Strabo; yet it is certainly both low in position and level in surface, when compared with the crags and precipices that surround it. It is an area in the bosom of a mountain, swelling into mounds and intersected with gullies; but the whole ground is of such a nature as may be conveniently built upon, and has neither ascent nor descent inconveniently steep. Within the actual circuit of the city there are two mounds, which seem to have been entirely covered with buildings, being still strewed over with a prodigious quantity of loose stones, tiles, and fragments of ancient ware, of a very light and delicate fabric. The bed of the river, taking its course to the N.W., flows between these two spots; the water has now sunk beneath the surface, and perhaps creeps through the rubbish which ages have accumulated in its bed; great part of it seems to have been arched over in the same manner as the stream at Philadelphia. Some of the principal edifices seem to have been on the low ground at the left bank of the stream. The first, to the N.W. from the theatre, was an archway of a very florid architecture, with pilasters, having panels enriched with foliage, in the manner of Palmyra: the whole is much ruined. This arch was the introduction to a great pile of building, standing nearly at right angles to it. The building had a door on one side; on the three others, it was decorated with a frieze of triglyphs, and large flowers in the metopes. Beams of wood are let in, at intervals, between the courses of the masonry, and continue, to this day, a strong proof of the dryness of the climate. The front had a portico of four columns. This part is much fallen into ruins. The interior of the edifice was divided into three parallel chambers, and there seem to have been several stories. This interior arrangement made us suspect that it was not a temple, but rather a palace or some private edifice. Whatever may have been its nature, it seems to have been intended for the same purpose as the ruined building at "Bait-el-Carm," which we afterwards saw from our camp above Dibdebar, and which is the only considerable work of masonry existing at Petra. Upon the summit of the other mound there is a mass of ruins of some solidity, but no very definite shape. The Nubian geographer says that the houses of Petra were excavated in the rock; now, that this was not universally true is evident, from the great quantity of stones employed for the lesser kind of edifices, which are scattered over the whole site; but it is also true, that there are grottoes in great numbers, which were certainly not sepulchral, especially near the palace; there is one in particular which presents a front of four windows, with a large and lofty door-way in the centre. In the interior, one chamber of about 60 ft. in length, and of a breadth proportioned, extends across three of the windows and the door; at the lower end, the fourth window seems allotted to a very small sleeping chamber, which is not brought down to the level of the floor of the great apartment, but has a chamber below it of the same size, receiving no light but from the entrance. This, which seems the most important of all the excavated residences, has no ornament whatever on the exterior; and the same observation applies to all the other excavations of this nature. The access to this house is by a shelf gained out of the side of the mountain;* other inferior habitations open upon it, and more particularly an oven, and some cisterns. These antique dwellings are close to an angle of the mountain, where the bed of the stream, after having traversed the city, passes again into a narrow defile, along steep sides of which a sort of excavated suburb is continued, of very small and mean chambers, set one above another, without much regularity, like so many pigeon-holes in the rock, with flights of steps or narrow inclined planes leading up to them. The main wall and ceiling only of some were in the solid rock; the fronts and partitions being built of very indifferent masonry with cement.

Following this defile farther down, the river re-appears, flowing with considerable rapidity. Though the water is plentiful, it is with difficulty that its course can be followed, from the luxuriance of the shrubs that surround it, obstructing every track. Besides the oleander, which is common to all the water-courses in the country, one may recognise among the plants which choke this valley, some which are probably the descendants of those that adorned the gardens and supplied the market of the capital of Arabia; the carob, fig, mulberry, vine, and pomegranate line the river side; a very beautiful species of aloe also grows in this valley, bearing a flower of an orange hue, shaded to scarlet; in some instances it had upwards of one hundred blossoms in a bunch.

Amongst the niches for votive offerings in the mountain's side, some of which are cut to the height of 30 ft., are pyramids and obelisks; and in one instance there is an altar between two palm trees. The position of the theatre has been mentioned; it is the first object which presents itself to the traveller on entering Petra from the eastward. It is entirely hewn out of the rock; the diameter of the podium is 120 ft., the number of seats thirty-three, and of the cunii three. There was no break, and consequently no vomitories. The scene, unfortunately, was built, and not excavated; the whole is fallen, and the bases of four columns only remain on its interior face. The theatre is surrounded by sepulchres; every avenue leading to it is full of them, and one may safely say, that a hundred of those of the largest dimensions are visible from it; indeed, throughout almost every quarter of this metropolis, the depositories of the dead must have presented themselves constantly to the eyes of the inhabitants, and have almost outnumbered the habitations of the living. There is a long line of them not far from the theatre, at such an angle as not to be comprehended in the view from it, but forming a principal object from the city itself.

The largest of the sepulchres had originally three stories, of which the lowest presented four portals, with large columns set between them; and the second and third, a row of eighteen Ionic columns each, attached to the façade. The rock being insufficient for the total elevation, a part of the story was grafted on in masonry, and is for the most part fallen away. The four portals of the basement open into as many chambers, very dissimi-

* "He that heweth him out a sepulchre on high, and that graveth an habitation for himself in a rock." Isaiah, xxii. 16.

lar, both in distribution and arrangements, but all sepulchral, and without any communication with each other. In one were three recesses, which seem to have been ornamented with marble, or some other extraneous material. Almost contiguous to this extensive front, is another somewhat smaller but equally rich, the design of which has a great analogy, especially in the circumstance of the half pediment and the circular lantern in the centre, to the beautiful temple of the eastern approach. Though a general symmetry pervades this piece of architecture, yet there are irregularities observable in its doors and windows, which may be explained by the circumstance of their opening into apartments no way connected with each other, and intended apparently for different families. A little further to the S.E., an area is gained upon the slope of the mountain by excavating it, so as to form three sides of a square. Two of these have been formed into Doric porticoes. The third, which is the loftiest, being that which abuts against the body of the mountain, is occupied by a lofty front, decorated with four columns of the same order, but without triglyphs. A pediment surmounts the frieze, supporting an urn, in all respects similar to that on the temple at the eastern approach. A doorway with a window over it, fills the centre, and there are three windows in the attic, the centre one of which exhibits two half-length figures in basso-relievo. In the approach to this tomb there were arched substructions of great extent, now fallen into ruins. It is surprising to reflect that monuments of so vast a scale should be executed subsequent to the Roman conquest, since after that period we can look upon them as no more than the tombs of private individuals. It is difficult to conceive whence should come so much wealth, and such a taste for magnificence after the country had lost its independence. It is possible, however, that a trade by the Red Sea with India, or even the caravan trade with the spice country, may have imported such riches into the place, as to give the inhabitants the same fondness for ostentation and ornament as at Palmyra, which owed its wealth to the same source. Yet to consider a mausoleum of upwards of 70 or 80 feet high, with lateral porticoes, and flights of terraces upon arched work leading up to it, as resulting from the vanity of some obscure individual in a remote corner of the Roman Empire, has something in it surprising and almost unaccountable. The interior consisted of one large and lofty chamber, having six recesses, with grooves in them at the further end.

On the establishment of Christianity these six recesses have been converted into three, for the reception of the altars, and the whole apartment has been made to serve as a church. The fastenings for the tapestry and pictures are still visible in all the walls, and near an angle is an inscription in red paint, recording the date of consecration. These were the only vestiges of a Christian establishment that we were enabled to discover throughout the remains of Petra, though it was a metropolitan see.

Diodorus Siculus has a long account of the expedition sent by Antigonus against the Nabatæi. He mentions that their riches were very great in gold and spices, and that such of them as were feeble and infirm were left at Petra, which he calls afterwards a place of prodigious natural strength, but without any walls; and distant two days' journey from any inhabited place. In the second expedition, it is said there was but one way of access to it, which was artificial. The loftiness of the post is afterwards mentioned. It is difficult to apply this description to Wady Mousa. Upon some of the high points of rock that rise about the skirts of the city, and tower above them, the remains of walled forts are visible from below; and as it is probable there was an acropolis, it must be looked for in some of these.

Two days were spent upon these ruins, from day-break until dusk, and yet it will be evident from what has been said, that this time was very insufficient to complete an examination of them. It was impossible to remain any longer, for although Abou Raschid attended personally with us the whole time, yet having forced us to decline in so abrupt a manner to visit Abou Zetoun, and having but few attendants, he was never at his ease, and constantly urged us to depart. On the first afternoon, we undertook the ascent to the little edifice, which is visible from all the country round, being upon the very highest and most rugged pinnacle of this range of mountain, and is called "the Tomb of Aaron." The Tomb of Moses has been so grossly misplaced by the Mussulmen, who shew it half a day's journey beyond Jordan to the westward, that we might look with some suspicion at that assigned to his brother, were it not that Josephus expressly says of the place of his decease, that it was near Petra.* Comparing the name Mosera, as given by Moses, with Mousa, it seems that the monument and the ruins mutually authenticate each other. We had no doubt, therefore, that the height which we were going to ascend, is the Mount Hor of Scripture. The base of the highest pinnacle of the mountain is a little removed from the skirts of the city to the westward. We rode to its foot over a rugged and broken track, passing in the way many sepulchres, similar to those which have been described. A singular monument presents itself upon the left hand. An obtuse cone, produced by the coils of a spiral, stands on a vast square pedestal or altar, the whole being cut out of one of the peaked summits of the rock. Not far from thence, close to the way side, and within a niche, is the same representation in relievo which we have described in speaking of the eastern approach, the form of the recess which surrounds the altar rises into the figure of a sugar-loaf. Nowhere is the extraordinary colouring of these mountains more striking than in the road to the Tomb of Aaron, where the rock sometimes presented a deep, sometimes a paler blue, and sometimes was streaked with red, or shaded off to lilac or purple; sometimes a salmon-colour was veined in waved lines and circles, with crimson and even scarlet, so as to resemble exactly the colour of raw meat. In other places there are livid stripes of yellow or bright orange, and in some parts all the different colours were ranged side by side in parallel strata. There are portions also where the tints are paler, and some quite white, but these last seem to be soft, and not good for preserving the sculpture. It is this wonderful variety of colours observable throughout the whole range of mountains, that gives to Petra one of its most characteristic beauties. The façades of the tombs, admirably as they are sculptured, owe much of their imposing appearance to this infinite diversity of hues.

We engaged an Arab shepherd as our guide, and leaving Abou Raschid with our servants and horses, where the more difficult part of the ascent commences, we began to mount the track, which is extremely steep and toilsome, and affords but an indifferent footing. In most places the pilgrim must pick his way as he can, and frequently on his hands and knees. At the steepest points there are flights of rude steps, or inclined planes, constructed of stones laid together, and

* "Take Aaron and Eleazar his son, and bring them up unto Mount Hor. And Moses stripped Aaron of his garments and put them upon Eleazar his son. And Aaron died there on the top of the mount."—Numb. xx. 25, 28. ——"And the children of Israel took their journey from Beeroth of the children of Jaakan, to Mosera: there Aaron died, and there he was buried."—Deut. x. 6.

"But after the army (that had so long mourned the dead sister of the general) were thus purified, he led them through the desert, into Arabia; and arriving in a place (which the Arabians account for their metropolitan city, in times past called Arce, and at this present, Petra) which is environed with a high mountain, Aaron ascended the said mountain, and Moses showed him the place where he should yield up his soul unto God; and in the sight of all the army standing on a high place, he put off his stole, and gave it to his son Eleazer, to whom, by eldership, the succession appertained; and thus, in the sight of the people, he died in that very year wherein he lost his sister, on the one hundred and thirty-third year of his age, in the month of August."—Vide Josephus's Antiquities, book iv. ch. 4.

here and there are notches cut in the rock, to receive the foot; the impression of pilgrims' feet are scratched in the rock in many places, but without inscriptions. Much juniper grows on the mountain, almost to the very summit, and many flowering plants which we had not observed elsewhere: most of them are thorny, and some are very beautiful. On the top there is an overhanging shelf in the rock, which forms a sort of cavern; here we found a skin of extremely bad water suspended, and a pallet of straw, with the pitcher, and the other poor utensils of the sheikh who resides here. He is a decrepit old man, who has lived in this place during the space of forty years, and occasionally encounters the fatigue of descending and re-ascending the mountain. The tomb itself is inclosed in a small building, differing not at all in external form and appearance from those of Mahommedan saints, common throughout every province of Turkey. It has probably been re-built at no remote period; some small columns are bedded in the walls, and fragments of granite and slabs of white marble are lying about. The door is near the S.W. angle, within which is a tomb, with a pall thrown over it; it is patched together out of fragments of stone and marble that have made part of other fabrics. Upon one of these are several short lines in the Hebrew character cut in a slovenly manner; we had the copy which we made of them translated at Acre, and they proved to be merely the names of a Jew and his family who had scratched this record, as it is not probable that any professed Jew has visited the spot for ages past, perhaps not since the period of the Mahommedan conquest; it may lay claim to some antiquity, and in any case is a curious appendage to the testimony of Josephus on this subject. There are rags and shreds of yarn, with glass beads and paras, left as votive offerings by the Arabs. Not far from the N.W. angle is a passage, descending by steps to a vault or grotto beneath, for we were uncertain which of the two to call it. It is covered with so thick a coat of whitewash, that it is difficult to distinguish whether it is built or hollowed out; but the whole is rude, ill-fashioned, and quite dark. The sheikh, who was not informed that we were Christians, a circumstance which our guide was not aware of, furnished us with a lump of butter. Towards the farther end of this dark vault lie the two corresponding leaves of an iron grating, which formerly prevented all nearer approach to the tomb of the prophet; they have, however, been thrown down, and we advanced so as to touch it; it was covered by a ragged pall. We were obliged to descend bare-footed, and were not without some apprehension of treading on scorpions or other reptiles.

The view from the summit of the edifice is very extensive in every direction; and although the eye rests upon few objects, which it can clearly distinguish, an excellent idea is obtained of the general face and features of the country. The chain of Idumean mountains, which form the western shore of the Dead Sea, seems to run on to the southward, though losing considerably in their height; they appear from this point of view barren and desolate. Below them is spread out a white sandy plain, seamed with the beds of occasional torrents, and presenting much the same features as the most desert parts of the Ghor. Where this desert expanse approaches the foot of Mount Hor, there arise out of it, like islands, several lower peaks and ridges of a purple colour, probably composed of the same kind of sand-stone as that of Mount Hor itself, which, variegated as it is in its hues, presents in the distance one uniform mass of dark purple. Towards the Egyptian side there is an expanse of country, without feature, the limits of which are lost in the distance. The lofty district which we had quitted in our descent to Wady Mousa, shuts in the prospect on the S.E. side; but there is no part of the landscape which the eye wanders over with more curiosity and delight than the crags of Mount Hor itself, which stand up on every side in the most rugged and fantastic forms: sometimes strangely piled one on the other, and sometimes as strangely yawning in clefts of a frightful depth. In the midst of this chaos of rocks, there rises into sight one finished work, distinguished by profuseness of ornament, and richness of detail. It is the same which has been described as visible from other elevated points, but which we were never able to arrive at; it bears N.E. half N. from this spot, but the number and intricacy of the valleys and ravines, which we hoped might have led us to it, baffled all our attempts. No guide was to be found. With the assistance of the glass we made out the façade to be larger to all appearance than that of the temple at the eastern approach, and nowise inferior to it in richness and beauty. It is hewn out of the rock, and seemed to be composed of two tiers of columns, of which the upper range is Ionic; the centre is crowned with a vase of a gigantic proportion. The whole appeared to be in a high state of preservation; it may perhaps be an ornament to the northern approach to the city, similarly situated to that on the eastern side. Petra is intercepted and concealed by the prominences of the mountains. An artist who would study rock scenery in all its wildest and most extravagant forms, and in colours, which, to one who has not seen them, could scarcely be supposed natural, would find himself rewarded should he resort to Mount Hor for that sole purpose.

We had employed just one hour in the ascent, and found that our return to the place where we had left our horses occupied the same time. As the day was closing, we were reconducted by Abou Raschid close to the palace, and from thence proceeding in a N.E. direction quitted the ruins. On leaving Petra the track rises considerably, and is slippery and dangerous. Our attention was particularly excited by remarking with how much care the scanty soil had been banked up into terraces, and disposed into fields and gardens. Every nook that could furnish room for a single plant is turned to account, proving that Strabo was not mistaken in speaking of the horticultural advantages of this city, of which the inhabitants seem to have made the most. At present, the barren state of the country, together with the desolate condition of the city, without a single human being living near it, seem strongly to verify the judgment denounced against it.* It appeared to have been our chief's intention to have carried us for the night to some camp at a greater distance. However, it so happened that we had scarcely quitted the district of the tombs, when we passed near a small camp, consisting of a few tents only. Two men rushing out from them with impetuosity seized our bridles, and carried us by main force to lodge with them. Before we could dismount they had contrived to loose the corn bags from behind our saddles, and were fighting with one another, disputing who should fill them. The contest was so much in earnest that the most elderly of the persons engaged was thrown down, and the corn bags which he had secured, snatched from him by force. It will hardly be credited that the object of so much contention was the furnishing necessaries from their own stock gratuitously, to persons whom they had never seen before. A sheep was slain, and we supped in the usual style. Thus finished our first day's visit to the ruins of Petra.

Little more than a general survey had been taken, and that imperfectly. When we proposed returning, the principal objections that were started, were the difficulty of finding provisions for ourselves, and provender for our horses: this, however, was remedied by the purchase of a sheep on our part, together with whatever else was necessary for the ensuing day. It will appear strange to those who have had no experience in Arabian manners, that the same people who had fought with one another a few hours before, for the privilege of providing what we wanted at their own expense, from the moment that payment was talked of, and money

* "Edom shall be a desolation." Jeremiah, xlix, 87. See also Ezekiel, xxxv. and xxxvi.

shown to them, became greedy and imposing to the highest degree, and resorted to every method of extortion that they could devise. This is, however, entirely in accordance with the Arab character. Generous, and prone to hospitality at first, and as long as there is no talk or appearance of a recompense, but from the moment it is discovered that anything can be got, they not only lose sight of liberality, but even of common honesty, and a scene of fraud, double-dealing, and extortion begins ; so that, in fact, a poor man may pass better, and upon a more friendly footing, than a rich one. The result of the second day's operation has been thrown into the preceding description of Petra. We remained there till night, and took our last farewell with reluctance, leaving unexplored the great temple which we had seen from Mount Hor, the arch thrown over the chasm of the eastern entrance, the obelisk on one of the commanding heights, many of the ravines and valleys in the entrances of which were tombs, and which seemed especially worthy of examination, the insulated and conical mount with steps, the height which we supposed to have been the acropolis ; and in short, enough to have employed us four days more at least, but we could not obtain a further extension of the time allotted. We returned to the same camp where we had passed the previous night.

There were great apprehensions of robbers carrying off our horses in the dark. It was said they would probably be the Annasee Arabs, who are continually lurking about in the neighbourhood ; and it was reported in the morning that two fellows had been seen, but as persons were on the watch, they made no attempt to seize the horses.

May 26.—At day-break we quitted the camp and proceeded towards Shobek. The weather throughout the day was excessively cold. An European would find it difficult to believe, that on the 26th of May, in a latitude more southern than the Delta of Egypt, and with a wind from the westward, we should have suffered great inconvenience from cold. The very elevated situation we were on was in some measure the cause of this, but does not seem quite to account for it. The gusts were so violent, and the cold so bitter, that our people halted in the middle of their route for the purpose of kindling a fire. Arriving at Abou Raschid's camp, no impatience was expressed at our delay. Here we were joined by Sheikh Yousouf and Sahlem ; and taking leave of Abou Raschid, who sent his mace-bearer with his iron mace, to ensure for us the same reception as if he was himself of our company, we proceeded to Shobek. We gave our intrepid friend four hundred piastres, and Mr. Legh presented him with a brass blunderbuss, having a spring bayonet, with which he was much pleased. He kissed us all at parting.

May 27. — In the morning we quitted Shobek. On our route this day, we passed a swarm of locusts that were resting themselves in a gully. They were in sufficient numbers to alter the appearance of the rock on which they had alighted, and to make a sort of cracking noise while eating, which we heard before we reached them (Volney compares it to the foraging of an army). Our conductors told us they were on their way to Gaza, and that they pass almost annually. In the evening we arrived at Ipseyra, sometimes called Bsaida ; it is a miserable village, and the people a fanatical and surly set. We here met the man who had conducted Sheikh Ibrahim to Wady Mousa, as old Yousouf would not attend him farther than this place. He told us that Burckhardt made a very hasty survey of the ruins.

May 28.—We went to the tents of Sheikh Sahlem, passing on our way the village of Tafyle, and several others in the district of Djebal; most of them very picturesquely situated.

May 29.—In the morning we took our leave of Sheikh Sahlem. On our road we passed several shepherds' boys, who were playing on double pipes similar to some of those represented in the tombs of Egypt. We descended into the Wady El Ahsa, and bathed in the hot spring, which the Arabs call the bath of Solomon the son of David. Crossing the deep ravine and river El-Ahsa, we entered into the district of Kerek. El-Ahsa is probably the Zared of Scripture, the boundary of the Edomites and Moabites. On our ascent from the valley of the El-Ahsa, which occupied two hours, we killed, by the road side, a black scorpion, at least four inches long. About noon we reached a camp belonging to the father of Old Yousouf's bride. He is the sheikh of a village called Khanzyre, less than a mile from the camp. The next day we proceeded to Kerek. As we entered Yousouf's quarters, the throats of three kids ranged in a line were cut before us, to celebrate our return. The people were employed bringing in the harvest. We found the sheikh's house very full of Annasee Arabs, who were come with their camels from the eastward to procure corn. They had brought a mare as a present to old Yousouf, who had not of late been on good terms with their tribe. He gave, in his turn, six camel loads of wheat and six of barley, a sword of value, and a benish for the chief. The wife of the sheikh's brother was apparently dying of a fever, in a little room which opened into the court, and which was thronged to excess. She was lying on the floor speechless, and round her were women and girls, some squatting, and others leaning over her, so thick together that they could not move without treading on one another, or on the sick person, who was hardly visible from the numbers that surrounded her. The whole multitude were uttering the most piercing and piteous cries, nearly the same as at a funeral. Old Yousouf and another male of the family were seated in silence at the lower end of the room towards the door. At our particular request, the troop of mourners were expelled, and the woman left quiet. Knowing of no other remedy, and hearing that she was weak from fasting, Mahommed, the soldier, prescribed chicken broth, upon taking which she recovered surprisingly.

To the S.W. of the castle of Kerek, about a mile distant, is a spring, the name of which is a memorial of the occupation of this country by the crusaders; it is called Ain-el-Frangee, or the Franks' Fountain.

June 1.—In the forenoon we set out on a journey for the purpose of examining the southern extremity of the Dead Sea, under the guidance of an old man of the family of Yousouf Magella, who made us pay him 30 piastres, under the pretence that an escort of three was necessary, at 10 piastres each. We left the town by a more easy descent than that by which we first arrived. At the bottom we fell in with a small caravan of horses and mules, who were setting out for Hebron and Jerusalem. We pursued the same road by which we had arrived at Kerek from Hebron. A spot was pointed out to us by Soliman as the scene, many years before, of the slaughter of 30 men of Kerek. We could not learn the story very distinctly, but it seemed to be the result of a civil war amongst them. It was not far from where we had ourselves been accosted by the armed men, whom we had supposed robbers, and certainly a fitter place for an attack of thieves could not easily be found. We had previously passed many camps; in one of these we were desired to observe a very large herd of cattle collected, which we were informed was a spoil just brought in from the Haouran, near Djebal-El-Druze, where they had been stolen by some men in Ismayel's employ.

As soon as we came to the pass, which commands an extensive prospect of the Dead Sea, we could observe the effect of the evaporation arising from it, in broad transparent columns of vapour, not unlike water-spouts in appearance, but very much larger. We did not deviate at all from our old route, as far as the brook Dara; here the little Hebron caravan halted for a few hours. They implored us in the most earnest manner, as we valued their safety, not to mention in the huts of the Ghorneys below, that we had seen them, as it would infallibly lead to their being assaulted and robbed; adding, that so small a company could seldom pass that way with safety. From this point we began to take a new course, making a pretty direct descent towards the plain of the Ghor. An open grove of the acacia and doom-tree was thinly sprinkled on the first portion of our way; of these a great number were apparently either dead or dying, from what cause we did not learn, possibly their foliage had been stripped by locusts. All this tract might be irrigated, for it would be easy to dam up the brook, and conduct it in almost every direction. Probably it was so at a former period, for the divisions of fields, and even the marks of furrows, are to be seen; and some ruins, like those of cottages, or of a small hamlet. Lower down there is, very clearly, an ancient site; stones that have been used in building, though for the most part unhewn, are strewed over a great surface of uneven ground, and mixed both with bricks and pottery. This appearance continues without interruption, for the space of at least half a mile, quite down to the plain, so that it would seem to have been a place of considerable extent. We noticed one column, and we found a pretty specimen of antique, variegated glass; it may possibly be the site of the ancient Zoar. Near these remains the Dara opens from its glen into the plain to the northward, by a nook, where there is a wall of rude brick, with an arched door-way, which, as it seemed not to promise much, we did not examine.

The brook so far fertilizes this part of the plain, that it is scattered over with thickets of the acacia and doom-plant; we observed another shrub also, the branches of which have an inclination downwards, and are of a dull green, with little or no foliage; it bears a fruit about the size of an almond in its green husk, and not very dissimilar in colour, but having several seams or ribs like those on the fruit of the green pippin. When it ripens, the skin retains its roughness without, but becomes soft and juicy like a greengage, and has a degree of sweetness mixed with a strong bitter; by culture it might perhaps be improved and rendered an agreeable fruit; some said it was eatable, but others asserted that it was poisonous, and that children were frequently disordered, or even died, after eating it; there is a stone within it, and the smell is sickly and disagreeable. The hare and the partridge of the desert abound throughout this thicket, portions of which are cleared and cultivated. In the very heart of it, not visible in any direction beyond a few yards, unless by the smoke issuing from it, is the village of the Ghorneys, who are by profession Mahommedans, but are looked on by the faithful as little better than absolute infidels, as they seldom, if ever, exercise the forms of their religion. They hire themselves out as herdsmen and shepherds, and are notorious robbers. Their abode has more the appearance of a village in India or the South Seas, than of any we have seen in these regions. The weather being now excessively hot, the people were nearly naked; the children quite so. We were well received and few questions asked of us, but our guide shewed great mistrust of our hosts, laying all our goods together close to our heads, where we lay down to sleep.

June 2.—On the first dawn we left our guide, who wished to purchase tobacco to take to Kerek, and turning rather to the eastward of north, made our way through the thicket towards the sea-beach. We were here surprised to see, for the first time, the oskar plant grown to the stature of a tree, its trunk measuring, in many instances, 2 ft. or more in circumference, and the boughs at least 15 ft. in length, a size which far exceeded any we saw in Nubia; the fruit also was larger and in greater quantity. There is very little doubt of this being the fruit of the Dead Sea so often noticed by the ancients as appearing juicy and delicious to the eye, while within it is hollow, or filled with something grating and disagreeable in the mouth. The natives make use of the filaments, which are inclosed in it, and which somewhat resemble the down of a thistle, as a stuffing for their cushions; and they likewise twist them into matches for their guns, which they assured us required no application of sulphur to render them combustible. Nearer the sea, the vegetation consists principally of the tamarisk and cane, so high and so thickly set, as to render many parts wholly impassable. The rotten and marshy ground, formed probably by the stagnation of deposited water, during the winter season especially, renders the passage very difficult. The foliage has a salt dew hanging upon it, which causes on the hand the same greasy sensation and appearance that is produced by dipping it in the sea itself.* We saw frequent tracks of the wild boar.

A narrow, pebbly beach separates the jungle from the sea; it is very hard and firm to the tread, and continues so along the edge of the water, which here turns westward, and forms a bay. As the land lies lower here than in other places, the water encroaches more or less on the shore according to the season; the highest point which it ever reaches being marked by an extensive deposit of timber of all sizes. It dries off into shallows and small pools, which in the end deposit a salt as fine and as well bleached, in some instances, as that in regular salt pans. The western horn of this bay is formed by a sharp promontory, projecting forward into the sea, in a direction nearly from south to north; that is to say, such is the relative bearing of the extremities —for between them there is a considerable concavity in the line of shore where the salt water stagnates and evaporates. We found several persons engaged in peeling off a solid surface of salt, several inches in thickness; they were collecting it and loading it on asses. Towards the same part the ground is treacherous and deep, and only glazed over with a thin crust, not unlike the sediment of mud which the Nile, in some parts, leaves on its shores. The promontory is not entirely of high land; a steep, white ridge runs, like a spine, down the centre, presenting steep, sloping sides, seamed and furrowed into deep hollows by the rains, and terminating at the summit in sharp, triangular points, standing up like rows of tents ranged one above another; the whole is of a substance apparently partaking of the nature of soft and broken chalk and slate, and is wholly unproductive of vegetation. The height of the ridge varies from 10 to 30 ft., becoming gradually lower towards its northern extremity. At its foot, all round, is a considerable margin of sand, which varies in length and breadth according to the season, being much narrower in summer than it is in winter, when, in rough weather, at least, it is probable that the waves almost wash the base of the cliff. At the northernmost point of the cape some rotten branches are standing up, so encrusted with salt deposited upon them by the spray, or the evaporation, that they have the appearance of straight branches of fine white coral. The total length of this promontory, or horn of the bay, may be about four miles, computed from the fact, that we employed an hour and twelve minutes in riding along it at a walking pace. Following the line of coast round the angle, the same cliff presents an opposite face of similar appearance and equal height, running two miles in a direction S.W. by S. Here we first collected lumps of nitre and fine sulphur, from the size of a nutmeg to that of a small hen's egg: it was evident from their situation that they must have been brought down by the rain, and that their great deposit must be sought for in the cliff.* It is probable that persons come to collect these substances; at least, it was the only mode that occurred to us of accounting for the numerous prints of

* In the Phil. Trans. Vol. xcvii., p. 269, Dr. Marcet gives the following analysis of the water of the Dead Sea:

Muriate of Lime	3.920
„ Magnesia . .	10.246
„ Soda	10.360
Sulphate of Lime . . .	0.054
	24.580

* "The whole land thereof is brimstone and salt." Deut. xxix. 23.

human footsteps which we saw here, and those of asses somewhat farther on; for this place does not fall into any ordinary line of communication. We quitted the foot of the cliff, where the sand is in some places deep and distressing to the horse, and followed the edge of the beach, which diverges from the cliff to the S.W. As the water subsides—which, being always shallow towards the strait, retires rapidly in this part—a very considerable level is left, which is encrusted with a salt that is but half dried and consolidated, appearing like ice at the commencement of a thaw. All this space is soft, and gives way nearly up to the ankle when it is trodden on. We reached the narrowest part of the channel of communication between the sea and the back-water (which we have called the strait) in just two hours after leaving the foot of the cliff, our direction having been about S.W. The strait is formed by a low promontory projecting from the opposite or western shore. Just as we arrived at the narrowest part, where the ford is indicated by boughs of trees, we observed the small caravan from Kerek landing on the opposite side; and as we could discern the species of animal, as well as the people on their backs, we all agreed in estimating the distance about a mile. The depth of the water cannot be great, as the asses of the caravan were able to pass the ford. We searched for the shells mentioned by Seetzen, as proving that there are living creatures in the lake, but found none, excepting snail shells, and a small spiral species, which we invariably found to be without any fish, and having no appearance of having had any for a long time. Dead locusts were found in very great numbers; they had not become putrid, nor had they any smell, as is the case when they are cast up by any other sea; they were completely penetrated and incrusted with salt, and had lost their colour. The sight of such a multitude of carcasses of creatures who had perished in passing over these waters, might seem to lend some countenance to the account of the ancients, "that no living thing could attempt the passage over it with impunity," were this not a spectacle sufficiently common upon other shores, as in Sicily, and about El-Arish: and we had another still better proof to the contrary; first, in a pair of Egyptian geese, and afterwards in a flight of pigeons, which passed over the sea. It is, however, remarkable how few living things, such as birds, insects, or reptiles, are to be seen on this lake; the want of vegetable matter and of fresh water is probably the reason.

Leaving the narrowest part of the strait, we followed it to its southern extremity, where it opens into the back-water, and passed along the shore of the back-water itself to some distance. The high water-mark was at this season a mile distant from the water's edge. We were told that this back-water never entirely dries up, and that the ford is not at any season impassable.

Having returned from the edge of the back-water we ascended the cliff, which is steep but practicable, and gained a broad table-land on its top, where we fell in with the track of those who had passed from Kerek to the ford. In two hours we reached the banks of the Dara, where we found our guide. Late in the evening we arrived at some tents, where Sheikh Yousouf was encamped. We found here a man from Szalt, and two men from Herak in the Haouran, near the Druze country, who had come to reclaim the cattle stolen from them by Ismayel's people. In the morning we removed to Ismayel's tents, when the cause of the stranger was pleaded, but it was before a most partial and interested tribunal, for Yousouf was the accused as well as the judge and arbitrator. He decided accordingly; offering, at the utmost, to restore half the number that had been stolen. He accused them of having been, in some shape, the aggressors, but explained himself so little, that we did not learn what provocation he alluded to; there was much arguing and prevarication. We were surprised to find, that two places lying so very wide of each other, should have any such disputes to settle. Towards noon we returned to Kerek.

June 5.—In the afternoon we proceeded on our journey to the northward, accompanied by Sheikhs Yousouf and Ismayel, Daoud, his nephew, and the two men of Herak, together with the man from Szalt. We passed over a fine country, flat, and higher than Kerek, keeping in a N.N.E. direction; the reapers were at work, and the corn was luxuriant in all directions. Several sites which we passed proved that the population of this country was formerly proportioned to its natural fertility. In about two hours we reached Rabba, formerly Rabbath Moab, afterwards Areopolis; the ruins are situated on an eminence, and present nothing of interest, except two old ruined Roman temples, and some tanks. The whole circuit of the town does not seem to have exceeded a mile, which is a small extent for a city that was the capital of Moab, and which bore such a high sounding Greek name. We were surprised not to find any traces of walls about it. We passed the night at a camp near the ruins; it is the only *Christian camp* we have ever been in; they told us there were altogether five encampments of Christians. They were poor people, but connected with families in Kerek; occasionally they take their turn in the town, and send others to take theirs in the camp. A deep gully behind their tents led to the Dead Sea. This evening, about sun-set, we were deceived by a dark shade on the sea, which assumed so exactly the appearance of an island, that we entertained no doubt regarding it, even after looking through a telescope. It is not the only time that such a phenomenon has presented itself to us; in two instances, looking up the sea from its southern extremity, we saw it apparently closed by a low, dark line, like a bar of sand to the northward; and, on a third occasion, two small islands seemed to present themselves between a long sharp promontory and the western shore. We were unable to account for these appearances, but felt little doubt that they are the same that deceived Mr. Seetzen into the supposition that he had discovered an island of some extent, which we have had opportunity of ascertaining, beyond all doubt, does not exist. It is not absolutely impossible, however, that he may have seen one of those temporary islands of bitumen, which Pliny describes as being several acres in extent, and from which, he adds, the Egyptians drew their store of resinous matter for embalming their mummies.

June 6.—This morning we visited the ruins of Beit-Kerm, distant from Rabba about one mile and a half to the north. The principal feature of them is a great building, evidently Roman, resembling that which we took to have been a palace at Petra; perhaps this is the temple of Atargatis, at Carnaim, as it is called in 1 Maccabees, v. 43; or Carnion, b. 2, xii. 26. A great number of tanks prove that it was once a populous place. There were four camps near the ruins; we lodged in one; the men of Herak renewed their discussions and remonstrances with Yousouf, for having returned to them but forty head of their cattle. These were driven along the same road by which we travelled, and the drivers generally halted when we did. Two hours and a half north from Beit-Kerm there is a slight eminence, which forms a conspicuous object from all the country round, and is called "Sheikh Harn."

June 7.—During this day we visited several elevated heights, each commanding very fine views of the Dead Sea, comprehending the back-water at one end, and the Plains of Jericho at the other. Jerusalem and the Frank Mount were also discernible, and from the different bearings which we made, we clearly ascertained, that the length of the lake Asphaltes, including the back-water, does not exceed thirty miles at the utmost, though the ancients have assigned to it a length of from seventy-five to eighty miles. From the first height the bearings were as follows: Jerusalem, N. W. ¾ N.; Frank Mount, N. W. ¾ W.;

Jericho, N. by W.; east end of the back-water, S. W. by S. From the second height, Sheikh Harn, E. $\frac{1}{4}$ S.; the first-mentioned hill, N. N. E. $\frac{1}{2}$ E.; the Strait leading to the back-water, W. S. W. $\frac{3}{4}$ W.; the village of the Ghorneys, S. W. by W. $\frac{1}{4}$ W.; the hollow of the bay, W. S. W. $\frac{1}{4}$ W.; Jericho, N. $\frac{3}{4}$ W.; the extremity of the back-water, S. W. $\frac{1}{2}$ S.

On reaching the tents we found the men of Herak out of all patience at Yousouf's injustice in making so little retribution; they called us aside to assure us that he was no better than a robber, and hoped that we would publish and confirm their complaints at Damascus. "We will drag him," said they, "by the beard to Mezeereeb." But it would be no easy task to force the lord of Kerek out of his district.

June 8.—We proceeded to the northward, and in about two hours arrived upon the brink of the Wady Modjeb, the ancient Arnon; on looking down, it has more the appearance of a precipice than a road, and, although the Roman way coincides with the modern track, very near to the brink, and again about half way down it, it must have been formerly very different from that by which we descended, and which is not only extremely steep, but so interrupted with rocks and stones, that we were obliged to dismount and lead our horses full half the way down. About mid-way the declivity is more earthy and shelving; hereabouts we recovered the Roman highway. It is not here as above, completely paved, but at regular intervals a line of stones is carried across the road in the manner of a step, to prevent the washing away of the earth from above, and to serve as a resting place in the descent. On the right hand of the road, a shallow tank, of considerable size, walled round with thick and good masonry, is placed on the side of the hill; and below it, at only a few yards distance, are the remains of a large square building, which we took to be a Roman military station; there was another above on the brink of the precipice. We found several mile-stones; all those which were legible were of the time of Trajan.

The valley of the Arnon is less covered with shrubs, than that of most of the other streams in this country, which is probably owing to the violence and frequency of the torrents. There are, however, a few tamarisks, and here and there an oleander growing about it; it is not more than three paces wide where the Roman road comes down upon the stream, and there remains a single arch, measuring 28 feet 9 inches in perpendicular height, and 31 feet 6 inches in span; the remnants of the other arches of the bridge have all disappeared. The descent occupied one hour and a half. In our ascent up the opposite side, we followed, for the most part, the ancient road, and found some more Roman mile-stones; one of the time of Marcus Aurelius. We found the road on this side as steep as on the other, and it was remarkable in this pass, that looking from either side to the other, there appeared no possible mode of ascent. We had now passed from the land of the Moabites into that of the Amorites. As far as the eye could follow the course of the stream from the heights, the valley is neither of a size or nature that could ever have admitted of cultivation, or have given room for the placing of any village or city on its banks; which makes it probable, that the places, supposed to have stood upon the river, were in reality in the adjacent district.

We found the territory of the Amorites a flat down, of smoother and evener turf than that of Moab, and with much fewer stones scattered over it. We soon recovered the ancient road, and in forty-five minutes reached Diban, the Dibon of Scripture.* The extent of these remains is considerable, but not so large as Rabba. The ruins present nothing of interest. In the afternoon we arrived at a camp in the Wady Wale, pitched on the banks of the river, which this year seems to have swollen to a prodigious degree. The oleanders are here more numerous than we have ever seen them; one species, which is very rare, bore a white flower; the rushing of the waters

* Numbers, xxi. 30; and Jeremiah, xlviii. 18.

had rooted many of them up, and the whole were thrown aslant by the course of the torrent, the marks of which were seen upon them to the height of fifteen feet. On the left bank stands a stone about ten feet high, four feet wide at the base in its broadest part, and not more than one foot at the narrowest; it has been set up by art, being placed contrary to the natural direction of the strata, very near the bank, and at right angles to the stream. We supposed it to be one of those ancient boundary-stones of which we read so frequently in Scripture.* Across the stream, but at a greater distance from its channel, is a similar stone, bearing obliquely on the path, its broad side parallel to the stream. There are no signs of sculpture on them, nor is there any appearance of their having ever been wrought. There is in this same valley another rude work, that may be referred to a remote period; it is about a quarter of a mile higher up than the two boundary-stones. A knoll, of very moderate height, rises detached near the centre of the valley, upon the right bank of the rivulet. On its summit are the remains of a very large quadrangular platform, constructed of rude stones laid together without cement. It is possible that this may be one of the "altars of the high places." It is still a place in some measure consecrated; there is a tomb at the top with paltry Bedouin votive offerings hanging about it. About a mile lower down the valley, are the remains of a Roman bridge of five arches; all is fallen, and nothing is left but the foundation of the piers. Near this bridge are other ruins. From hence we passed upwards out of the valley. Near the ancient paved road there were several mile-stones, one of which was of the time of *Severus*. We passed at the foot of Djebal Attarous, which probably may be Nebo, although it is far from opposite Jericho. We now entered a fertile plain, covered with corn, and stopped at a camp near the ruins of Mayn, which both its name and the neighbouring hot springs, seem to identify with the Baal Meon of Scripture; it stands on a considerable eminence. In the afternoon, we went to a height which commands a fine view of the Dead Sea, and is very nearly on a parallel with its northern extremity. Here we took the following bearings; Jericho, N. W. ¾ N.; Mouth of the Jordan, N.W ½ N.; Rama of Samuel, N.W. by W.; Djebal Attarous, S.W.; Frank Mountain, W. N. W. ¾ W.; Sheikh Harn, S. ½ W. Below us was a square ruin which we could not get to; from its position we thought it might possibly be Herodium. At sunset we returned to the camp near Mayn, from whence there are a great number of ruined sites visible, and amongst the rest, Heshbon, bearing N.E. ¾ N.

We engaged a guide from the tents, who undertook to carry us to the hot springs: our route was S.W.; in less than half an hour we reached a tall stone, set up apparently as a boundary-mark, like those in the Wady-el-Wale. The direct track is continued round the southern side of a rocky knoll rising to some height, and in a great measure detached from the surrounding hills. Some remarkable objects, of which we got a glimpse, induced us to pass round on the other side of this knoll; they are rude sepulchral monuments of the same nature as those we discovered on our road from Szalt to the Jordan, on our last tour; yet, as these are rude throughout, without any mark whatever of the tool about them, whereas the others have universally a door in one of the smaller ends, it is possible that they may date from a remoter period, or have belonged to a still ruder people. Their proportions vary considerably, as does their aspect, though the construction is uniform; one flat stone is laid at the bottom, and this, there can be little doubt, covers the grave of the deceased; and, as there is no appearance of the tombs ever having been violated, it probably protects them to this day. They would be a highly interesting object for excavation, as it might possibly lead to the ascertaining of the form of some of the weapons and warlike apparel mentioned in Scripture. It is worthy of notice, that however remote may be

* "And the border went up to the stone of Bohan." Joshua, xv. 6.

the period to which these sepulchres are to be referred, the stature of those buried in them is so far from gigantic, that it seems not to have exceeded the middle height of modern times.

Not only is the rocky eminence, upon which we first observed them, covered over on all sides with these barbarous structures, but there are also some few scattered in the fields upon a lower level, and a great many upon the sides of the surrounding hills, insomuch that not less than fifty were in sight at one time. We were puzzled to think to what city this necropolis belonged. Mayn being more than a mile off, in a straight line, would seem too distant. Some which we had passed on our left hand the day before, at a place called Dher, were now visible, upon an eminence at no great distance to the north. Passing on, we found ourselves in an ancient highway, not paved, but edged with stones, and possibly prior to Roman times. Arriving at the brink of a deep descent, towards the Zerka Mayn, we found the track steep, long, and winding. In about two hours from Mayn we reached the bed of the Torrent Zerka Mayn, which we crossed, and kept along it in a westerly direction. We saw some animals which the Arabs called Meddn or Beddn. They are of the goat species, as large as asses, with long knotty horns which stand upright. Some had beards. In colour they resembled the gazelle. In four hours from Mayn we reached the place where it was necessary to dismount, the appearance beyond being that of a precipice. Here a narrow path has been contrived in a zig-zag direction, which makes the descent tolerably safe. In the last stage of the path there is a fine view of the Dead Sea at the end of the ravine, with the Frank Mount and Bethlehem beyond it; the former bearing N.N.W. Looking down into the valley of Calirrhoe, it presents some grand and romantic features. The rocks vary between red, grey, and black, and have a bold and imposing appearance. The whole bottom is filled, and in a manner choked up with a crowded thicket of canes and aspines of different species, intermixed with the palm, which is also seen rising in tufts in the recesses of the mountain's side, and in every place whence the springs issue. In one place a considerable stream of hot water is seen precipitating itself from a high and perpendicular shelf of rock, which is strongly tinted with the brilliant yellow of sulphur deposited upon it. On reaching the bottom we found ourselves at what may be termed a hot river, so copious and rapid is it, and its heat so little abated. For some way the temperature is kept up by the constant supplies of water of the same temperature which flow into the river. In order to visit these sources in succession, we crossed over to the right bank, and ascending by the mountain side, we passed four abundant springs, all within the distance of half a mile, discharging themselves into the stream at right angles with its course. We judged the distance from the Dead Sea, by the ravine, to be about one hour and a half. Macbean says, that there was a city of the same name in the valley of Calirrhoe; in which we think he must be wrong, since there is not space for a town in the valley as far as we saw it. That Herod must have had some lodging when he visited these springs is true, and there are sufficient remains to prove that some sort of buildings have been erected. The whole surface of the shelf, where the springs are, is strewed over with tiles and broken pottery; and what is most surprising, within a very few minutes, without any particular search, four ancient copper medals were found by our party. All were too much defaced to be distinguishable, but they appeared to be Roman. Our Arab guide here took a vapour bath according to the practice of the country. A bed of twigs and broom was laid across a crevice, whence one of the springs issued at the height of a foot or two from the water. On this he laid himself, wrapped in his Abba, and only remained a few minutes. The effect of the steam upon him was soon very evident. We observed another of these sweating beds a little further down. We had no thermometer, but the degree of heat in the water seemed very great. Near the source it scalds the hand, which cannot be kept in it for half a minute. The deposit of sulphur is very great, but the water is tasteless to the palate. A very singular plant grows near the hot springs, of the bulk and stature of a tree. Its foliage does not seem to differ from that of the common broom. It bears a pod hanging down from it, about a foot or 14 inches in length, fluted with convex ribs from the end to the point. We never met with this before. After bathing, we returned by the same road, and passing our old camp at Mayn, proceeded to the great encampment of the Benesuckhers, near Madeba. We arrived at night-fall. There were more than 200 tents scattered over a great extent of ground. We alighted at that of the chief Ebn Fayes, which was at least 100 feet long. The chief, and his brother, the same who was with us on our former Djerash expedition, and from whom we escaped to Szalt, received us outside their tent. They were dressed in handsome silk caftans from Damascus. Sheikh Yousouf had previously been invested with an ermine pelisse, and presented an odd figure, having his red-tanned sheep-skin underneath it. The three closed sides of the tent were allotted to the visitors, the two chiefs sitting on the open side, scarcely within the cove- of the tent. The elder brother, who has a hair lip, called for his one-stringed fiddle and played to us, singing at the same time. On our inquiring the purport of his song, he said it was on "the death of his father," who we learned had been killed in battle. The notes, though but little varied, were plaintive and harmonious. There was within the tent a messenger from Damascus, whom we had once seen at Kerek. He had arrived in the course of the afternoon to summon or invite Ebn Fayes to go to Damascus to the pasha. It was supposed his object was either to make some arrangement with the Benesuckhers for the safe conduct of the hadj to Mecca, as the Annasees under Sheikh Narsah were in rebellion; or to endeavour to reconcile the divisions which had taken place among the Benesuckhers, that they might be a check against the Annasees. To the accidental presence of this man, the favourable reception we met with was probably owing; and we were lucky in the absence of Abdel Khader, the prime minister, our former enemy. The wooden dish in which our supper was served, was of such a size as to require four iron handles, and was brought in by three persons.

June 11.—This morning we were told that Ebn Fayes was already on his way to Damascus; his brother remained with us. We requested of him a guide for Oom-i-Rasass; after some hesitation, and a good deal of talk about danger and enemies, one was promised, and an agreement made as to payment. We were to pass by Madeba as we advanced; after breakfast we proceeded. At Madeba, the only object of interest was an immense tank.* At three we reached Oom-i-Rasass (Mother of Stones); we found the ruins very extensive, and evidently Christian. There were the remains of a stone wall which inclosed the whole city; the cross is often to be met with, but there is no architectural remnant worthy of notice. Mr. Bankes, attended by his janissary, went over them a second time, in search of inscriptions, while we remained under the wall. While walking about the ruins, an armed Bedouin made his appearance and robbed him of his abba.

June 12.—We reached Heshbon in the evening, where we found Sheikh Yousouf, the man from Szalt, and the young prince of the Benesuckhers. Our first object was to see the ruins, and to inspect the celebrated pools; but just as we were starting, we received a message from Ebn Fayes, demanding payment for permission to proceed. We sent word in reply, that

* Madeba is noticed in Numbers, xxi. 30: "And we have laid them waste unto Nophah, which reaches unto Medeba." And in Isaiah. xv. 2: "Moab shall howl over Nebo, and over Medeba."

we had already paid him on a former occasion. "Tell them," said the young man in reply, "that the first that moves from the tent receives this ball (presenting a pistol) through his body." The firman was now mentioned; he said he cared nothing for firmans; that he considered them only fit for those who were weak enough to obey them; that *he* was Grand Seignior, and everything else here; and that we must pay. After some delay, Ebn Fayes, seeing we were not inclined to give in, sent word that we might proceed. We found the ruins uninteresting; and the only pool we saw was too insignificant to be one of those mentioned in Scripture. In two of the cisterns amongst the ruins, we found about three dozen of human sculls and bones.

June 13.—We left Heshbon, passing a stream which, if followed, would probably have led to the pools. We then proceeded along the road to Szalt, and in about four hours arrived at a place called by the natives Arrag-el-Emir. Here are the ruins of an edifice constructed of very large stones, some of which are twenty feet long, and so broad that one stone constitutes the thickness of the wall. The ruin is situated upon a square platform or terrace, of some extent, with a stream below. From the situation, and from the circumstance of large beasts, in relievo, being sculptured about it, Mr. Bankes believed it to be the palace of Hircanus, who, according to Josephus, being driven across the Jordan by his brother Alexander, king of Jerusalem, had built a palace in this neighbourhood, surrounded by hanging gardens, traces of which are yet visible. There are many artificial caves in a large range of perpendicular cliff near it; some of these are in the form of regular stables, in which feeding-troughs still remain, sufficient for thirty or forty horses, with holes cut in the rock for the head fastenings. Some of the caves are chambers and small sleeping apartments, probably for servants and attendants. There are two rows of these chambers: the upper one has a sort of projecting balcony across the front of the chambers. There is one large hall finely proportioned, with some Hebrew characters inscribed over the doorway; the whole is approached by a sort of causeway. We spent the remaining part of the day here, and slept at an adjoining camp. On the hill, immediately above the palace, are the remains of a small temple, much in ruins.

June 14.—We advanced to Szalt, passing through a richly wooded and picturesque country; we arrived early in the afternoon, and lodged in the castle. We remained at Szalt until the 16th, when we proceeded for three hours in the direction of Amman. Near this place we passed the night in a camp belonging to the party of the Benesuckhers hostile to Ebn Fayes, and we employed the chief part of the next day in examining the ruins of Rabbath Ammon, afterwards called Philadelphia, and now Amman. They stand in a long valley; a stream runs through them, which has been arched over. The ruins are extensive, but there remains nothing of much interest excepting the theatre, which is very large and perfect, and a small odeum close to it. There are the vestiges also of many other Roman edifices, as well as of Christian churches. We did not find any inscriptions.

June 17.—We passed the night at an Arab camp, about three miles distant on the road to Djerash. Here old Yousouf was again accused of having stolen cattle from the people; it was said to have happened four years ago. After much dispute he ended the argument by saying, that "he was one of those people who never returned anything after it was once in his power."

June 18.—At dawn of day we advanced; in about two hours Yousouf took leave of us to return to Kerek. He had made strong demands for money, both for himself and his nephew Daoud, though at Szalt we had made him a present of two hundred piastres over and above his agreement. He also tried to make us give an exorbitant sum to the guide who accompanied us to Djerash, but failed. Notwithstanding all this, it must be admitted that he strictly and honestly adhered to his contract with us; and it is doubtful whether we should ever have succeeded in reaching Wady Mousa, if it had not been for him. His only dishonesty towards us was borrowing money from Mr. Bankes, and refusing to repay it; but where all are rogues, and cheating and imposition are reckoned honourable and fair, one must not expect too much.

About noon we crossed the Zerka, the Jabbok of Scripture,* the northern boundary of the Amorites, and at 2 P.M. reached Djerash. We employed this and part of the next day in making those measurements of the public edifices which we had left unfinished before; most of them were Christian churches. Among many new inscriptions which we found, was one recording the dedication of one of the churches to a Christian saint. Macbean, quoting Eusebius, says, "that the Christians, just before the siege of Jerusalem by Titus, were divinely admonished to fly to Pella;" and Strabo notices, "that it abounded in water;" from Ptolemy he adds, "that Pella was situated thirty-five miles to the N.E. of Gerasa." Macbean also quotes from Ptolemy and Josephus, "that Gerasse was at the east side of the sea of Tiberias;" these authorities seem to show that the ruins at Djerash are those of Pella rather than of Gerasa.

June 19.—Intending to proceed to the valley of the Jordan by a place called Rajib, where we expected to find the ruins of Ragaba, we quitted Djerash in the afternoon, and passed through Katty. About half an hour after, we traversed another village, in the mosque of which there are some Roman remains. We entered a very picturesque country, most beautifully varied with hanging woods, mostly of the Vallonia oak, laurestinus, cedar, common arbutus, arbutus Andrachne, &c. At times the country had all the appearance of a noble park; indeed, nothing could exceed the beauty of this day's ride; there were some few spots cultivated with corn. As we advanced, the wood became more dense; and at dark we stopped at a small open space covered with high grass and weeds. We went with our guide a short distance to endeavour to shoot some wild boars; we hid ourselves close to the water, where all the trees were marked with mud, left by the hogs in rubbing themselves. We plainly heard some of these animals advancing towards us; but one of the horses unluckily making a noise, they all ran off. On returning to our bivouac, our guide refused to go for water, fearing the serpents in the high grass. Mr. Legh, in the night, feeling something move under him, rose to see what it was, and found an adder coming up to him from under the edge of his blanket, attracted no doubt by the warmth of his body, as the night air was very cold; having a knife by him, he cut the reptile in halves. In the morning we found another close to our sleeping place.

June 20.—We started at dawn, and descending through a thick wood, arrived, at ten, at the village of Rajib, which contains no ruins whatever; though we had previously passed in the wood a Roman architrave, on a small open space, where our guide told us there had once been a village; no other vestiges of it remain. Rajib is situated a little without, and below the woodlands. At noon we began a rapid descent towards the valley of the Jordan, and reached it in two hours. We saw nine wild pigs in our way; they were all in one herd. Four hours more, in a northerly direction, brought us to the Bysan ford, and we arrived at that town after dark.

June 21.—We went to Tiberias, and the 23rd visited Mount Tabor on our way to Nazareth. Maundrell overrates the view from this eminence; we saw nothing striking except the beautiful plain of Esdredon. In a cave, amongst the ruins of the town, on the top of Tabor, we noticed many travellers' names, and, amongst others, that of Mr. Wright, who visited this place, when first lieutenant of the

* "Even unto the river Jabbok, which is the border of the children of Ammon." Joshua, xii. 2

Tigre, with Sir Sydney Smith, and who afterwards died in the Temple at Paris; Sheikh Ibrahim's name was also there.

On the *25th June* we went to Acre. During our stay there we witnessed an instance of great barbarity: on going to breakfast at the consul's, we found his Greek servant, who had been very ill for some days before, lying outside the door; and actually expired on the floor before us as we entered the room—unattended by any medical man, and unheeded by every one. The corpse lay neglected for some time before any one could be found to take it away, all refusing to touch it, lest they should be at the trouble and expense of burying it. At last the Turkish authorities interfered and the body was removed.

As we have now been much amongst the Arabs, and have had better opportunities of studying their manners and habits than on our former short journey to Palmyra, some further observations upon them may not be considered out of place. The love of liberty created in the wandering Bedouin, by his erratic habits, is instinctively cherished by him from his earliest infancy. Impatient of every species of control, and proud of his independence, he disowns and scorns the Arab that cultivates the soil. We found these people still deserving of their character for hospitality; but we never heard of the celebrated story of *bread and salt*, mentioned by Volney. If the mere eating of bread and salt with an Arab was a security from imposition, Sheikh Sahlem, when threatening us, would have said, "Had you not eaten bread and salt with me," &c., instead of "Had you not Sheikh Yousouf with you;" for we had feasted with Sahlem in his own tent, before we had the quarrel with him. Mr. Bankes was imprisoned, and Sir Wm. Chatterton robbed, at Palmyra, after eating bread and salt; and we had feasted with Ebn Fayes at Heshbon, before his ill treatment of us. It would certainly be a most noble commendation to advance in their favour were it true. There is a great deal of good breeding amongst them: a sheikh arriving at another's tent, seats himself opposite his friend to avoid all appearance of pre-eminence, so that either side of the tent is occupied, while the end, the "post of honour," remains vacant. When Mr. Bankes presented the Sheikh of Souf with a dress, he immediately sent it into the harem, without looking at it in the presence of the donor; and the people of Kerek, on our arrival, although our appearance must have been so novel to them, abstained from asking any questions. But although civil, they had a great contempt for us; and observing how awkwardly we ate with our hands—for we never, during the whole tour, saw a spoon, or knife, or fork—they remarked amongst themselves, "Poor fellows! they don't even know how to eat; they eat like camels." If an Arab chief gives you coffee first, he takes none, not choosing to drink after a Christian. Thieving, pilfering, low cunning, lying, and cheating, are not considered as dishonourable acts amongst them. We were all of us robbed of some of our effects. On one occasion, Mr. Bankes's drawing of the grand temple at Petra was purloined, and after some days' negotiation he was allowed to purchase it back again, they having confessed all the time that they had it. Mr. Legh's Bible was also pilfered in the same manner, and never recovered. Mr. Bankes's two paint-boxes were also stolen, and many other articles were lost. Our diet, while we were with them, varied according to the wealth or poverty of the tribe: sometimes we had pillaw of rice, or of wheat, mixed with leban; sometimes mutton, boiled the moment the animal is skinned, and generally in leban, a custom alluded to in Scripture.* This mode of cooking renders the meat very delicious and tender—far preferable to meat boiled in water: the milk, enriched with the juice of the meat, is poured on the pillaw of rice or wheat. Sometimes we had melted butter, and bread baked on an iron plate in the form of a pan-

* "Thou shalt not seethe a kid in his mother's milk." Exodus, xxiii. 19.

cake to dip into it. The staple of the Arab's food, however, is leban and bread. The milk was usually presented in a wooden bowl, and the liquid butter in an earthenware dish.* The party being seated round, dipped their bread in, endeavouring to make it *imbibe* as much as possible. The Arabs were very expert at this, pinching the thin cake in such a form as to make a sort of spoon of it. This mode of eating is alluded to in Scripture.† Occasionally, a bowl of milk only was presented to us, which was passed round in rotation. Once we had milk sweetened and curdled to the consistency of liquid jelly, too thick to be drunk, and very awkward to take up with the hands, though it was the only method of eating it. A rich dish of rice and cream was once given us as a great treat. All the way between Kerek and Petra, we had meat served up alone, without bread or even pillaw of rice or wheat. We could not at all reconcile ourselves to this diet, which we found used in this district only. When the Arabs have an over supply of leban, they have a method of preserving it by pressing out the liquid parts, and drying the curds, which may then be kept for some time. This substance has the appearance of soft chalk; when mixed with water it makes an agreeable acid drink.

When we had pillaw of grain, it often served also for a candlestick, the candle being fixed in the middle of the dish. An Arab, when he wishes to pay you very particular attention, pulls your meat to pieces with his fingers, and throws it to you. We never saw roasted meat among the Arabs, except in Narsah's tent at Palmyra. They have no fruits or vegetables; their wandering life depriving them of such enjoyments. It is their custom, from time immemorial, to lodge and feed all travellers and their horses for one night free of all expense; as the practice is general, it is equally beneficial to all. We never once paid for food or corn during the whole of our journey; and the expenses of the whole party, eleven persons and as many horses, amounted to 1500 piastres; a piastre is worth nine-pence of our money: this was from the 5th of May to the 25th of June. Each owner of a tent takes it by turns to feed the strangers that may arrive. Their jokes were sometimes rather rough: on one occasion an Arab put a live scorpion inside my jacket; shortly afterwards, I had occasion to make the usual daily search for vermin, and then I discovered the reptile. At the Ghor, when we asked if a poisonous fruit was good, they said it was, though well aware of its bad qualities.

The women weave carpets and cloth for their tents, which are mostly black, and curtains, which are striped white and black. Goats' hair is manufactured for this purpose.* The women have to do all the hard work; they grind the corn with a hand-mill, bring the water and wood, cook, and in short do all the drudgery, while the men sit down and smoke all day. The children guard the flocks, the girls always having a bundle of wool at their backs for spinning. The form of the tents is oblong. We frequently observed negroes in their camps, apparently not slaves; and some had the short woolly hair of the Africans. It may not be amiss here to mention, that, though we never had any apprehensions of personal danger from the Arabs, yet there are some grounds for the dread these people are held in throughout Syria, as we met with many dead bodies concealed in the country frequented by them; we saw 20 in one of the Roman tombs near Nablous, the mouth of which had been shut up with stones; 3 in one of the theatres at Om Keis; 24 skulls, &c. in the theatre at Bysan, and subsequently 22 in the ruins at Heshbon. Whenever we inquired about them, the Arabs always owned they were the remains of people whom they had murdered, and they did not appear to be in the least ashamed of the deed. To keep

* "She brought forth butter in a lordly dish." Judges, v. 25.

† "He that dippeth with me in the dish." Matt., xxvi. 23.

* "And he made curtains of goats' hair." Exodus, xxxvi. 14.

your arms on in a tent, is considered very ill-bred, as implying a distrust in the protection of the roof you are under; and whenever we forgot to disarm, the Arabs always requested us to do so. These people are frequently without water, and sometimes that which they have is dirty and bad; but then they are "lords of the desert," pay no tribute, and have nothing whatever to do with governors of any description. The desert, as an ancient author, I think Diodorus, observes, is their fort, whither they retire as to a place of certain safety on any appearance of attack. The state and equipage of the sheikhs is maintained by means of a revenue derived from a tithe which they exact for all the cattle, camels excepted. This tenth of the innumerable herds and flocks, yields the chiefs a very handsome income. The supper in the tents of Sheikh Narsah and Ebn Fayes was bountiful in the extreme; and, as this profuse hospitality is extended to all strangers, there must needs be ample store to meet so great a demand.

It is surprising, that in so monotonous a life, they have no amusements, no games, no athletic employments, to make some little change in their custom of squatting down and smoking all day. All their carpets, cushions, sacks, and in short, everything they have, are covered with vermin, so that it is impossible to avoid them. We used to kill from off our clothes from 40 to 100 every day; and of a night, we frequently observed the Arabs searching and shaking their linen over the fire, the vermin making a crackling noise as they fell into the flames. Old Yousouf used to make a singular figure, with his sword drawn, striking them from off his back.

July 12.—We embarked on board an imperial brig belonging to Venice for Constantinople, as all with whom we spoke on the subject agreed in opinion, that it would have been madness to have gone to the coast of Asia Minor at this season of the year, when the pestilential air forces all the inhabitants of the coast to quit their habitations, and retire to the mountains during the summer. We have, therefore, deferred this part of the tour for a short time. Our friend Mr. Legh left Acre for Constantinople by land a short time before we did, intending to visit Palmyra, Baalbec, Damascus, and Aleppo. Mr. Bankes went by water to Egypt, with the intention of penetrating into Abyssinia by way of the second cataract.

THE END.

LONDON: BRADBURY AND EVANS, PRINTERS, WHITEFRIARS.

MR. MURRAY'S

COLONIAL AND HOME LIBRARY.

THE main object of this undertaking is to furnish the Inhabitants of Great Britain and her Colonies with the highest Literature of the day, consisting partly of original Works, and partly of new editions of popular Publications, at the lowest possible price. It is called for in consequence of the Acts which have recently passed the British Parliament for the protection of the rights of British authors and publishers, by the rigid and entire exclusion of foreign pirated editions. These Acts, if properly enforced, will, for the first time, direct into the right channel the demand of the Colonies for English Literature: a demand of which our authors and publishers have hitherto been deprived by the introduction of piracies from the United States, France, and Belgium. In order, therefore, that the highly intelligent and educated population of our Colonies may not suffer from the withdrawal of their accustomed supplies of books, and with a view to obviate the complaint, that a check might in consequence be raised to their intellectual advancement, Mr. Murray has determined to publish a series of attractive and useful works, by approved authors, at a rate which shall place them within reach of the means not only of the Colonists, but also of a large portion of the less wealthy classes at home, who will thus benefit by the widening of the market for our literature: and the 'Colonial Library' will consequently be so conducted that it may claim to be considered as a 'Library for the Empire.' Owing to the very low price placed upon the numbers of this Series, the undertaking can succeed only if it meets with strenuous support from the Colonial Government at home and abroad, in giving effect to *the law*, and in supporting the just rights of British genius, industry, and manufactures, by preventing illicit importation of foreign reprints. It is also necessary for its progress and success that it be favoured with the patronage of the Reading Public in all parts of the British dominions, and the chief aim and object of the publisher will be to render it worthy of their countenance.

Mr. Murray's 'Colonial Library' will furnish the settler in the backwoods of America, and the occupant of the remotest cantonments of our Indian dominions, with the resources of recreation and instruction, at a moderate price, together with many new books within a short period of their appearance in England; while the student and lover of literature at home, who has hitherto been content with the loan of a book from a book-club, or has been compelled to wait for its tardy perusal from the shelves of a circulating library, or perhaps has satisfied his curiosity by the scanty extracts in magazines or reviews, may now become possessed of the work itself, at a cost little beyond that entailed by either of the methods above mentioned. He may at the same time lay up a permanent Library in a condensed and portable form.

The series of Works designed to appear in Mr. Murray's 'Colonial and Home Library' will be selected for their acknowledged merit, and will be exclusively such as are calculated to please the most extensive circles of readers. They will be printed most carefully, in a superior style, and on good paper.

Works already Published.

Nos. 1 and 2.

BORROW'S BIBLE IN SPAIN;

OR, THE

JOURNEYS, ADVENTURES, AND IMPRISONMENTS OF AN ENGLISHMAN IN AN ATTEMPT TO CIRCULATE THE SCRIPTURES IN THE PENINSULA.

Price 2s. 6d. each; or bound in cloth, 6s.

"Difficulties!! were they to be deterred from proceeding on that account? Let them look at Mr. Borrow; why, if he had suffered himself to be prevented from circulating the Bible in Spain by the difficulties he met with, he could never have spread such enlightenment and information through that country."—Sir Robert Peel, *in the House of Commons.*

Nos. 3 to 6.

BISHOP HEBER'S JOURNAL IN INDIA.

Price 2s. 6d. each; or 2 vols., bound in cloth, 12s.

*** "Bishop Heber's Journal forms a monument of talent, sufficient, singly and alone, to establish its author in a very high rank of English literature. It is one of the most delightful books in the language."—*Quarterly Review.*

"We remember Bishop Heber's Journal as one of the most perfectly charming books we ever read; gentle, tolerant, humane, and full of wisdom; a religious book in the best sense of the word, because full of charity. It is lively without effort, and abounds in valuable judgments of men and things, without one harsh, sarcastic, or illiberal word. We envy those who have it now in their power to read it for the first time."—*Examiner.*

TO BE FOLLOWED BY

1. A LIFE OF LORD CLIVE.

2. LIFE OF CRABBE, THE POET.

3. THE MANUFACTURING DISTRICTS OF ENGLAND;

THEIR CANALS, RAILROADS, MINES, MILLS, AND WORKS.

4. LIFE OF WILLIAM PITT.

And other Attractive Works, at intervals of One Month.

VII.

HISTORY OF ENGLAND,

From the Death of Queen Anne to the Reign of George the Second.
By LORD MAHON. *Second Edition.* 3 vols. 8vo, 36*s.*

VIII.

HISTORY OF PAINTING,

From the Age of Constantine the Great to the Present Time.
THE SCHOOLS OF ITALY,
Translated from the German of KUGLER,
By a LADY; and Edited, with Notes, by C. L. EASTLAKE, R.A. Post 8vo, 12*s.*

BIOGRAPHY.

I.

LIFE OF SIR SAMUEL ROMILLY,

WRITTEN BY HIMSELF; WITH HIS LETTERS AND POLITICAL DIARY,
EDITED BY HIS SONS.
Third Edition. Portrait. 2 vols. fcap 8vo, 12*s.*

II.

LIFE AND VOYAGES OF SIR FRANCIS DRAKE.

By JOHN BARROW, Esq. 8vo, 14*s.*

III.

LIFE OF EDWARD GIBBON;

WITH SELECTIONS FROM HIS CORRESPONDENCE, &C., AND NOTES.
By Rev. H. H. MILMAN. Portrait. 8vo, 9*s.*

IV.

LIFE OF LORD BYRON,

WITH HIS LETTERS AND JOURNALS.
By THOMAS MOORE, Esq. *New and Cheaper Edition.* Portraits. 8vo, 15*s.*

V.

LIFE OF CRABBE, THE POET;

With his Letters and Journals. By his SON. Plates, fcap 8vo, 7*s.* 6*d.*

VI.

LIFE OF SIR DAVID WILKIE;

With his Letters, Journals, and Critical Remarks on Works of Art
During his Tours in France, the Netherlands, Italy, Spain, Germany, Turkey,
Egypt, and the Holy Land.
By ALLAN CUNNINGHAM, ESQ. Portrait. 3 vols. 8vo, 42*s.*

VII.

LIFE OF ROBERT BURNS.

By JOHN GIBSON LOCKHART, Esq. *Fourth Edition.* Portrait. Fcap 8vo, 6*s.* 6*d.*

VIII.

LIFE OF THE LATE LORD HILL,

COMMANDER OF THE FORCES.
From Authentic Documents, supplied by his Family and Friends.
By Rev. EDWIN SIDNEY. 8vo. (*Nearly Ready.*)

IX.

LIVES OF GALILEO, TYCHO BRAHE, AND KEPLER,

THE MARTYRS OF SCIENCE.

By Sir DAVID BREWSTER, LL.D., Principal of St. Andrews. 12mo, 7*s*.

X.

LIFE OF JAMES WATT.

By M. ARAGO. Translated from the French, by J. P. MUIRHEAD, M.A. 8vo, 8*s*. 6*d*.

XI.

LIFE OF BELISARIUS.

By LORD MAHON. Map. 8vo, 12*s*.

RELIGION.

I.

THE BOOK OF THE CHURCH.

With Notes, containing References to the Authorities, and an Index.

By ROBERT SOUTHEY, LL.D. *Fifth Edition*. 8vo, 12*s*.

II.

ILLUSTRATIONS OF THE LITURGY AND RITUAL OF THE CHURCH;

Being Sermons and Discourses selected from the Works of eminent Divines who lived during the Seventeenth Century.

By JAMES BROGDEN, M. A. 3 vols. post 8vo, 27*s*.

III.

EVIDENCES OF CHRISTIANITY.

By WILLIAM SEWELL, B.D., late Professor of Moral Philosophy at Oxford. Fcap 8vo, 7*s*. 6*d*.

IV.

PARISH SERMONS;

On the Lessons, the Gospel, or the Epistle, for every Sunday and Principal Festival in the Year.

By the late BISHOP HEBER. *Fifth Edition*. 2 vols. post 8vo, 16*s*.

V.

HYMNS FOR THE CHURCH SERVICE.

Adapted for every Sunday in the Year.

By the late BISHOP HEBER. *Eleventh Edition*. 16mo, 2*s*.

VI.

THE NESTORIAN CHRISTIANS, OR LOST TRIBES;

With SKETCHES OF TRAVEL IN OOROOMIA, KOORDISTAN, ANCIENT ASSYRIA, and MEDIA.

With Illustrations of Scripture Prophecy, and evidence of their identity with the Lost Tribes of Israel.

By ASAHEL GRANT, M.D. *Third Edition*. Map. Fcap 8vo, 6*s*.

VII.

PSALMS AND HYMNS FOR PUBLIC WORSHIP,

Selected and arranged, and adapted to the various Solemnities of the Church.
By Rev. W. B. HOLLAND, M.A., Perpetual Curate of Walmer.
24mo, cloth. Price 1*s*. 6*d*.

*** *Clergymen wishing to introduce this Selection will have an allowance made them.*

VIII.

EXPLANATION OF THE SACRAMENTS,

And the occasional Rites and Ceremonies of the Church of England.
By A LADY. Fcap 8vo, 5*s*. 6*d*.

IX.

ON THE SACRAMENT OF THE LORD'S SUPPER,

With Directions as to the proper Mode of Receiving it.
By Rev. F. SULLIVAN, A.M. 16mo, 1*s*.

X.

HISTORY OF JOSIAH.

By the Author of "GIDEON, THE MAN OF MIGHTY VALOUR." Fcap 8vo, 4*s*. 6*d*.

POETRY.

I.

LORD BYRON'S POETICAL WORKS.

With Portrait and Plates. 10 vols. 18mo, 2*s*. 6*d*. each.

II.

LORD BYRON'S POETICAL WORKS.

With Portrait and View of Newstead Abbey. Complete in one volume.
New and cheaper Edition. Royal 8vo, 15*s*.

III.

LORD BYRON'S TALES.

(POCKET EDITION.)

1. GIAOUR.
2. BRIDE OF ABYDOS.
3. CORSAIR.
4. LARA.
5. SIEGE OF CORINTH.
6. BEPPO.
7. MAZEPPA.
8. ISLAND.
9. PARISINA.
10. PRISONER OF CHILLON.

2 vols. 24mo, 5*s*.; or separately, 6*d*. each.

IV.

LORD BYRON'S DRAMAS.

(POCKET EDITION.)

1. MANFRED.
2. MARINO FALIERO.
3. HEAVEN AND EARTH.
4. SARDANAPALUS.
5. TWO FOSCARI.
6. DEFORMED TRANSFORMED.
7. CAIN.
8. WERNER.

2 vols. 24mo, 7*s*.; or separately at 6*d*. and 1*s*. each.

V.

LORD BYRON'S CHILDE HAROLD.

(POCKET EDITION.)

With Engraved Title-page. 24mo, 2*s*. 6*d*.

VI.

THE POETICAL WORKS OF CRABBE.

Containing The Library, The Borough, Parish Register, Tales of the Hall, The Village, Posthumous Tales,

With his Letters and Journals. By his Son. Plates. 8 vols. fcap 8vo, 40s.

VII.

BEAUTIES OF THE BRITISH POETS;

With Biographical and Critical Notices, and an Essay on English Poetry.

By Thomas Campbell, Esq.

Third and Cheaper Edition. Portrait and Vignette. Royal 8vo, 15s.

VIII.

PALESTINE, EUROPE, THE RED SEA,

AND OTHER POEMS.

By the late Bishop Heber. *Second Edition.* Portrait. Fcap 8vo, 7s. 6d.

IX.

FALL OF JERUSALEM, BELSHAZZAR, MARTYR OF ANTIOCH, SAMOR, ANN BOLEYN,

AND OTHER POEMS.

By Rev. H. H. Milman. *Second Edition.* With Notes and Illustrations.
3 vols. fcap 8vo, 18s.

POPULAR TRAVELS.

I.

THE BIBLE IN SPAIN;

Or, the Journeys, Adventures, and Imprisonments of an Englishman in an Attempt to Circulate the Scriptures in the Peninsula.

By George Borrow, Esq., late Agent to the British and Foreign Bible Society.
Fifteenth Thousand. Post 8vo, 6s.

II.

LETTERS FROM CANADA AND THE UNITED STATES;

Written during a Journey in North America.

By John Robert Godley, Esq. 2 vols. post 8vo.

III.

FOREST SCENES AND INCIDENTS IN THE WILDS OF CANADA.

By Sir George Head. *Second Edition.* Post 8vo, 10s.

IV.

RAPID JOURNEYS ACROSS THE PAMPAS AND AMONG THE ANDES.

By Sir Francis B. Head, Bart. *Third Edition.* Post 8vo, 9s. 6d.

V.

LETTERS FROM MADRAS;

Or, First Impressions of Manners and Society in India, during a Three Years' Residence.

By a Lady. Post 8vo, 9s. 6d.

VI.

FIFTY DAYS ON BOARD A SLAVE-SHIP

IN THE MOZAMBIQUE CHANNEL.

By Rev. PASCOE GRENFELL HILL, Chaplain of H.M.S. *Cleopatra*. With a Map. Fcap 8vo, 3*s*. 6*d*.

VII.

MODERN EGYPT AND THEBES:

Being a Description of Egypt; including the information required for Travellers in that Country.

By Sir GARDNER WILKINSON. Woodcuts and Map. 2 vols. 8vo, 42*s*.

VIII.

VISIT TO THE IONIAN ISLANDS, ATHENS, AND THE MOREA.

By EDWARD GIFFARD, ESQ. With Views. Post 8vo, 12*s*.

IX.

A BACKWOODSMAN'S ACCOUNT OF UPPER CANADA;

FOR THE USE OF EMIGRANTS. *Third Edition*. Fcap 8vo, 1*s*. 6*d*.

X.

A JOURNEY THROUGH ARABIA PETRÆA, MOUNT SINAI, TO THE EXCAVATED CITY OF PETRA, THE EDOM OF THE PROPHECIES.

By M. LEON DE LABORDE. *Second Edition*. Plates. 8vo, 18*s*.

XI.

TRAVELS IN NEW ZEALAND:

With Contributions to the Geography, Geology, Botany, and Natural History of the Islands.

By ERNEST DIEFFENBACH, M.D., Naturalist to the New Zealand Company. With Plates. 2 vols. 8vo, 24*s*.

XII.

EXCURSIONS IN NEWFOUNDLAND:

With an Account of the Cod Fishery—Fog Banks—Sealing Expeditions, &c.

By J. B. JUKES, Esq., Geological Surveyor of Newfoundland. With a Map. 2 vols. Post 8vo, 21*s*.

XIII.

JAPAN IN THE NINETEENTH CENTURY.

Described from the Accounts of Recent Dutch Travellers. Post 8vo, 9*s*. 6*d*.

XIV.

JOURNAL OF AN AFFGHAN PRISONER,

With a Narrative of the Military Operations at Cabul, which ended in the Retreat and Destruction of the British Army, January, 1842.

By Lieut. VINCENT EYRE, Bengal Artillery.

Seventh Thousand. With a Plan of the Cantonments. Post 8vo, 12*s*.

XV.

A JOURNAL OF THE DISASTERS IN AFFGHANISTAN.

By LADY SALE. *Eighth Thousand*. With Plan. Post 8vo, 12*s*.

XVI.

VOYAGE TO NEW SOUTH WALES

IN AN EMIGRANT SHIP, WITH A RESIDENCE IN SYDNEY AND THE BUSH, AND THE ROUTE HOME BY WAY OF EGYPT AND INDIA.

By JOHN HOOD, Esq. 8vo, 14*s*.

XVII.

BUBBLES FROM THE BRUNNEN OF NASSAU.

By Sir FRANCIS B. HEAD, Bart. *Sixth Edition*. 16mo, 5*s*.

XVIII.

A HOME TOUR THROUGH ENGLAND, SCOTLAND, AND IRELAND,

THE CHANNEL ISLANDS AND THE ISLE OF MAN.

By Sir GEORGE HEAD. *Third Edition*. 2 vols. post 8vo, 12*s*.

XIX.

A NARRATIVE OF TRAVELS THROUGH INDIA,

WITH NOTES UPON CEYLON, &c.

By the late BISHOP HEBER. *Fifth Edition*. 2 vols. post 8vo, 12*s*.

ART AND SCIENCE.

I.

HAND-BOOK OF NEEDLEWORK.

Being a Complete Guide to every kind of Decorative Needlework, Crochet, Knitting, and Netting, with a brief Historical Account of each Art.

By MISS LAMBERT. *Third Edition*. 115 Woodcuts. Post 8vo, 10*s*. 6*d*.

II.

MY KNITTING-BOOK.

Containing Examples selected with the greatest care, and arranged so as to render them easy to a novice in the Art.

By MISS LAMBERT. Authoress of the "Hand-book of Needlework."

Third Edition. Woodcuts. 16mo, 1*s*. 6*d*.

III.

CONNEXION OF THE PHYSICAL SCIENCES.

By MARY SOMERVILLE. *Sixth Edition*. Fcap 8vo, 10*s*. 6*d*.

IV.

FACTS TO ASSIST THE MEMORY IN VARIOUS SCIENCES.

New Edition. Fcap 8vo, 6*s*. 6*d*.

V.

CHEMICAL MANIPULATION;

Being Instructions to Students in Chemistry, on the Methods of performing Experiments of Demonstration or Research, with accuracy and success.

By MICHAEL FARADAY, F.R.S. *Third Edition*. 8vo, 18*s*.

AGRICULTURE.

I.

THE FARMER'S ANNUAL ACCOUNT BOOK,

ARRANGED ON NEW AND EASY PRINCIPLES.

By the Author of "British Husbandry." Imperial 4to, 10*s*.

II.

LAND DRAINAGE, SUBSOIL, PLOUGHING, AND IRRIGATION.

By the Author of "British Husbandry." *Second Edition.* 8vo, 2*s*.

III.

THE MUCK MANUAL, FOR THE USE OF FARMERS.

A PRACTICAL TREATISE ON THE CHEMICAL NATURE AND VALUE OF ANIMAL AND VEGETABLE MANURES.

By F. FALKNER, Esq., and the Author of "BRITISH HUSBANDRY."

"Muck is the Mother of Money."

Fcap 8vo, 6*s*. 6*d*.

NATURAL PHILOSOPHY.

I.

ON THE PHILOSOPHY OF THE MORAL FEELINGS.

BY JOHN ABERCROMBIE, M.D. *Sixth Edition.* Fcap 8vo. 5*s*.

II.

ON THE INTELLECTUAL POWERS AND THE INVESTIGATION OF TRUTH.

BY JOHN ABERCROMBIE, M.D. *Tenth Edition.* Post 8vo, price 8*s*. 6*d*.

NATURAL HISTORY.

I.

NORTH AMERICAN GEOLOGY;

WITH A JOURNAL OF A TOUR IN 1841-2. BY CHARLES LYELL, Esq.
With Illustrations. 8vo.

II.

ELEMENTS OF GEOLOGY;

OR, THE ANCIENT CHANGES OF THE EARTH AND ITS INHABITANTS.
By CHARLES LYELL, F.G.S.
Second Edition. With 400 Woodcuts, &c. 2 vols. 12mo, 18*s*.

III.

PRINCIPLES OF GEOLOGY;

OR, THE MODERN CHANGES OF THE EARTH AND ITS INHABITANTS.

By CHARLES LYELL, F.G.S.

Sixth Edition. With 250 Woodcuts, &c. 3 vols. 12mo, 24*s.*

IV.

SCENES & TALES OF COUNTRY LIFE,

WITH RECOLLECTIONS OF NATURAL HISTORY AND LOCAL SCENERY.

BY EDWARD JESSE, Esq. Woodcuts. Post 8vo, 12*s.*

V.

GLEANINGS IN NATURAL HISTORY.

WITH ANECDOTES OF THE SAGACITY AND INSTINCT OF ANIMALS.

By EDWARD JESSE, Esq.

Fifth Edition. With Woodcuts. Fcap 8vo, 6*s.* 6*d.*

VI.

JOURNAL OF A NATURALIST.

Fourth Edition, with Woodcuts. Post 8vo, 9*s.* 6*d.*

SPORTING.

I.

THE CHASE—THE TURF—AND THE ROAD.

By NIMROD. *Second Edition*, with Plates by ALKEN and GILBERT. Post 8vo, 9*s.* 6*d.*

II.

ART OF DEER-STALKING;

ILLUSTRATED BY A FEW DAYS' SPORT IN THE FOREST OF ATHOLL.

BY WILLIAM SCROPE, F.L.S. Plates by EDWIN and CHARLES LANDSEER, R.A.

Second Edition. Royal 8vo, 2*l.* 2*s.*

III.

DAYS AND NIGHTS OF SALMON FISHING IN THE TWEED.

With a short Account of the Natural History and Habits of the Salmon.

BY WILLIAM SCROPE, F.L.S.

With Illustrations by SIR DAVID WILKIE, EDWIN and CHARLES LANDSEER, WILLIAM SIMSON, and EDWARD COOKE, &c.
Royal 8vo, 2*l.* 2*s.*

IV.

MAXIMS AND HINTS ON ANGLING, CHESS, SHOOTING, AND OTHER MATTERS.

By RICHARD PENN, F.R.S. *Second Edition.* With 24 Plates. Fcap 8vo, 5*s.*

V.

SALMONIA; OR, THE DAYS OF FLY-FISHING.

By the late SIR HUMPHRY DAVY. *Fourth Edition.* Fcap 8vo, 12*s.*

VI.

THE MOOR AND THE LOCH;

WITH PRACTICAL HINTS ON HIGHLAND SPORTS, AND THE HABITS OF THE DIFFERENT CREATURES OF GAME AND PREY;

With Instructions in River, Burn, and Loch Fishing.

By JOHN COLQUHOUN, Esq. *Second Edition.* Plates. 8vo, 9*s.* 6*d.*

RURAL AND DOMESTIC ECONOMY.

I.

FARMING FOR LADIES;

Or, INSTRUCTIONS FOR REARING ALL SORTS OF DOMESTIC POULTRY:

Together with the best mode of Managing the Dairy and Piggery, and useful Hints on the Rural Economy of Small Families.

By the Author of "BRITISH HUSBANDRY." Woodcuts. Fcap 8vo, 8*s.*

II.

GARDENING FOR LADIES.

With Practical Instructions and Directions for every Month in the Year; and a Calendar of Operations.

By MRS. LOUDON. *Sixth Edition.* Woodcuts. Fcap 8vo, 6*s.*

III.

MODERN BOTANY FOR LADIES.

A POPULAR INTRODUCTION to the NATURAL SYSTEM and CLASSIFICATION of PLANTS.

By MRS. LOUDON. With 150 Woodcuts. Fcap 8vo, 8*s.*

IV.

NEW SYSTEM OF DOMESTIC COOKERY,

Suited to the present advanced state of the Art, but founded upon principles of economy and practical knowledge, and adapted to the use of Private Families.

By MRS. RUNDELL.

The 67th Edition, improved by the addition of 900 *new Receipts, and a Chapter on Indian Cookery.* By the late EMMA ROBERTS. Fcap 8vo, 6*s.*

*** *Of this Work more than* 310,000 *copies have been sold.*

V.

NEW FAMILY RECEIPT-BOOK;

A Collection of a Thousand valuable Receipts in various Branches of Domestic Economy.

New Edition. Fcap 8vo, 5*s.* 6*d.*

WORKS OF AMUSEMENT & INSTRUCTION,

ADAPTED FOR YOUNG PERSONS.

I.

MRS. MARKHAM'S HISTORY OF ENGLAND,

From the First Invasion by the ROMANS, to the end of the Reign of WILLIAM THE FOURTH.

Tenth Edition, with Woodcuts. 2 vols. 12mo, 12*s.*

II.

MRS. MARKHAM'S HISTORY OF FRANCE,

From the Conquest of Gaul by JULIUS CÆSAR, to the Reign of LOUIS-PHILIPPE.

Fifth Edition, with Woodcuts. 2 vols. 12mo, 12*s.*

III.

BERTHA'S JOURNAL

DURING A VISIT TO HER UNCLE IN ENGLAND.

COMPRISING A VARIETY OF INTERESTING AND AMUSING INFORMATION.

Fifth Edition. 12mo, 7*s.* 6*d.*

IV.

PHILOSOPHY IN SPORT MADE SCIENCE IN EARNEST;

Or NATURAL PHILOSOPHY explained by the aid of the ordinary Toys and Sports of Youth.

Fifth Edition. With 100 Woodcuts. Fcap 8vo, 8*s.*

V.

THE JEWESS:

A TALE, FROM THE SHORES OF THE BALTIC.

By a LADY. *Second Edition.* With Portrait. Fcap 8vo, 4*s.* 6*d.*

VI.

PUSS IN BOOTS.

Suited to the Tastes of LITTLE AND GROWN CHILDREN. By OTTO SPECKTER, the German Artist. With 12 Illustrations. Small 4to, 7*s.* 6*d.*

VII.

STORIES FROM THE HISTORY OF ENGLAND,

FOR CHILDREN.

Thirteenth Edition. 18mo, 3*s.*

VIII.

ELEMENTS OF GEOGRAPHY FOR CHILDREN.

By the Author of "STORIES FOR CHILDREN."

Third Edition. 12mo, 2*s.*

IX.

GOSPEL STORIES;

An Attempt to render the chief Events of the Life of OUR SAVIOUR intelligible to Young Children.

Second Edition. 18mo, 3*s*. 6*d*.

X.

LITTLE ARTHUR'S HISTORY OF ENGLAND.

By the late Lady CALLCOTT.

Sixth Edition. With Woodcuts, 18mo, 3*s*.

XI.

YEAR BOOK OF NATURAL HISTORY.

ARRANGED FOR EVERY MONTH.

By Mrs. LOUDON. With 40 Woodcuts. 18mo, 4*s*.

XII.

HISTORY OF THE LATE WAR;

With Sketches of NELSON, WELLINGTON, and NAPOLEON.

18mo, 2*s*. 6*d*.

XIII.

SENTENCES FROM THE PROVERBS,

IN ENGLISH, FRENCH, ITALIAN, AND GERMAN.

ARRANGED FOR THE DAILY USE OF YOUNG PERSONS.

By a LADY. 16mo, 3*s*. 6*d*.

SCHOOL BOOKS.

I.

INTRODUCTIONS TO THE STUDY OF THE GREEK CLASSIC POETS,

By HENRY NELSON COLERIDGE, M.A. *Second Edition.* Fcap 8vo, 7*s*. 6*d*.

II.

PUBLIC & PRIVATE LIFE OF THE ANCIENT GREEKS.

Translated from the German of HENRY HASE. Fcap 8vo, 5*s*. 6*d*.

III.

GREEK VERBS, THEIR FORMATIONS, IRREGULARITIES, AND DEFECTS.

By A. N. CARMICHAEL, Classical Master of the Edinburgh Academy. Post 8vo, 8s. 6d.

IV.

MATTHIÆ'S SHORTER GREEK GRAMMAR.

Translated by Blomfield.

Seventh Edition, revised, by EDWARDS. 12mo, 3s.

V.

GRÆCÆ GRAMMATICÆ RUDIMENTA IN USUM SCHOLARUM.

Fifth Edition, including the Syntax. 12mo, 5s.

VI.

GRÆCÆ GRAMMATICÆ RUDIMENTA IN USUM SCHOLARUM.

Pars posterior, sive *Syntaxis.* 12mo, 2s.

VII.

RUDIMENTA GRÆCA MINORA IN USUM SCHOLARUM.

Editio altera ad disciplinam Etonensem accommodata. 12mo, 1s. 6d.

VIII.

LATINÆ GRAMMATICÆ RUDIMENTA.

12mo, 3s. 6d.

This Grammar is intended to serve also as an ENGLISH LATIN GRAMMAR and a LATIN EXERCISE BOOK; and being based on that enjoined by the Royal Founder of so many noted Grammar Schools in England, and many of his Successors, is called KING EDWARD VIth's Latin Grammar.

It is printed in the same size as the GRÆCÆ GRAMMATICÆ RUDIMENTA, to which references are made throughout the volume.

X.

ENGLISH NOTES FOR LATIN ELEGIACS;

Designed for early proficients in the Art of Latin Versification, with Prefatory Rules of Composition in Elegiac Metre. By the Rev. W. OXENHAM, M.A., Second Master of Harrow School. 12mo, 4s.

X.

GRAMMAR OF THE GERMAN LANGUAGE,

For Beginners as well as the more advanced Learner. By G. M. HEILNER. 12mo, 10s.

MR. MURRAY'S
HAND-BOOKS FOR TRAVELLERS.

Malta and the East.

THE IONIAN ISLANDS, GREECE, TURKEY, ASIA MINOR, AND CONSTANTINOPLE. With Maps. Post 8vo, 15*s.*

Modern Egypt and Thebes.

BEING A DESCRIPTION OF EGYPT, THEBES, & OTHER PLACES. With Directions for Travellers. By Sir GARDNER WILKINSON. With Map. 2 vols. 8vo, 42*s.*

Northern Italy.

STATES OF SARDINIA, GENOA, THE RIVIERA, VENICE, LOMBARDY, AND TUSCANY. With Map. Post 8vo, 12*s.*

Central Italy and Rome.

THE PAPAL STATES, AND THE CITIES OF ETRURIA. With Map. Post 8vo, 15*s.*

Italy.

GUIDE TO SCHOOLS OF ART AND COLLECTIONS OF PAINTINGS ON THE CONTINENT. Italy—From the Age of Constantine the Great to the Present Time. From the German of KUGLER. Post 8vo, 12*s.*

Spain.

ANDALUSIA, GRANADA, CATALONIA, &c. With Maps. 2 vols. post 8vo. (*Nearly Ready.*)

France and the Pyrenees.

NORMANDY, BRITTANY; THE RIVERS LOIRE, SEINE, RHONE, and GARONNE; the FRENCH ALPS, DAUPHINÉ, PROVENCE, and the PYRENEES. With 5 Maps. Post 8vo, 12*s.*

Switzerland.

THE ALPS OF SAVOY AND PIEDMONT. With Map. Post 8vo, 10*s.*

Northern Germany.

HOLLAND, BELGIUM, PRUSSIA, and the RHINE to SWITZERLAND. With Map. Post 8vo, 12*s.*

Southern Germany.

BAVARIA, AUSTRIA, TYROL, SALZBURG, STYRIA; AUSTRIAN and BAVARIAN ALPS; the DANUBE, from ULM to the BLACK SEA. With Map. Post 8vo, 10*s.*

Northern Europe.

DENMARK, NORWAY, SWEDEN, AND RUSSIA. With Maps and Plans. Post 8vo, 12*s.*

[BRADBURY AND EVANS, PRINTERS, WHITEFRIARS.]